The Power of Positive Dog Training

Josie. (Photo by Pat Miller)

Other Books by This Author:

Positive Perspectives: Love Your Dog, Train Your Dog
(Dogwise Publishing, 2004)

Positive Perspectives 2: Love Your Dog, Train Your Dog
(Dogwise Publishing, 2008)

The Power of Positive Dog Training

2nd Edition

Pat Miller

Wiley Publishing, Inc.

Howell Book House
Published by Wiley Publishing, Inc., Hoboken, New Jersey

Library of Congress Control Number: 2008001313
ISBN: 978-0-470-24184-4
Printed in the United States of America

10 9 8 6 5 4 3 2
Second Edition

Book production by Wiley Publishing, Inc. Composition Services

This book is dedicated to the hundreds of thousands of homeless dogs who were my teachers during my two decades of animal protection work at the Marin Humane Society in Novato, California; to the millions who still wait for homes at shelters around the country; and to my beloved husband, Paul, who is, always, the wind beneath my wings.

Contents

Epilogue

Acknowledgments

I will be forever and deeply grateful to the many people who have encouraged my obsession with animals over the years, which has led me down life's path to this book. The list by rights begins with my parents, Janet and Hal Nieburg, who indulged my childhood demands for every kind of animal companion imaginable, from mice and rabbits to dogs, cats, and horses; and it certainly includes my husband and best forever friend, Paul, who continues to indulge those demands to this day.

Also at the top of that list is Nancy Kerns, my *Whole Dog Journal* editor, who believed in me as a writer long before I believed in myself.

Thanks also to the following people, for being there during those times in my life when I needed guidance and illumination: Diane Allevato, Ray Hill, Lynn Dahmen, Joyce Turner, Betsy Dischel (and Simchah), Karen Pryor, Trish McConnell, Karen Overall, Jean Donaldson, Kim Kilmer, my sister Meg, and, last but never least, my irrepressible dog, Josie.

Foreword

When many of us began dog training, almost every available book spoke of the human-dog relationship in ominous terms such as *discipline*, *dominance*, and *punishment*; or they used euphemistic terms such as *corrections*, with dogs needing to be made *responsible*. If you looked up how to solve a behavior problem, the range of options consisted of different flavors of punishment. There were all kinds of frowning discussions about which implements to use (throw chains, keys, booby traps, noxious chemical sprays, one's hands or fists), where on the dog's body to strike him (on the muzzle, the backside, under the chin so he doesn't see it coming, on the part of his body that committed the "crime"), and what sort of collar to put around the dog's neck in order to deliver pain efficiently and to startle.

If dogs could read, such books would all seem like some sort of dark science fiction. Dogs are, like all living organisms, just trying to get through their days accessing as much pleasant stuff as possible and avoiding as much unpleasant stuff as possible. In *The Power of Positive Dog Training*, the book you're about to read, Pat Miller speaks eloquently of her epiphany, the beginning of her crossover to positive training methods. This is the most profound realization a trainer can have—that gaining control of the *reinforcers*, the pleasant stuff in the dog's environment, is as effective a means of behavioral control as administering pain and startle. What a great day it is for dogs whenever a trainer crosses over. And what an especially great day it was when Pat Miller decided to trade in her choke collar for a clicker. Her words and work have inspired so many more who have come after her.

I first encountered Pat's ideas in her many outstanding articles in *Whole Dog Journal*—always technically sound, always carefully researched, and always demonstrating a keen empathy for the dog and, somewhat remarkably, for the dog's owner, a party so often trampled on. There are many dog trainers who, in their heart of hearts, view the dogs as victims, the owners as perpetrators (or hapless middlemen), and the trainer as the hero in the play. The truth is that dogs have not been the only victims.

Owners have been victims of the dearth of correct and accessible information about dogs—about the true propensities of breeds, about the amount of time and effort involved in training, about the basics of management and training. Phone six trainers at random with the same training questions. The range of answers would leave any consumer confused and in despair. In fact, if the same quality of consumer information existed about, say, cars, people might well be told by different car "authorities" to never change the oil, change the oil every day, or replace the oil with lemon juice. Is it any wonder that so many dog owners continue to fall prey to collar enthusiasts? Pet dog behavior counselors have been victims of the poor quality or low relevance of much of the trickled-down information from the pet dog training "ancestor" endeavors: traditional, militaristic training; competitive obedience training; and academics.

In spite of this spotty history, however, pet dog training and behavior counseling has blossomed. Pat Miller embodies all that is right in this thriving specialty. She is tireless in her championing of training techniques that, first and foremost, do no harm and, almost as importantly, are based on sound, well-understood learning principles, rather than the gut-level intuition and hocus-pocus that seduces so many in this field.

Dogs have intrinsic value in addition to their value to us, and this dictates the use of the most benign techniques available to educate them. There are few trainers who have a better handle on this than Pat Miller, or who can impart these techniques with grace, honesty, and humor to the audience most in need.

—Jean Donaldson
April 2001

Pat's Positive Training Principles

The training journey that you and your dog are about to embark upon is guided by four concepts that are fundamental for positive learning. You will read more about them in the text, and I will often refer to them where they illustrate a point.

CONCEPT 1: All Living Things Repeat Behaviors That Are Rewarding and Avoid Behaviors That Are Not

If you remember this one simple concept, you can teach every behavior that you want your dog to do and change every behavior that you don't want. You do not have to punish your dog in order to make a behavior "not rewarding." You just have to figure out how to make the right behavior rewarding enough that your dog will choose to do that behavior instead of an inappropriate one. You accomplish this by rewarding the behaviors you want and ignoring or preventing those you don't want.

CONCEPT 2: Your Dog Already Knows Everything You Are Going to Teach Him

Your dog already knows how to sit, and he knows how to lie down. He can walk quietly by your side, he can come bounding to you from a distance, and he can stay in one place for long periods of time—when he wants to. All you're going to do is teach him the English words for those behaviors and make them very rewarding and fun for him so he will want to do them when you ask him to. Of course, he always has a choice. If you're a good trainer, you'll program a pattern of responses in his brain so that he will want to do them and will choose to do them when you ask.

CONCEPT 3: Dogs Can Learn Only One Behavior for Any Particular Cue

Dogs don't understand that a word can have several different meanings. For the best training success, have everyone in the family agree on which words will be the cues for which behaviors, and make sure that these cues are used consistently by everyone.

CONCEPT 4: Think in Terms of What You Want Your Dog to Do, Not What You Want Him Not to Do

This is the Peaceable Paws formula for modifying unwanted behavior. All you have to do is figure out how to prevent your dog from being rewarded for the behaviors you don't want and rewarded consistently and generously for the behaviors you do want.

PART I

Partners in Training: Laying the Relationship Foundation

Training is about trust and relationships. (Photo by Elizabeth Dodd)

Chapter 1

Dogs Just Want to Have Fun

So you're going to train your dog. At least you're thinking about training, or you wouldn't be reading this book. Congratulations! You are taking an important step toward ensuring that you and your dog will share a lifetime of fun, companionship, love, and respect. If you make a firm commitment to training your dog, you'll have a loyal friend for life—and you could be saving your dog's.

From 1995 to 1996, the National Council on Pet Overpopulation conducted a study to determine why dogs are surrendered to shelters and found that 96 percent of the dogs given up by their owners had not received any obedience training. Sadly, millions of potentially great dogs are euthanized at animal shelters in the United States every year simply because no one took the time to train them. But you can make sure this doesn't happen to *your* dog.

Great dogs don't happen by accident. When you see an owner playing in the park with a dog who is playful and exuberant, yet at the same time attentive, responsive, and obedient, you can be sure that the owner has spent lots of quality time with his dog. When you train your dog, you establish a powerful bond that helps to cement the relationship. This bond is the critical difference between an unfortunate dog who ends up at a shelter because her owner is moving and can't keep her and a dog whose owner would live in his car or on the street before he would consider giving up his faithful four-legged friend. Every dog has the power to be great. Will yours? It's up to you. Both you and your dog bring the power to succeed in the training adventure. You bring the power to teach; your dog brings the power and eagerness to learn what you teach.

Few couples get married intending to divorce later on. By the same token, no one adopts a dog with the intention of getting rid of her several weeks, months, or years down the road. When you adopt a dog, you enter into a social contract, whether you buy one from a breeder, find a stray on the street, rescue a puppy from a cardboard box in front of the supermarket, or select a homeless hound from the local shelter. You agree to provide for your dog's needs for the rest of her life in exchange for her companionship and unconditional love. Given that unconditional love is pretty hard to come by in this world, you're getting the better end of this bargain, by far!

If you want to uphold your part of the contract, you must teach your dog the social skills necessary for her to adapt to the human world. You need to teach her good manners. Training takes a commitment of time and energy, but it's easier—and more fun—than you might think.

So why don't more people train their dogs? Surely everyone wants a well-mannered canine companion, and a new dog owner's intentions are usually good. Many dog owners make a genuine effort to train their dogs, only to give up because they find that training is more work or harder than they had expected.

Training, however, can be fun. Learning how to communicate with your dog can be a joyful and awe-inspiring experience of mutual empowerment. It doesn't have to feel like work, especially now that a whole new generation of dog trainers are teaching with positive reinforcement methods.

Positive reinforcement training opens the door to your dog's mind. It gives you and your dog the keys to understanding each other's alien cultures. By receiving rewards for desired behaviors, your dog learns how to choose to do the right thing, rather than just how to avoid doing the wrong thing. She learns how to think. As you train your dog, you create a relationship based on trust and understanding. You will also be thrilled and amazed by your dog's unlimited learning potential and positive attitude. She can learn at the speed of light, and, if you choose to teach her, you will realize that she is capable of performing incredibly complex behaviors. If you want to use positive methods to train your dog for the precision of obedience ring competition, high-speed agility, or canine freestyle competitions, you can do that, too. Both of you will have loads of fun in the process.

Once upon a time, I trained dogs using traditional "jerk and pull" choke-chain methods. And I was good at it. My dogs won competitions, achieving scores in the upper 190s out of a possible perfect 200 points. My teachers insisted that a little pain was necessary and a small price for my dogs to pay in order to ensure that they would be well-behaved, good canine citizens. I believed them.

Then I learned about positive training methods. I discovered that I don't have to hurt my dogs to teach them. I crossed over to the positive side of training. Whether you have never trained a dog before, or you, too, are thinking about becoming a crossover trainer, you are about to embark on an amazing journey. Open your eyes, your mind, and your heart. Sign on the dotted line of your canine social contract, make a commitment to having fun, and get ready to discover your dog. That's the power of positive dog training.

It's not worth destroying the trust for points and trophies.
(Photo by Paul Miller)

Chapter 2

Train with Your Brain, Not Pain

Just a few years ago, most positive trainers began their dog-training careers using force-based methods—jerking on choke chains and otherwise physically or verbally intimidating their dogs into submission. Happily, more and more trainers today are "first-generation" positive trainers, growing up in a world where dog-friendly training is readily available and never experiencing the trainer who insists that they have to hurt dogs in order to train them.

Most trainers who started their training careers using coercive methods but who have since crossed over to positive training had an epiphany at some point, often triggered by an experience with one of their own dogs. Mine occurred in the early 1990s, thanks to our terrier mix, Josie. Josie was always a joy to train. Although terriers are generally known for being strong-willed, Josie had always been willing to work very happily with me and showed little of the independence that is a characteristic trait of the feisty Terrier Group.

Heeling, coming when called, and staying were no problem for her. She breezed through her CD (Companion Dog) title with ease, never scoring below a 192 out of a possible perfect score of 200 points. (A dog can earn an obedience title at each level by passing, with a score of 170 points or higher, three separate competitions scored by three different judges. The dog/handler team enters the ring with a perfect score of 200 points, and the judge deducts points for errors as he instructs the team to perform the various exercises.) But we hit a bit of a stumbling block when we began working on her CDX (Companion Dog Excellent); Josie was never what trainers call a natural retriever. In the Open class, dogs must retrieve a dumbbell on the flat as well as over the high jump. Josie simply wasn't interested in picking up the dumbbell.

My trainer at the time convinced me to use the *ear pinch*, a training technique that involves pinching the ear over the choke chain until the dog opens her mouth to protest, then popping the dumbbell in her mouth and releasing the ear. This is a classic example of the learning principle that behaviorists call *negative reinforcement*, where the dog's behavior (opening her mouth) makes a bad thing (the pain in her ear) go away.

Josie, being smart as well as sensitive, soon learned to pick up the dumbbell on command in order to avoid having me pinch her ear. That obstacle conquered, she excelled in the Open competition and earned her CDX in three shows, including at least one High in Trial and an impressive best score of 197.5.

The retrieve problem came back to haunt us, however, as we prepared for Utility. This class includes a scent discrimination exercise in which a dog must select from among a group of similar articles the article that her owner has touched. The exercise is done twice—once with leather articles, once with metal. The leather articles presented no problem for Josie. In no time she could easily find the article with the proper scent from among a group of several. But she hated the metal articles. She refused to put them in her mouth. We tried coating them with plastic spray to make them less offensive, but she still refused. My trainer urged me to pinch Josie's ear harder, so pinch I did. Still, she refused. Then one afternoon when I got out the training equipment, Josie, who had always been a happy and willing worker, hid under the deck and refused to come out.

Josie's behavior was a rude awakening for me. What was I doing to my dog? Were a few scraps of satin ribbon and a certificate to hang on the wall worth the damage I was doing to Josie's psyche, our relationship, and my soul? I quit training and didn't do any serious training for several years. Then I started hearing about a new method that used treats, not choke chains. I checked it out for myself and liked it. I was back in the training game.

Josie never got her Utility title. Somehow it never again seemed that important. We said sad farewells to her in the spring of 2001, when old age took her from us. In the last years of her life, however, when I got out her training toys, her eyes again sparkled and she would dash in happy circles around the yard. She was always a willing worker, even when I used old-fashioned methods. But after she eloquently showed me the errors of my methods and I learned new, gentler ways, she was again my joyful partner in training.

I've realized that ribbons and trophies are just not as important to me as they once were. One of these days you may see me in the obedience ring again with another canine partner, maybe even on the agility course, in the rally ring, or the canine freestyle dance floor. We may even win a ribbon or a trophy or two. But that won't be our goal. Our goals will be to have fun and to enjoy each other's company. That's worth far more than all the trophies in the world.

OPERANT CONDITIONING

Over the last few decades, modern trainers have increasingly utilized positive training techniques based primarily on two of the four principles of learning developed in the 1930s by behavioral scientist B. F. Skinner. Before you start your positive training, it's important that you have a basic understanding of Skinner's theories.

Skinner defined the principles now known as *operant conditioning,* called that because the subject (the dog you are training) can operate on (or manipulate) his environment by his behavior. He can make things happen, either good or bad, by choosing behaviors that are either rewarded or punished.

In describing the principles of operant conditioning, behaviorists use the words *positive, negative, reinforcement,* and *punishment.* In common usage, *positive* usually means good, and *negative* means something bad. *Punishment* is considered bad and often involves the use of physical force, and *reinforcement* means making something stronger.

To behaviorists, the terms have somewhat different connotations. To a behaviorist, *punishment* is something that reduces the likelihood of a behavior being repeated, while *reinforcement* is something that increases the likelihood of a behavior being repeated. When something is added, it is called *positive,* whether that something is desirable—such as a treat or a toy—or whether it's undesirable—such as a verbal or physical correction. Conversely, when something is taken away, it is referred to as *negative,* whether that something is desirable (a toy, the owner's attention, or a privilege) or undesirable (a collar that chokes or a pinch to the ear).

When you combine those terms, you get the following four principles of operant conditioning:

- **Positive Punishment.** The dog's behavior makes something *undesirable* happen, and a behavior decreases as a result. The puppy pees in the house, so the owner yells at him and throws him outside. Yelling and tossing the dog outside might reduce the likelihood of the puppy peeing in front of the owner the next time. But it won't necessarily reduce the likelihood of the puppy peeing in the house!

- **Positive Reinforcement.** The dog's behavior makes something *desirable* happen. As a result, the behavior is likely to increase. The puppy pees outside in his designated bathroom spot, so the owner says "Yes!" in a happy tone of voice and feeds the dog a cookie. Giving the dog a treat in immediate proximity to the act of peeing outside will increase the likelihood of the puppy peeing outside in his bathroom spot the next time.

- **Negative Punishment.** The dog's behavior makes something *desirable* go away, and the behavior is likely to decrease as a result. The puppy jumps up to get his owner's attention, and the owner turns his back on the puppy. The puppy is less likely to keep jumping up if the behavior makes the owner's attention go away from the puppy.

- **Negative Reinforcement.** The dog's behavior makes something *undesirable* go away. The behavior is likely to decrease. The dog is gagging at the end of his leash because the choke chain is strangling him. He stops pulling on the leash and the choking stops—as long as the owner doesn't tighten the leash. The dog is more likely to stop pulling on the leash the next time (unless the reward of getting to go where he wants with a tight leash outweighs the reward of not choking).

All animals, including dogs and humans, can learn through any and all four of these principles of operant conditioning. We all want to make good stuff happen, and to make bad stuff go away. Coercive methods that use large doses of positive punishment and negative reinforcement have persevered over the last century because they worked well enough with enough dogs to be considered successful. Force-based training comes with a number of pitfalls, however, and because of these pitfalls, there are lots of dogs and owners for whom punishment-based methods don't work well. Because people care about their dogs, they feel bad when they punish them. Positive methods help you feel good about training your dog, *and* they work!

THE PITFALLS OF POSITIVE PUNISHMENT

A lot can go wrong when you use positive punishment as one of your primary training tools. Punishment can cause aggression and fear. Punishment doesn't provide your dog with enough information on which to act. It also isn't specific to the behavior that you actually desire, and it might only work to stop the behavior in your presence. Furthermore, you, as the trainer, must time punishment perfectly in order for it to be effective at all. Plus, a corrective punishment must be one that you don't have to repeat over and over, because some dogs can become so tolerant of or so damaged by the punishment that it becomes completely ineffective. Let's briefly examine each of these problems with positive punishment.

Positive punishment can cause aggression. Your dog can easily associate you with the punishment and learn to fear you. Fear is a primary cause of aggression, and your dog may start biting in anticipation of or as a reaction to the punishment. The more you punish the aggression, the more fearful your dog becomes and the more he fights back in self-defense. If your dog is confident and assertive rather than fearful, he may resent your efforts of physical force, and resist aggressively, setting up a dangerous and escalating cycle of conflict that may end up with someone getting hurt.

Positive punishment doesn't provide very much information. Let's say your dog is standing at the front window, wagging his tail and barking. You punish him by yelling at him for the barking. But how does he know whether he's being punished for the barking, the standing at the window, or the tail-wagging? Let's say your brand-new puppy squats and pees in front of you on the living room rug. You grab him, spank him, and throw him outside. You think you just taught him not to pee in the house. But what you really taught him was that peeing in front of you isn't safe. Next time, he'll run to the back bedroom to pee, and in the future he may be very reluctant to pee in front of you when you take him for a walk on-leash to relieve himself.

Positive punishment may only work in your presence. Dogs are pretty smart and can learn to associate punishment with the person who delivers it. Let's say you've punished Sleeper numerous times for getting on the sofa. When he sees you enter the room, he quickly jumps off the sofa. *You* think he's being sneaky, getting on the sofa when you're not there. Obviously he knows better, because he jumps off and looks guilty when he sees you. Or does he? What Sleeper has really learned is that it's not safe to be on the sofa when you're in the room because you get violent. His "guilty" look is actually appeasement behavior, not guilt—he knows you're angry, and he's using body language that has a good chance of turning away anger. However, rather than understanding he's not *ever* supposed to be on the sofa, he knows it's quite safe—and comfortable—to be on the sofa when you're not there, because bad things never happen if he gets on the sofa when you're gone.

Positive punishment isn't very specific. When you punish your puppy for peeing in front of you, you are only telling him what you *don't* want him to do: "Don't pee in front of me!" There are still a lot of places in the house where he can pee that you wouldn't approve of. If you housetrain through punishment, it could take a long time to punish him in every spot he's not supposed to pee in. It is better, and faster, to teach him through positive reinforcement what you *do* want him to do. "Pee over here, puppy. Yes! Here's a cookie for peeing in the *right* place!"

The proper timing of positive punishment is critical. In order for any correction to be effective, it must be given *during or immediately after* the behavior that it is intended to change. "Immediately after" means within one to two seconds. If the correction is too late, your dog won't make the connection to the misbehavior, and you will be punishing the wrong thing.

Let's say you walk in the front door after work and find that Rambo has ripped the sofa cushions to shreds. He runs up to you, happy to see you, tail wagging furiously. Angry at him for ripping the cushions, however, you grab him, shake him, hit him with the limp cushion, and yell a few choice words.

Then you drag him to the back door and throw him outside. You have just punished him for greeting you happily at the door and taught him that you are very dangerous when you first come home from work. You've taught him nothing about chewing up sofa cushions.

By the way, a correction is positive punishment. Pretending that it isn't is just another way of trying to make you feel okay about hurting your dog. Feeding your dog a cookie *after* you punish him is not training with positive reinforcement, as some trainers might have you believe.

Of course, the timing of your rewards is important to successful positive training too. The difference is that an occasional poorly timed or too-generous treat does no harm, whereas a single poorly timed or overly strong correction can do serious, even permanent damage to the relationship between you and your dog.

An effective correction must also be strong enough that it requires no more than one or two applications. A collar correction is a quick jerk on the leash. This abruptly tightens, then releases the choke chain around the dog's neck. It is used to punish the dog for inappropriate behavior, such as moving out of heel position, and, if done properly, should be hard enough to stop the behavior without causing permanent physical or mental damage to the dog. Therein lies the dilemma. How do you know how hard is hard enough for a particular dog? When you have jerked *too* hard, the damage is already done.

Dog personalities range from very compliant (or soft) to very tough and assertive. Dogs in the middle of the range seem to be relatively capable of tolerating coercion-based training methods. The very soft dogs, however, are easily damaged—mentally—by the application of positive punishment, and when they have been overcorrected, regaining confidence and trust can be extremely difficult.

At the other end of the range are the tough dogs. These dogs don't give in easily. In fact, when corrected physically, they are likely to fight back. What do you do when your 150-pound Mastiff decides he didn't like the collar correction and lets you know in no uncertain terms? Plenty of small dogs won't put up with physical force, either. They aren't quite as intimidating as big dogs, but they can still do plenty of damage!

Some old school, force-based trainers insist that you have to overpower the dog with force, using things like scruff shakes (where the handler grabs the sides of the dog's neck and shakes him) and alpha rolls (where the handler flips the dog onto his back and holds him there until he stops resisting) or, if necessary, by hanging the dog with a choke collar until he submits or collapses into unconsciousness. Most owners, thankfully, are unwilling or unable to inflict this kind of abuse on their dogs. These abused dogs frequently end up biting or becoming enough of a threat that they are surrendered to animal shelters, where they are usually euthanized as dangerous and incorrigible. Sadly, if these dogs had been trained with nonconfrontational methods, they might have been fine.

THE BENEFITS OF POSITIVE REINFORCEMENT

Sunny was a 12-week-old Golden Retriever puppy whose owners had called me in a panic. Their veterinarian had told them that the pup was dangerously dominant and that they needed to put him in his place now or he would grow up to be an aggressive adult. The vet had told them to use the scruff shake and alpha roll on Sunny. Now Sunny was growling and snapping at them. They were terrified of their 3-month-old puppy—and he was terrified of them!

When I did an in-home consultation with them, I found a normal Golden Retriever puppy whose personality leaned toward the assertive end of the temperament range. Sunny was just confused and frightened of his owners, who had suddenly turned unpredictably dangerous. The little pup thought he was fighting for his life. As soon as his owners stopped forcing and punishing Sunny and started showing him what they wanted (and rewarding him for it), he eagerly responded.

Positive trainers believe that it is our challenge, as the supposedly more intelligent species, to get our dogs to voluntarily offer us the behaviors we want without the use of force. When they offer the desired behavior, we reward it, thereby increasing the likelihood that the behavior will be repeated. Eventually, we can put the behavior on cue so our dogs will offer it when we ask for it. Finally, when the behavior is rock-solid, we can reduce or phase out the use of food as a reward.

The question, then, is this: Would you rather hurt your dog to train him—or feed him treats? Seems obvious, doesn't it? Yet, for years trainers have told owners that you couldn't train dogs using food. If you train with treats, they declared, your dog would only work when there were treats present or when he was hungry. Both of these claims were wrong. People have been sold a whole philosophy of dog training that says dogs are power-hungry dictators who will take over your household if you don't force them into submission. Heaven forbid you allow your dog on the furniture. Next thing you know, old-fashioned trainers would have you believe, you'll be sleeping on the floor while your dog stretches out on the comforter in the master bedroom! My own dogs are allowed on the furniture, and they are permitted to sleep on the bed. And they haven't taken over the house yet.

We've been told that our dogs should do what they are told because they know they have to and because they love us. They need to know they don't have a choice—they *have* to do what we say or bad things happen. This is just plain bunk. First of all, your dog always has a choice. Plenty of force-trained dogs choose not to do as they are told and are willing to suffer the consequences. If punishment worked all that well, you'd never have to punish your dog more than once. In fact, one of the keys to effective punishment is that it must work with just one or two applications. If you have to punish your dog for the same behavior over and over, you are just teaching the dog to tolerate punishment, and you will have to punish him harder and harder for it to have any effect. Ongoing punishment is abusive.

The majority of dogs you see in today's obedience competitions are compulsion trained, at least to some degree. Fortunately this situation is changing. If you've ever watched an obedience trial, you've seen plenty of those compulsion-trained dogs choosing not to do what they are told.

Of course, if any trainer tells you she can make your dog 100 percent reliable, run away fast and find another trainer. Dogs are not machines—they are living, thinking creatures. We humans—the supposedly more intelligent species—are not 100 percent reliable. We make mistakes. Should our dogs have the right to bite us on the ankle when we do? Of course not. But then why on earth should we have both the right to expect our dogs to be perfect and claim the right to hurt them when they are not? Like us, our dogs have good days and bad. Sometimes they're tired or in pain and can't do what we ask. Sometimes they are easily distracted, and sometimes they'd just rather play their own games than ours.

DOGS JUST WANT TO HAVE FUN, REDUX

Dogs just want to get good things and avoid bad things. Through pain and force, you can teach your dog that if he does what he is told, bad things don't happen. On the other hand, you can teach him without pain that if he chooses to do as he is asked, *good* things *do* happen.

Take jumping up on people, for example. Lots of dogs jump up. Jumping up is one of their most annoying behaviors. Why do dogs jump up? To greet people, because face-to-face greetings are natural dog behavior, and because it's exceptionally rewarding to them. They get to touch you, and you pet and hug them in return. Sometimes, however, when their feet are muddy and you have on your favorite business suit, they get yelled at. Still, even yelling is attention, and they are rewarded often enough that it's always worth a try.

Old-fashioned methods for teaching a dog not to jump up include kneeing him in the chest, stepping on his hind paws, hitting him on top of the nose, and holding his paws until he struggles to get away. Some of these methods may work for some dogs. Other dogs, however, may think a knee in the chest is an invitation to a rousing game of rough-and-wrestle. Hitting a dog on top of the nose may make him hand-shy, and stepping on his fast-moving hind paws may lead to an injury. Paw-holding teaches your dog that hands on paws is a bad thing, which doesn't make it any easier when you or anyone else tries to clip your dog's nails. I want *my* dogs to associate me and my hands with good things, not bad.

Reread the Concept 1 section of "Pat's Positive Training Principles" in the beginning of the book. **Remember:** You want to reward the behaviors you want, and ignore or prevent the behaviors you don't want. Instead of physically punishing your Jumping Jack, ignore him by not making eye contact, by not speaking to him, and by turning your back on him—until he does something good, like sits, and then you reward with treats and attention. If you do this consistently, Jack will learn to run up to you and sit as hard as he can for attention. Dogs repeat behaviors that are rewarding to them.

Sometimes, of course, you can't ignore an inappropriate behavior. If Jack is a 90-pound black Labrador and he is about to jump on 93-year-old Aunt Martha, you obviously have to intervene and manage his behavior to prevent immediate damage to Aunt Martha until Jack is better trained.

Yes, the Miller dogs are allowed on the bed! (Photo by Paul Miller)

Chapter 3

How Can I Answer If I Don't Understand the Question?

People tend to forget that dogs aren't born knowing English. When your puppy is young, you think that she knows the word *come* because she runs toward you when you encourage her to. All a puppy really knows, however, is that she is dependent on you and wants to be with you, so she comes when she is invited. She doesn't know that *come* means that she should come to you even if there are more interesting things to sniff, chase, or see.

All mammals are designed to become more independent as they reach adolescence. When your puppy gets older, she is naturally compelled to explore the world around her. You become less important and interesting as she finds other exciting things to investigate. When you call her and she doesn't come, it's not because she is deliberately defying you. It's because she has found something more rewarding to her at that moment in time.

SOFT FEATHERS on a DUCK

Remember the Concept 2 section of "Pat's Positive Training Principles" at the beginning of the book? Your dog already knows all the behaviors you are going to teach her. Training is the process of teaching your dog the verbal cues and hand signals that go with the behaviors she already knows how to do, and motivating her to voluntarily offer those behaviors when you ask for them by routinely making those behaviors very rewarding. When you have programmed a reliable response to a cue, you no longer have to reward the dog regularly with treats. You will still reward her occasionally with treats, but more frequently you will reward her with other things that she likes such as petting and praise, playing with a toy, making eye contact, opening the door, or throwing the ball. While some of these may not seem very rewarding to you, remember that it's only a reward if your dog likes it—it doesn't matter what *you* think of it!

It really doesn't matter which words you use as cues. People usually use the word *sit* when they want their dogs to sit because that word has meaning for people. It has no meaning whatsoever for the dog, though—at least not until you give it meaning. You could just as easily teach Shep that *peanut butter* means "sit." It's a good idea, however, to use words that make sense and are easy for you to remember so that you don't get confused. In appendix V, "Glossary of Training Cues and Terms," I list the words that I commonly teach as behavior cues, but you are free to use any words you want.

One Cue, One Action

Dogs don't understand that a word can have several different meanings. To humans, the word *down* can mean "Lie on the ground," "Get off the sofa," "Don't jump on me," "I'm feeling a little depressed today," or "soft feathers on a duck."

If you want the word *down* to mean "Lie on the ground," but your spouse uses it to mean "Don't jump on me" or "Get off the sofa," your dog will be confused. She won't learn to lie down reliably when you give the cue because it doesn't always mean "Lie down." Similarly, the term *sit down* literally means "First sit, then lie down." Consistency in the way your cues are used by *everyone* who regularly interacts with your dog is critically important to her learning process. That is the essence of the Concept 3 section of "Pat's Positive Training Principles." Training success is best ensured when everyone in the family is in agreement as to which words will be the cues for which behaviors; then everyone uses the cues consistently. I recommend to my clients that they write down their own vocabulary list and post it on the refrigerator so that everyone in the family can be consistent with the cues they use.

Your dog isn't the only one who needs to learn a new vocabulary. Old-fashioned training is loaded with vocabulary words that imply the use of force. The relationship between dog and owner is perceived as a power struggle—one that the owner must win by any means. You go to *obedience* class. You give your dog a *command*. You *make* her do it. Your trainer tells you to *jerk* on the leash to give your dog a *correction*. Dogs are portrayed as sneaky, belligerent, rebellious, ornery, contrary, intractable, dominant, defiant, devious, and deceitful. How sad.

In positive reinforcement training, however, the relationship between dog and owner is a partnership of mutual empowerment. Training classes are designed to educate dog and owner—both to open the lines of communication between the two of you and to help you work *together*. You *teach* your dog the cues you will use to elicit various behaviors, which the dog will offer voluntarily, without being forced, if you teach her well. You don't *make* her do things; you *help* her do them and reward her so that she will do them again. If she makes a mistake, take into consideration that you may have communicated poorly, that she didn't know the cue as well as you thought she did, or that you made the mistake of asking for a behavior when you didn't have her attention or before she was ready.

A DOG'S-EYE VIEW OF TRAINING

Dogs are not moral creatures, at least not by the human definition of morality. They don't have an innate, ethical sense of right and wrong. When you come home from work, for example, and find that your dog has knocked over the kitchen garbage and strewn debris around the house for the umpteenth time, your dog may seem to be groveling at your feet on the hall rug. She is *not* feeling guilty, however. Dogs are masters at reading body language. Your dog can probably tell that you're upset, and she is being submissive in an effort to appease your anger.

If she connects your behavior to the garbage at all, it is only because she has learned that the presence of garbage on the floor turns you into an unpredictable, dangerous human, and she is attempting to avert your wrath. She doesn't really understand your attitude about this—to a dog, garbage on the floor is a very good thing. When she was frolicking in the garbage three hours earlier, she wasn't thinking about how bad she was being, nor was she anticipating that she would get a beating when you got home. She was having a wonderful time, enjoying the great and satisfying rewards of garbage-play.

You may still wonder why, given the number of times you have punished her for getting into the garbage, she hasn't learned to leave it alone. The answer is: She likely thinks she is being punished for you coming home, not for getting into the garbage. My question to you is: Given how many times your dog has gotten into the garbage, why haven't you figured out a way to secure the lid or place it in a closet so that she can't get into it? We are, after all, supposed to be the more intelligent species.

Team "You and Your Dog"

When you use positive methods to train your dog, you build an entirely different kind of relationship than that formed by old-fashioned training methods—a bond based on a foundation of cooperation and trust rather than on coercion and fear. The goal of positive reinforcement training is to develop the dog's learning potential. You encourage her to solve problems and help her learn to control her own behavior. You also encourage her to offer behaviors and to discover which ones are successful. Positive training opens up a dog's mind. With modern training, you create a joyful, self-confident partner who almost trains herself and who eagerly looks for opportunities to receive a reward. If that's what you want, then welcome to positive training!

Positive training requires a major mental shift for most dog owners. Even if you never wanted to train your dog using pain, our culture has been immersed in a training philosophy that claims that we must dominate our dogs.

When you change the way you talk about dogs, from a force-based vocabulary to a positive vocabulary, it helps you to change your thinking. Dogs aren't bad—they just make mistakes.

When your dog makes a mistake, instead of saying "No, bad dog!" say "Oops" or "Too Bad" and then show her the right way to do it. When one of my clients says, "But she *knows* she's not supposed to get on the sofa. When I enter the room, she jumps off and looks guilty," I answer that if she *knew* she wasn't supposed to do it, she wouldn't. What she knows is that being on the sofa is very rewarding because it is comfortable. But the consequence of being on the sofa *in your presence* is that you get upset. At best, she has learned that she's not supposed to be on the sofa *in your presence*. So when you enter the room, she jumps off and tries to appease your anger with submissive body language. To her, that's an entirely different scenario than being on the sofa *in your absence*.

One of the benefits of changing your perspective regarding your dog's behaviors is that you get angry at her less. Instead of blaming your dog for her mistakes, you realize that she is just being a dog. Dogs like being comfortable, and it's more comfortable on the sofa than on the floor. Want to keep your dog off the sofa? Give her her own bed that is just as comfortable or more so. Reward her for sleeping on her own bed. Prevent her access to the sofa when you aren't present by shutting her out of the room or by putting boxes on it.

Want to keep your dog out of the garbage? Don't put the turkey carcass in the garbage can. Cover the can so she can't get into it. Prevent her access to the garbage can when you aren't present by putting it where she can't get to it. Positive training is all about simple management. You just have to remember to be the more intelligent species. Train with your brain.

Dogs are masters at understanding our body language. If only we could read theirs as well as they read ours! (Photo by Pat Miller)

Chapter 4

Let Me Hear Your Body Talk

Your positive training program will go much more smoothly if you're good at interpreting what your dog is saying to you and communicating to him in a way that he can easily understand. Dogs are, first and foremost, superior body language communicators. They do have the ability to communicate vocally, but they are much more articulate with their subtle body movements, and much more intuitively able to understand ours. As Patricia McConnell says in the introduction of her excellent book, *The Other End of the Leash*, "All dogs are brilliant at perceiving the slightest movement that we make, and they assume that each tiny movement has meaning."

The students in my classes who tend to be most successful are those who are most consistent with their body movements. Consistency allows your dog to attach a specific meaning (and response) to the movement. The more inconsistent your movements, the harder it is for your dog to connect your random motions to a specific behavioral response.

It is *because* of a dog's use of body movement as a first language that we can train so successfully using lure-and-reward methods and so easily teach hand signals. However, the importance of understanding and responding appropriately to your dog's body language goes far beyond formal training. Body talk can make everyday life with your dog easier, enhance your relationship, and help you overcome some of the canine behaviors that are giving you grief.

CROSS-SPECIES COMMUNICATION

One reason our dogs coexist so beautifully with us is that we are both social species—we live in groups and create social rankings within those groups. Both species intuitively understand the concept of a "group leader" (Pack Leader = Head of Household, Employer, President of the United States); both species have members in their various groups who lead more naturally than others; and in both groups, ranking (or status) is fluid: You might be the head of your household, but subordinate to your father or to a colonel in the Army or your professor at college. Your dog might be the leader of your own personal dog

24

pack, but he might have very low status among the bunch who play together after your Good Manners class.

However, canine and primate body talk have very different vocabularies, which can cause serious conflict between our species.

In the canine dictionary, direct eye contact is an assertion or a threat. The dog on the receiving end either (preferably) looks away, a sign of submission—in order to avoid a fight—or takes offense and engages in agonistic (aggressive) behavior in response. The other dog backs off or a fight occurs. This is one reason why so many children are bitten. They tend to stare at dogs, and the more strangely (aggressively) the dog behaves, the more a child stares—exactly the wrong response. Adults who insist on direct eye contact with strange dogs also tend to get bitten. Better to look away when a dog is staring at you with hard eyes than try to stare him down!

We naturally face another person we are speaking to, and our force-based culture encourages us to get more strident if a subordinate fails to comply with our requests. We were once taught to call our dogs by standing squarely facing them, arms at our sides, and saying "Come!" in a commanding tone of voice. Our voices got louder, more insistent, perhaps even angry, if our dogs failed to come. Dogs see a full-frontal communication as a threat, and they see loud, firm, angry vocalizations as aggressive. Their natural response is to turn away in appeasement or, at best, to approach slowly in a submissive curve, rather than respond with the speedy, enthusiastic straight-line recall that we strive for.

We often reach for our dogs' collars over the top of their heads. They see this as a direct threat; they duck away in submission (or they bite) and learn to avoid us when we are trying to catch them. We follow or chase them, intimidating them further or, alternatively, teaching them that if they take the lead, we follow. The more we try to catch them, the more they avoid us.

We bend over them to pet them on the tops of their heads, or to cuddle them. Again, we are unwittingly offering a posture of threat and intimidation. Primate hovering is a very off-putting posture for dogs. Dogs back away in fear or submission or, worse, bite in an aggressive response.

Prompted by ill-advised old-fashioned thinking, some humans still use force (alpha rolls and scruff shakes) to overpower and dominate their dogs. Most dog body language is very subtle and in large part ritualistic, including the belly-up position, which is usually offered voluntarily by the subordinate pack member, not forced by the higher-ranking one. Dogs experience the alpha roll as a violent, terrifying attack, and some will respond aggressively out of a likely belief that they are fighting for their very lives.

THE GOOD NEWS

If you think about it, it's surprising that we get along with our dogs as well as we do. The good news is that both of our species are highly adaptable. We can teach our dogs to appreciate some of our bizarre primate behaviors, and we can learn to use canine body talk to our advantage.

We humans pretty much insist on hugging our dogs. Touch is so important to us that as much as we may intellectually understand our dogs' resistance to such close body contact, our hearts overpower our heads and we just have to hug them. Many dogs learn to tolerate, even enjoy this odd human behavior because hugs are often paired with other things that dogs *do* like—treats, scratches behind the ear, tummy rubs.

I hug some of our dogs—and not others. Katie, our geriatric, creaky, arthritic Australian Kelpie, hates hugs. She's never been snuggly, but now she hurts, which makes hugs even more aversive to her. I don't even try to hug her. Dubhy, our Scottish Terrier, thinks hugs are okay because they come packaged with tummy rubs, and he adores tummy rubs. I hug him sometimes. Bonnie, our Scorgidoodle (Scotty/Corgi/Poodle), is a total cuddler and can't get enough hugs. She loves them. I hug her a lot.

When a dog reacts badly to being hugged, it's often an innate response, not a conscious decision. The dog doesn't sit next to the hugger, ponder his options, and make a deliberate decision to bite. Rather, the hug triggers a subconscious response—"Threat! Fight or Flee!" If the dog can't flee—because he is being hugged—or is one of those dogs whose fight response is stronger than his flight response, he bites.

It's easiest to teach a dog to accept hugging if you start associating gentle restraint with something yummy when he is very young. Using counterconditioning and desensitization to change his natural association with close contact from bad (Danger! Run Away!) to good (Oh, yay! Cheese!), you can convince the part of his brain that reacts subconsciously that being hugged is a very good thing.

To do this, hold the dog at a level of restraint with which he is very comfortable—perhaps just a light touch of your hand or arm on his back. Feed him a tiny tidbit of something wonderful, and remove your hand. Repeat this step until he turns his head eagerly toward you in anticipation of his tidbit when he feels your touch.

Now, very slightly increase the intensity of your touch, either by holding your hand on his back longer and feeding him several treats in a row, by pressing a tiny bit harder on his back, or by moving your arm a little farther over his back so your hand brushes his ribs on the other side. The more your dog accepts your touch, the more quickly you will be able to move through the counterconditioning and desensitization process.

Note: Increase intensity of only one stimulus at a time. For example, work on length of time until your dog is perfectly comfortable with long "hand rests," then shorten the time while you work on increased pressure. When he is comfortable with each new stimulus, add them together. When he can handle more pressure happily, start applying more pressure for longer periods of time. Then ease up on both of these while you work on moving more of your arm over his back.

At the same time, of course, it is vitally important to teach children (and uninitiated adults) not to hug dogs unless they know the dog very well and are totally confident that the dog is fully comfortable with such intimate contact. Even then, young children should never be left unattended with *any* dog.

The same approach used to teach your dog to appreciate a hug works with many other culture-clash behaviors. If you want your dog to love having his collar grabbed, pair the action with cheese or a hot dog or chicken. This particular exercise should be taught to every dog. Perhaps *you* know that the safest way to take hold of a dog's collar is gently, under the chin. But if a friend tries to grab the collar over your dog's head, it would be nice if she doesn't get bitten for her primate behavior because your dog has learned to accept it.

You can also teach your dog that eye contact is a good thing by encouraging him to look into your eyes and rewarding him when he does. (The clicker [see chapter 6] is very useful here.) In fact, we reinforce this behavior strongly in Good Manners training and for obedience competition—we want our dogs to know that direct eye contact is a very good thing and makes lots of good stuff happen. Have your dog practice this with other humans as well as with you if you want him to be comfortable with that pervasive and offensive primate penchant for staring rudely into canine eyes. And remember to teach your children *not* to stare into a strange dog's eyes.

A TWO-WAY STREET

While you are teaching your dog to understand and accept primate language, you can also learn and use canine body language. This will greatly enhance your relationship and your training program, since your dog can respond very quickly when he realizes you are speaking Dog.

McConnell describes a process that she calls body blocking, which simply means taking up the space to prevent your dog from doing so. Let's say your dog is watching you while you are cooking in the kitchen and you drop a fried drumstick on the floor. Duggy starts to move to get it. Rather than grab at him or yell "Stay!" simply step forward into the space he was about to occupy. Like magic, he settles back into his Sit/Stay. McConnell reminds us that the *sooner* you react, the better, and she says that once you get good at it, you can simply lean forward an inch or two to express your intent to occupy the space.

Caution: This is *not* a good strategy to use with a dog who is a resource guarder—willing to get aggressive to claim or keep a valuable resource. (See chapter 23 for more on working with resource guarders.)

You can also use body blocking with dogs who jump on you. Next time you are sitting in a chair and your wild Westie makes a running charge for your lap, clasp your hands against your stomach and lean slightly forward, blocking the space with your shoulder or elbow. It also helps to look away, rather than make eye contact. You may have to do several repetitions of this, especially if your dog has had much practice lap leaping, but it can be very effective if you are consistent. He can learn to wait for permission to jump up—on your lap or on the sofa next to you.

I used body blocking for years without thinking about it or defining it as clearly as McConnell does. When our four dogs are all doing a Wait at the door, I can release them one by one, by name, in part because I use subtle body blocking movements to indicate which dogs are to remain in place. As with the Stay blocking, the more you do it, the more subtle the movements can become because dogs are *so* good at reading tiny body language signals.

This is just one example of the many ways you can make the canine/primate difference work *for* you as you build a relationship with your dog based on mutual trust and respect, and as you encounter other dogs. Move (run!) *away* from your dog when you want him to come rather than toward him. He will follow the leader, instead of move away from an intimidating direct approach. Look away from the challenging stare of an aggressive dog instead of sending your own direct–eye contact challenge back, and you are more likely to escape from the experience bite free.

We, with the more developed brains and higher intelligence, should be able to understand and forgive canine behaviors that clash with our human social expectations. It seems that our dogs are pretty darned good at understanding and forgiving ours, thank goodness. As you and your dog journey together through life, translating primate to canine and vice versa, appreciate the great gift of this cultural diversity.

Ears back, eyes soft and squinty, mouth relaxed . . . this dog
is inviting your attention. (Photo by Pat Miller)

Chapter 5

I Read You Loud and Clear

Paradigm shifts in the dog-training world in the last two decades have led people who care for and about dogs to pay closer attention to the interpretation and understanding of canine body language. Norwegian dog trainer Turid Rugaas identified more than thirty body gestures that dogs make in social settings—whether with members of their own species or with humans—that, she postulated, demonstrate an intent to get along with other pack members. Rugaas coined the term *calming signals* to collectively describe these gestures and their purpose, and the term has gained acceptance and everyday use as dog owners and trainers discuss dog behavior. Clumped behind that deceptively simple phrase is a complex constellation of behaviors that offer a much greater diversity of purpose than just calming.

Rugaas asserts that dogs purposely use calming signals to calm the other being with whom the dog is interacting. The suggestion is that the behaviors brought under this broad umbrella are deliberate.

Today, many ethologists (people who study animal behavior) speculate that much of the communication popularly identified as calming signals are often hardwired, automatic responses rather than deliberate ones, and are far more complicated than a simple attempt to *calm* a dog's social partners. They likely have more to do with the dog's own state of mind and/or an end goal to affect the *behavior* of the other dog or human for the purpose of self-preservation—rather than a necessarily deliberate intent to change the *state of mind* of the other being.

Communicative behaviors are adaptive in nature—helping canids maintain peaceful pack relationships without resorting to violence. Ethologists suggest that nonthreatening (showing deference) canine behaviors are more important in keeping the peace in packs than are dominance behaviors—that relations are primarily maintained by deference behaviors exhibited by subordinates toward high-ranking members, not dominance displays by high-ranking members. Canine social groups may more appropriately be described as *deference* hierarchies rather than dominance hierarchies.

The dozens of behaviors that have been dubbed calming signals can be separated into several subgroups: appeasement (active submission), deference (passive submission), displacement, stress signs, and threat (dominance) displays. By observing dogs and learning to recognize and respond to the various behaviors in this constellation, your relationships with canines will become richer, and your translations of dogspeak more accurate. Let's take a closer look at the submissive/subordinate behaviors.

As stated above, subordinate behaviors can be grouped into two general categories—*active submission (appeasement)*, characterized by increased activity and diminished posture, and *passive submission (deference)*, denoted by decreased activity and lowered body posture. The difference is that the dog offering the appeasement behavior desires attention from the higher-ranking individual, while deference behavior indicates that she'd prefer the attention she's receiving to go away.

Active submission may also be referred to as attention-seeking behavior: nuzzling, licking (including licking ears and lips), jumping up, paw lifts and pawing motions, "smiling," teeth clacking, crouching, pretzeling, play-bows, and sometimes excitement urination. Ears may be pulled back, and tail may be wagging expressively in wide, sweeping movements or in circles. These behaviors can often be seen during greetings between dog and owner, and between friendly, compatible dogs.

Passive submission usually involves a dramatic reduction in activity with a goal of diverting attention, and it is most often seen in a lower-ranking dog when threats are directed toward her by a higher-ranking member of the social group—dog or human. The dog's ears may be pressed flat against the head, with her tail tucked between her legs. The subordinate dog often freezes, averting eye contact and lowering head and body sometimes to the point of going "belly-up" on the ground. Passive submission may also be accompanied by submissive urination.

Read on for descriptions of several common submissive, stress, and threat behaviors, and suggestions for appropriate responses when the behavior is directed toward humans.

BODY PARTS

Your dog uses her various body parts to send the messages described in the following sections. The parts that tend to be the most expressive are her eyes, ears, tail, and body posture. When you observe a dog, it's important to look at the whole picture to get a sense of what she's saying. The more experience you have with dogs, the more quickly your brain will leap to a conclusion about the dog's message. This is why skilled dog-training and behavior professionals rarely get bitten—they don't have to stop and analyze what a dog's body parts are saying, they just *know!* But it's also useful to focus in on specific body parts to understand *why* we leap to the conclusions we do, and to help less experienced dog lovers learn how to understand what dogs are so clearly trying to tell us.

The following generalities are true:

- When a dog's posture is tall and forward—ears pricked; eyes open wide and making direct contact; tail erect and still or wagging stiffly; fur raised on neck, shoulders, and back—the dog is confident and could be friendly, curious, playful, aroused, or aggressive.

- When a dog's posture is low and back—ears flattened; eyes squinting or not making direct contact; tail low or tucked between the legs; fur raised on neck, shoulders, and back—the dog lacks confidence or is being appeasing or deferent, and could be friendly, playful, fearful, or defensively aggressive.

Subtle differences in those body parts will help you make important distinctions between friendly, playful confidence and confidently aggressive, or friendly appeasement and fear-related aggression. In general, the more extreme and tense the body part expression, the harder the eye contact, the more rapidly the tail vibrates, and the more firmly forward the ears are pricked, the more the dog is aroused and likely to be aggressive. The more quickly the dog moves away, the tighter the tail is tucked, and the more pronounced the avoidance of eye contact, the more fearful or appeasing the dog is being, and the more likely she is to be aggressive if pushed. The softer, more moderate the behaviors in either category, the more likely it is that the dog is safe.

If you want to communicate better with a dog, take the time to study her language. When you look at a photograph of a dog, look carefully at all the body parts and draw conclusions about what the dog might be saying. Of course, a photo is a moment frozen in time, so you won't know what followed or how accurate your assessment was. Watch videos so you can see body language in motion. Stop the video, make predictions about what the dog will do next, and then start the video again to see if you're right. If not, rewind and look for the clues you might have missed.

Finally, watch dogs in real life. Visit dog-training classes and canine sports events, go to dog parks, and watch dogs learning, working, and playing. See how keenly you can hone your dog-reading skills. If you're good, you might even be able to get a job as a translator!

Active Submission (Appeasement)

Some of the gestures exhibited by a dog who is demonstrating active submission can be irritating to us humans. With these behaviors, the dog communicates her recognition that you are a higher-ranking individual. Be a good leader and let her know how she can best appease you by redirecting her behavior to something less bothersome, rather than punish her for her attempts to appease you.

Nuzzling. Dog pushes nuzzle against you, perhaps under your arm or hand. If you respond by giving the dog attention (petting, making eye contact, speaking to her) you positively reinforce the behavior and it will continue or increase. This is fine if you like the behavior—and some people do. It can, however, become annoying if the dog is very persistent.

You may prefer to extinguish the behavior using negative punishment. When the dog nuzzles you, turn away or even walk away. The dog is seeking attention. If nuzzling consistently evokes the opposite response—attention goes away—the behavior will stop. Of course, you must educate all family members and visitors to respond in the same way, or the behavior will be randomly reinforced and will persist.

You could choose to put the behavior on cue, and teach the dog that nuzzling only works to elicit attention when you ask for it. You can also preempt the nuzzle by consistently asking the dog for an incompatible behavior that gains her the attention she seeks. A Sit or Down cue can serve as incompatible and polite attention-seeking behaviors if you consistently give your dog attention for those.

Licking. Dog licks your clothes and body parts, including your lips, ears, and nose. Again, if you like this behavior, you can encourage it with positive reinforcement by giving your dog attention when she licks. If you don't enjoy your dog's licking, use negative punishment (licking makes you go away) and install an incompatible behavior in its place. Having your dog hold a toy in her mouth when she approaches people is a great attention-eliciting behavior that's incompatible with licking.

Jumping up. Dog puts paws on human body, often projecting body against human with some force. A lot of small-dog owners don't seem to object to jumping up as an attention-getter, and a lot of small dogs are incorrigible jump-uppers as a result. Not all people with small dogs like this, however, and most people who cohabitate with medium-to-large dogs much prefer four-on-the-floor.

Jumping as an attention-getting behavior is positively reinforced by attention, even by attention that dog owners may offer to try to reduce jumping up such as pushing the dog away or telling her to get down. Once again, remove yourself from contact with the dog—take the attention away—to reduce the behavior, especially if you replace it by reinforcing an incompatible behavior such as Sit or Down. See the pattern yet?

Paw lifts and pawing motions. Dog lifts paw or paws at human. While uncontrolled pawing behavior can be annoying, a simple paw lift is a lovely behavior to put on cue and turn into a series of fun and useful behaviors. A paw lift on cue can become Shake, Wave, High-Five, or Salute, and pawing motions can be useful for turning appliances on and off, indicating found objects for dogs doing scent and search work, pushing a ball (canine soccer!), or playing an electronic keyboard. Persistent, annoying pawing is best extinguished by ignoring the behavior and putting an incompatible behavior, such as four-on-the-floor, or a gentle paw lift on cue.

Teeth clacking. Dog clicks or chatters teeth. This is an innocuous behavior and one that you can simply ignore—unless you're an avid trainer and want to encourage it by clicking and treating when the dog offers it, then putting it on cue.

Crouching. Dog lowers her body closer to the ground. This is also an innocuous attention-seeking behavior. If it bothers you, ignore it, and reinforce your dog when she approaches you standing taller. Training using positive methods will increase your dog's confidence and decrease incidents where she feels compelled to make herself smaller.

Pretzeling. Dog corkscrews her body into a C shape. This is also a harmless, kind of cute behavior that I'd be tempted to reinforce and put on cue!

Play-bowing. Dog lowers her forequarters while keeping her hindquarters elevated. This is a lovely behavior, and I can't imagine someone wanting to extinguish it. I'd reinforce and put it on cue.

Smiling. Dog lifts her lips into a grimace that is unaccompanied by other behaviors that would indicate a threat. I see no reason to try to make this behavior go away as long as humans around the dog understand that it's not an aggressive behavior. I think it's quite cute—I'd encourage it by clicking and treating when the dog offers a smile, and then put it on cue!

Passive Submission (Deference)

Deference behaviors are offered by a dog in response to a *perceived* threat—there doesn't have to be any intent to threaten on the part of the person interacting with the dog. For all of the deference behaviors listed here, the appropriate response is to determine how/why the dog perceives a human or humans as threatening, then to work to change the dog's perception through consistent positive associations with the perceived threat(s).

Normal human behaviors that can be perceived as threatening by a dog (thereby eliciting deference behaviors) include direct eye contact, full-frontal approach, loud voice, bending over the dog, and patting the dog on top of the head. Punishing or "correcting" a dog for offering a deference behavior is the worst thing you can do if you hope to modify the behavior. The dog will only intensify her deference in a futile attempt to convince you she's being subordinate. In a worst-case scenario, she may even become defensively aggressive if her deference signals aren't working. Instead, ignore the behaviors when they happen, and work to build your dog's confidence in relationships by being consistently nonthreatening, and insisting others do the same. You can also build confidence through positive training—when a dog has a better understanding of how to influence and predict her environment, her confidence increases.

A dog's deference behaviors may include any or all of the following:

- **Tail tucking:** Dog pulls her tail tightly against her belly to cover and protect her vulnerable underparts. Even dogs with gay tails (tails that curl over their backs) can do this when sufficiently threatened.

- **Freezing:** Dog ceases all motion as she attempts to convey her submission to the party threatening her—usually in conjunction with averting eyes.

- **Averting eye contact:** Dog shifts eyes to avoid making eye contact, or actually turns head away.

- **Lowering head and body:** Dog ducks head and/or crouches closer to the ground.

- **Belly-up:** Dog rolls over on back and exposes vulnerable underparts. (Can also be a simple invitation for a tummy rub when not accompanied by other deference behaviors.)

- **Submissive urination:** Dog urinates in response to perceived threat (not necessarily an actual threat) in a person's voice, touch, or approach.

MAJOR MISUNDERSTANDING

Humans have long misunderstood submissive behaviors in both categories, and have reacted inappropriately as a result. In many human cultures, failure to make eye contact is a sign of someone who is untruthful, shifty, and sneaky. Dogs displaying submissive behaviors such as averting eyes and lowering body posture (slinking) are often perceived as wimpy, cowardly, sneaky, manipulative, guilty, and disobedient—misinterpretations based on our familiarity with primate body language.

Unless wise to the ways of canid communication, humans tend to assume a dog offering lowered body-posture deference behaviors is expressing guilt—when in fact she's only responding to a perceived threat in her human's body language.

Sometimes, the more the dog acts guilty, the more righteously angry her human gets, the more submissive (guiltier) the dog acts, the angrier the human—a lose-lose cycle if there ever was one.

Submissive urination is another classic case in point. Dog owners who still live in the old-fashioned punishment dog-training paradigm may attempt to physically or verbally "correct" a pup for peeing submissively—the exact wrong thing to do.

A pup urinates submissively in response to a perceived threat—the assertive approach of a higher-ranking member of the social group. In the dog pack, this is a useful survival mechanism that effectively averts the wrath of most adult dogs who could otherwise do serious harm to a young subordinate.

Unfortunately, when the higher-ranking member is a human, the behavior (urination) that should avert wrath often initiates or escalates anger in the human. The pup's response is to urinate more, not less. The human gets angrier, the pup pees more, the human gets even angrier, the pup pees even more in a desperate attempt to turn off the anger—and another lose-lose cycle is born.

Even the submissive grin is misunderstood. Sadly, it can be mistaken for a snarl, and a dog may be labeled as aggressive who is actually anything but. It's also often perceived as a doggy version of a happy smile—a less damaging interpretation, but still a misperception of a clearly subordinate display.

Interestingly, the submissive grin is believed to be an imitation of the human smile, since dogs don't normally display this behavior to each other, only to humans. While some behaviorists consider the grin to be an attention-seeking appeasement gesture, others consider it more of a threat-averting deference signal. In any case, it's important to understand that the dog who grins is making a status statement—your rank is higher than hers—exhibiting neither an aggressive threat nor a relaxed, contented smile.

You can avoid misunderstandings, major *and* minor, by knowing what your dog is really trying to tell you with her wide variety of body language communications, reacting appropriately to them, and using them to your advantage in your positive training program.

STRESS AND THREAT SIGNALS

It's important to recognize signs of stress in your dog so you can help her before she gets into trouble. Stress is the primary underlying factor in almost all cases of aggression. If you can recognize that your dog is stressed and remove her from the situation, you can prevent her from feeling compelled to bite someone.

Common stress signals include:

- **Anorexia:** Stress causes the appetite to shut down.
- **Appeasement/deference signals:** These are not always a sign of stress but can be. They include:
  - Slow movement
  - Lip licking
  - Sitting, lying down, exposing underside
  - Turning head away, averting eyes
- **Avoidance:** Dog turns away, shuts down, evades handler's touch and treats.
- **Brow ridges:** Furrows or muscle ridges appear in dog's forehead and around eyes.
- **Digestive disturbances:** Vomiting and diarrhea can be a sign of illness *or* of stress.
- **Displacement behaviors:** Behaviors performed in an effort to resolve an internal stress conflict. They include:
  - Blinking (at a faster rate than normal)
  - Chattering teeth
  - Nose licking (dog's nose, not yours!)
  - Scratching
  - Shaking off (as if dog is wet, but she isn't)
  - Yawning
- **Drooling/Foaming:** This may be a sign of stress or a response to the presence of food or an indication of a mouth injury.
- **Excessive grooming:** Dog may lick constantly, even to the point of self-mutilation.
- **Hyperactivity:** Frantic behavior or just restless pacing, sometimes misinterpreted as ignoring or "blowing off" owner.
- **Immune system disorders:** Long-term stress weakens the immune system. Immune-related problems can improve if a dog's overall levels of stress are reduced.
- **Lack of focus:** The brain has difficulty processing information when stressed.

- **Leaning/clinging:** The stressed dog seeks contact with human as reassurance.
- **Lips pulled back:** Corners of the dog's mouth (commissure) are pulled back into a V shape, as if grinning.
- **Lowered body posture**: Slinking, acting "guilty" or "sneaky" (all misinterpretations of dog body language), can be indicators of stress.
- **Mouthing:** Willingness to use mouth on human skin can be puppy exploration or adult poor manners, but it can also be an expression of stress.
- **Obsessive-compulsive disorders:** Also packaged with a strong genetic component, behaviors such as fly snapping (biting at invisible, imaginary flies), tail chasing, light chasing, flank sucking, and more are usually triggered by stress.
- **Panting:** Rapid or shallow breathing can be a sign of stress if not a result of physical exertion.
- **Piloerection:** Hair is raised anywhere on a dog's back, from the neck down to and including the tail.
- **Stiff movement:** Tension can cause noticeable stiffness in leg, body, and tail movements.
- **Stretching:** Many dogs perform deep stretches to release stress-related tension in muscles (may also occur after sleeping).
- **Sweaty paws:** Damp footprints can be seen on floors, exam tables, or rubber mats.
- **Trembling:** May be due to stress (or cold!).
- **Whining:** This high-pitched vocalization, irritating to most humans, is an indication of stress.
- **Yawning:** Dog may be stressed—or tired.

Most (but not all) threat signals are generally more recognizable to adult humans than are many of the stress signals. But often children do not recognize threat signals, which is one of the reasons they are common victims of dog bites and why interactions between dogs and young children should *always* be closely supervised by an adult. When a dog is giving threat signals, she's doing her best to make you go away without actually biting you. Threat signals are a good thing (your dog is trying to *not bite!*) and should never be punished. Rather, you should back off (or have the person back off who is presenting the perceived threat), determine why the dog feels compelled to make threats, and work to modify her behavior. Common threat signals include:

- **Barking:** There are lots of different kinds of barks. The threat bark is usually a deeper sound and has a very distinct warning tone.
- **Freezing:** Dog stops all movement, including panting.
- **Growling:** Often but not always a precursor to a bite.
- **Hard stare:** Dog makes and holds direct eye contact with eyes wide open and hard.
- **Lips pulled forward:** Corners of dog's mouth (commissure) move forward into a C shape.
- **Nose bumping:** Dog makes a quick movement toward you with her mouth closed, bumps your skin with her nose instead of her teeth.
- **Snapping:** Dog moves as if to bite but connects with air instead of skin. Dog does not miss by accident—she *intends* to bite the air as a warning rather than make contact.
- **Snarling:** Lips pull up to reveal teeth.

It pays to take the time to observe dogs—yours and others—and become conversant in their body language. The better you are at understanding your dog, the better your training, communication, and relationship with her will be, and the more you'll enjoy your life together.

And now, let's get on with the training!

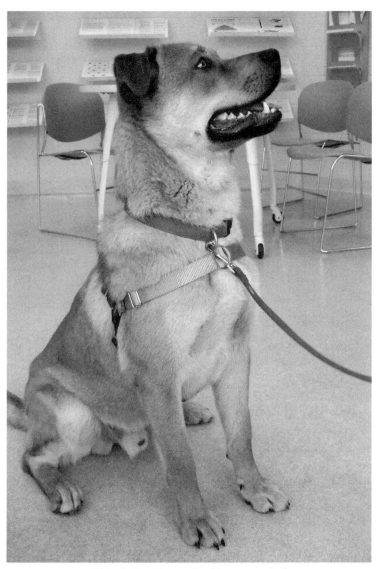

This shelter dog smiles his approval of
the front-clip control harness. (Photo by Pat Miller)

Chapter 6

A New Leash on Life

TRAINING EQUIPMENT

The equipment list for basic positive reinforcement training is short and simple: it includes motivators, reward markers, collars, and leashes. Make sure you have these basics before your dog's training begins.

Motivators

Also called *rewards*, motivators are anything that the dog likes and will work for. Food is a primary motivator because all living things need food to survive. I like to use food as a motivator in training because most dogs will work for food and because the dog can eat a treat quickly and get back to work. Food can also work as a lure. If your dog doesn't seem to be food-motivated, you may need to find a better motivator (see appendix II, "Delicious Treats and Delightful Rewards," for more information) or train just before his meal, when his appetite is sharper. If your dog works well for food at home but won't eat it elsewhere, he may be too stressed or distracted in new environments. (Not eating is a common sign of stress.) If your dog is too stressed or distracted to eat, slowly and gradually add new stimuli to his training sessions and desensitize him to new places until he can work with distractions.

You may be able to train with lower-value treats at home (ones he likes but that aren't his all-time favorites), and train with higher-value rewards in more distracting environments. For example, you may be able to use his regular dinner kibble for treats at home, but use small pieces of hot dog or freeze-dried liver for rewards when you're in a busy park.

Toys, play, petting, and praise are usually secondary motivators. You can also use them as rewards, replacing food treats when your dog has learned a behavior well. For some dogs, a toy can be a strong motivator—at least as motivating as food, if not more so. One drawback with using a toy as a reward is that you have to stop and let the dog play with it, so it takes longer to get back to training. An advantage to toys is that as long as you can get them back from your dog, you will never run out of them the way you may run out of treats.

Clicker and treat—your most important training tools (besides your dog and your brain).
(Photo by Tom Hanson)

Another advantage is that toys really let you and your dog combine play with training—reminding you to keep it fun, as it should be.

When you use food as a motivator, remember to subtract an equivalent amount of rations from your dog's food bowl so that he doesn't start looking too prosperous. Each treat should be just a tiny tidbit; you don't want him filling up too fast or consuming too many calories.

Reward Markers

The term *clicker* can actually refer to any reward marker. Clicker training is a generic term that means "training using a reward marker." By pairing a sound, such as the sharp *click!* of the clicker, with a reward—such as a tasty treat—you create a powerful training tool that you can use to immediately signal to the dog the instant he does something good. When the dog sits, you *click!*—and he knows he's earned a reward for sitting, even if he hasn't gotten the treat yet.

Clicker training was first introduced to the dog-training world in the 1980s by marine mammal trainer Karen Pryor through her landmark book, *Don't*

Shoot the Dog: The New Art of Teaching and Training. Pryor promoted the use of the clicker as a reward marker because it makes such a sharp, distinctive sound to which dogs seem particularly attuned. (With dolphins and other marine mammals, a whistle is used as a reward marker because the sound travels well under water.)

You can use other sounds as reward markers instead of clickers if you prefer. Some of my clients use mouth clicks, finger snaps, whistles, or the verbal marker "Yes!" or a verbal "Click!" or "Tick!" I recommend training new behaviors with an actual clicker, however, because the sound is so distinctive and effective, and because the *click!* is very consistent—it always sounds exactly the same—except when you get your thumb stuck! You always have the option of switching to a verbal marker after a behavior is learned, if you want. I teach my dogs both, conditioning them to a verbal marker after they've learned the clicker, because I like the versatility it gives me. I still use the clicker when teaching new behaviors or in formal training sessions, but the "Yes!" is sure handy when I'm out hiking with them, anytime I don't have a clicker handy, or when my hands are too full of leash, treats, target stick, and other training props to be able to grab the clicker.

It's easier to find your clicker when you need it if you attach it to your person. Some trainers use a plastic wrist coil or a neck cord to keep their clickers handy. You can buy clickers with a small elastic loop attached that slips over your finger for safekeeping. A fairly recent discovery for clicker-keeping (and my personal favorite) is the badge reel—a coiled cable that extends when you pull out the clicker and retracts when you let go, sort of like a retractable leash for your clicker! Badge reels are available from most office supply stores.

Some behaviorists theorize that the sound of the *click!* actually travels to a more primitive part of the brain called the amygdala, where it can be acted upon immediately, while a word must be processed through the cortex first, which might help to explain the clicker's effectiveness. The advantages of a verbal marker are, of course, that your mouth is always with you, and if you're like me, it usually works. You don't have to remember which jacket pocket you left it in, and it doesn't take an extra hand to use. A verbal marker, if used, should be a one-syllable word, such as "Yes!" and should be uttered only once per reward.

Reward markers should always be followed by a reward so that the dog learns to trust in the marker's message that a treat is coming. Every time you *click!* or say "Yes!" the dog should get a treat. My personal rule is that a *click!* always gets a food treat, while my verbal marker might be followed by a treat or, alternatively, by a high-value life reward such as the opportunity to chase a ball

A Word on Rewards

My clients often ask if positive training means that they will always have to feed their dogs treats. The answer is no—not if you don't want to. My dogs will certainly do what I ask them to most of the time, whether I have treats with me or not. Even though I almost always do have treats with me, they don't always get one. But I will continue to reward my dogs with treats on occasion for the rest of their lives for voluntarily doing what I ask. I look at it like this: I love the work that I do. But I wouldn't be nearly as enthusiastic about it if I didn't get paid occasionally for my efforts. My dog's job is to be my companion and to do what I ask him to do, when I ask him to do it. In order to keep him enthusiastic about doing his job, I make sure to give him an occasional paycheck—a yummy treat. So I keep cookies in the pockets of every jacket I own (which taught me to always hang my jackets up because my Pomeranian was very good at chewing the bottoms out of the pockets to get the treats). There is not a shred of doubt in my mind—I would much rather have cookies in my jacket pockets than a chain around my dog's neck.

or Frisbee, go for a walk or a ride in the car, or the chance to run outside to play with their dog pals. In the remaining chapters of this book, I use the term *click* to mean the application of whatever reward marker you decide to use.

Here's a dolphin-based explanation of why the reward marker is such an effective training tool. Let's pretend that we are dolphin trainers and that we want to train our dolphin to jump out of the water on cue. We can wait by the side of the pool until he jumps on his own accord, then quickly call him over to the side of the pool and feed him a fish. But wait—he now thinks he got the fish for swimming over to the side of the pool! How do we tell him the fish is his reward for the jump? We could try tossing the fish to him in midair, but that wouldn't be a very accurate or precise way to communicate, especially if our aim isn't very good!

There is a simpler way—we do it with the whistle. First, we condition the dolphin to the reward marker; that is, we teach him that the whistle means "fish." To do this, we simply blow the whistle, then feed him a fish. Blow the whistle, feed him a fish. Blow the whistle, feed him a fish. And we do this over and over again, until every time he hears the whistle, his brain thinks *fish*. Now we're ready. The next time he jumps out of the water, we blow the whistle when he's at the top of his leap, and his brain thinks *fish*. Even though he does not get the fish until he lands and swims over to the side of the pool, he knows that the fish was for the jump. The reward marker is an incredibly powerful training tool because it allows you to communicate instantly and clearly with your dog when he does something right.

You can't buy timing at the pet supply store, but it's also one of your most important training tools. The better your timing with the *click!* the faster your dog will understand which behavior is getting marked and rewarded. Behaviors are ideally marked the instant they happen, but at least within one second or quicker, in order for the dog to make the connection to the behavior you're trying to reinforce. One of my favorite things about clicker training is the "Aha!" moment—that instant in time when you see your dog's brain engage, when his eyes light up and he "gets it." The better your timing, the sooner you'll see the "Aha!" moment. The more you use clicker training with good timing, the faster that "Aha!" will come for each new behavior that you teach.

Collars

Nothing fancy is required here. I generally clicker train my dogs in a properly fitted plain buckle (or snap) collar. You should be able to fit one or two fingers between the collar and your dog's neck. If your dog pulls back and slips his collar, you can use a limited-slip collar, which is also known as a martingale or greyhound collar. These are designed to tighten slightly but not work on a choking action or pain principle as choke chains and prong collars do.

A harness is also acceptable if you're worried about a collar putting too much pressure on your dog's neck. A regular walking harness, however, may actually *encourage* your dog to pull because it is more comfortable for him to pull with pressure on his shoulders than on his neck. You may even want to teach your dog to pull in a harness. My Bloodhound, Otis, was a great hiking companion. I loved to take him hiking with me in California—he excelled at pulling me up those steep coastal hills when I asked him to. If you want to use a harness to help you teach polite leash walking, look for a front-clip control harness, where the leash attaches in front of the dog's chest rather than on top of his back. These go by brand names such as the Easy-Walk, SENSE-ation, SENSE-ible, or K9 Freedom Harness.

Leashes

In many areas dogs are required by law to be on-leash when they are off their own property. Even if you live in a rural setting and don't need to walk your dog on a leash regularly, it is an important skill for him to learn. There will be times when he must walk on a leash—for trips to the vet or maybe for a visit to your child's class for a session of show-and-tell after he's learned his good manners and a few entertaining tricks.

A six-foot leash is a good training choice. I prefer cotton canvas, but some trainers prefer leather. The brightly colored designer-nylon leashes are pretty, but if you have a dog who pulls, nylon can burn or cut your hands. Cotton and leather leashes are softer.

Leashes that extend and retract may be great for exercising your dog, but they aren't great for training—they are bulky to hold, and they don't help your dog learn to stay near you while walking. In fact, they actually reward the dog for pulling! Retractable leashes can be dangerous, too. There are documented cases of the thin, retractable cord getting wrapped around a finger and severing it when the dog charged to the end of the leash. I counsel all my clients not to use retractable leashes for training.

Despite my warnings, one of my California students arrived at the first session of class with one attached to his young Jack Russell Terrier's collar. As he was opening the gate to the training yard, the large plastic handle slipped from his hand and clattered to the pavement. The terrified pup took off full speed, dodging cars on a heavily trafficked avenue. Fortunately, he managed to avoid getting hit by a car, and we recovered him several blocks up the road. If you must use a retractable leash, don't use it for training, be considerate of others around you, and be sure you have a tight hold on the handle.

MANAGEMENT TOOLS

It is useful to have a number of behavior management tools on hand in addition to your basic training equipment. The better you are at managing your dog's behavior to prevent him from being reinforced for unwelcome behaviors, the easier it will be to teach him that *only* desirable behaviors make good things happen. If you do a good job managing your dog, you won't feel the need to yell at or otherwise punish him for being "naughty," because he won't have the chance to be naughty. These management tools are things that will make life with your dog run more smoothly while you are teaching him how to live in a human world.

Crates

A crate is an invaluable management tool. It is an artificial den for your dog—a box made of plastic, fiberglass, metal, or wood, with a door that you can close when you need to keep him contained. The crate also makes housetraining a breeze and gives your dog a safe place where he can stay when the stimuli in the environment are beyond his coping skills. These situations could be anything from your toddler's playgroup or the Super Bowl party to his own temptations of sofa-chewing while you are out shopping. The crate is your dog's den—a good place to be and *never* a place of punishment.

Your dog may adjust more easily to stays at the vet hospital or boarding kennel when he can take his own personal, portable bedroom with him. If he travels with you, many hotels and motels are much more amenable to allowing a dog in your room if you tell them that he will be crated. Most dogs love their

Teach your dog to love his den, and he will have his own personal,
portable bedroom he can take with him anywhere he goes.
(Photo by Pat Miller)

crates and enter them willingly when asked or when they want to give themselves a time-out.

Most puppies, even the majority of adult dogs, can be crate-trained with relative ease. However, a crate is generally not recommended for dogs with separation anxiety because they tend to panic in close confinement. If you believe your dog has a separation anxiety problem, consult a behaviorist or a trainer who has experience with this behavior.

A crate should be just large enough for your dog to stand up, turn around, and lie down comfortably. He doesn't need to be able to play football in it. If you want to get one large enough for your puppy to grow into, block off the back so that he has just enough room to be comfortable, and then increase the space as he grows. Cover the floor of the crate with a rug or soft pad to make it comfortable and inviting, and you're ready to begin training.

Start with the crate door open and just toss treats inside. If your dog is hesitant to go in after them, toss them close enough to the doorway so that he can stand outside and just poke his nose into the crate to eat them. Each time he eats a treat, click the clicker.

Gradually toss the treats farther and farther into the crate until he is stepping inside to get them. Continue to *click!* each time he eats a treat. When he is entering the crate easily to get the treats, *click!* and offer him a treat while he is still inside. If he is willing to stay inside, keep clicking and treating. If he comes out, that's okay too. Just toss another treat inside and wait for him to reenter. Don't try to force him to stay in the crate.

At this point in your dog's training, you can start using a verbal cue such as "Go to bed" as he goes in so that you will eventually be able to send him to his crate on just a verbal cue. When he is happily staying in the crate in anticipation of a *click!* and a treat, gently swing the door closed. Don't latch it. *Click!* and treat, then open the door. Repeat this step, gradually increasing the length of time the door stays closed before you *click!* Sometimes you can *click!* and reward without opening the door right away.

When your dog is staying in the crate with the door closed for at least ten seconds without any signs of anxiety, close the door and latch it. Then take one step away from the crate. *Click!*, return to the crate, reward, and open the door. Repeat this step, varying the time and distance you leave the crate. Don't always make it longer and farther—intersperse long periods with shorter ones so that it doesn't always get harder and harder for him. Sometimes you can *click!* and treat without opening the door, but remember that a *click! always* gets a treat.

When you aren't actively training, leave the crate door open. Toss treats and your dog's favorite toys inside when he's not looking, so that he never knows what good surprises he might find inside. You can even feed him his meals in the crate—with the door open—to help him realize that his crate is a truly wonderful place.

Some dogs and puppies can do the whole crate-training program in one day. Some will take several days, and a few will take weeks or more. If at any time during the program your dog whines or fusses about being in the crate, wait for a few seconds of quiet, then *click!* and reward him for being quiet. After this, back up a step or two in the training program. (If you let your dog out when he is fussing, you will teach him that fussing gets him free. If, however, he panics to the point of risking injury to himself, you must let him out. You may have a dog with a separation-anxiety challenge.)

When he is doing well at that level again, increase the difficulty in smaller increments and vary the times, rather than constantly making it harder. For example, instead of going from 5 seconds to 10 to 15, start with 5 seconds, then 7, then 3, then 8, then 6, then 4, then 8, and so on. Changing the time periods that you ask your dog to wait is an important part of a successful crate-training program.

Tethers

A tether is a three- to six-foot length of plastic-coated cable with snaps at both ends. You can use a tether to secure your dog to a particular spot when you are working on teaching him to be well-mannered. These spots should be set up with a soft bed and good chew toys so that a time-out on a tether is a pleasant experience, not a punishment.

Baby Gates

Designed to keep human babies out of trouble, a baby gate is every bit as useful for keeping canine babies, even adult dogs, restricted to areas that have been dog-proofed or where immediate human supervision can occur. You can use baby gates temporarily—for example, when you're housetraining your new puppy to keep him with you and make sure he can't wander into another room to poop, pee, or chew. When he gets a little older and can be trusted, you can remove the gate. Or you can use a gate to restrict access permanently to some parts of your house—to give your cats a dog-free part of the house, and keep cat food and litter boxes away from curious canines, for example, or to keep Buster on the other side of the threshold of the new baby's nursery.

Exercise Pen

Collapsible and portable, this is a sturdy wire pen that you can use to give your canine pal more room than a crate while still keeping him safely under wraps. It's good to use with a pup who must be left alone all day—too long to be crated, since you don't want him to soil his crate. You can put the crate in one corner of the pen, and papers or pee pads in the other, for his potty area. With very young pups, I put a tarp down, then a thick layer of newspapers, so they can go anywhere—as young pups tend to do. You can even get pens with tops, if you have a persistent climber. Be sure to get your pup comfortable with being confined to the pen *before* you leave him alone all day, so he doesn't panic, try to climb out, and get a leg caught between the wires.

Head Halter

The head halter is a tool that is intended for a dog who is a strong puller. It works on the negative reinforcement principle—when the dog stops pulling, the bad thing (the pressure on the dog's muzzle) stops.

The head halter works on the same principle as a halter on a horse—control the head and the body must follow. People learned centuries ago that they could control the horse, an animal weighing over 1,000 pounds, by putting a halter on his head. Only recently did people realize that this same tool could work for dogs.

At one time, the head halter was widely embraced by the positive training community, and indeed it appears far more positive than choke chains, prong collars, and shock collars. However, while some still use them routinely, many positive trainers are increasingly realizing that a good percentage of dogs find the head halter significantly aversive. Most dogs need to be introduced to the halter slowly, and they may resist unless it is done gently and gradually. Even then, some dogs never accept it, and others may only learn to tolerate it. Given the opportunity, most will still try to rub it off with their paws, on the grass, or on their owners' legs—which gives us a clue as to how much they *don't* like it. In addition, the head halter can act to suppress behavior, causing the dog to shut down, which actually interferes with his ability to learn and enjoy learning.

The author uses a treat as a lure to get Josie to offer a desired behavior. (Photo by Paul Miller)

Chapter 7

The Shape of Things to Come

There are five techniques that you can use to get a dog to offer a behavior so that you can mark and reward it, thereby increasing the chance that she will do it again. Two of them are *offered*—that is, the behavior occurs spontaneously, of the dog's own volition. The other three techniques are *elicited*—that is, you do something to encourage the dog to offer you the behavior.

OFFERED BEHAVIORS

Capturing. When a dog offers the complete, perfected behavior that you are trying to train all on her own, the behavior is *captured*. Capturing can be the fastest and easiest way to train simple behaviors. The Sit can often be captured, clicked, and rewarded because it is a behavior that dogs tend to offer very frequently. If the dog never offers the behavior you want, however, capturing could take forever!

Shaping. Trainers commonly use shaping to train more complex behaviors. To help a dog learn a complex behavior, the trainer breaks it down into small steps, then clicks and rewards each step repeatedly until the dog learns the entire behavior. Let's say you want to teach your dog to spin in a circle to the left. You could start by capturing a slight turn of the head to the left with a *click!* and treat. When the dog begins regularly offering left-head turns, you would then only *click!* and treat stronger left-head turns.

In any series of repetitions, some of the behaviors will be stronger, some will be weaker, and some will be average. As you begin to *click!* and treat only the average and stronger turns, the average behaviors will begin to shift toward the stronger end of the scale. Then you can raise the bar and only *click!* and reward turns when the body starts to follow the head or when the dog actually takes a step. In time, you can shape an entire circle to the left. Shaping can be quick and easy in some cases, but painstakingly slow in others. Even though it can sometimes take longer in the beginning for the dog to offer the desired behavior, many trainers believe that shaped behaviors are not only more reliable in the long run than elicited behaviors, but that the more shaping you do with your dog, the faster you will both become at shaping and learning.

ELICITED BEHAVIORS

Imitation. Birds and primates are masters at learning through *imitation* (watching and copying the behavior of others). The application of imitation in dog training, however, seems to be limited because most dogs don't tend to imitate humans easily. They are more likely to imitate another dog, in which case you can *click!* and treat a desired behavior.

True imitation involves having the dog simply watch another perform the behavior, and then be able to perform it on her own. At one time it was believed that dogs had difficulty learning simply through imitation.

Some early studies suggested that puppies might have some limited ability to learn this way. One study involved several pairs of litters of 8-week-old puppies. In each pair, one litter was given a wagon full of food. The wagon was outside the puppies' kennel, and they had to figure out how to pull the wagon into the kennel with the handle to get the food. The other litter was allowed to watch. It took an average of around twenty minutes for the initial litters to pull the wagon into the kennel. The litters who were allowed to watch took an average of about five minutes to get the food. In another study, young puppies of working mothers (i.e., drug detection dogs) who were allowed to watch their mothers at work reportedly performed better at the same task when they began training later on than puppies who were not allowed to watch their mothers working.

More recent research seems to indicate that adult dogs have a greater capacity to learn through imitation than we once thought. An Austrian study released in the spring of 2007 demonstrated not only that adult dogs were able to learn through imitation, but also that they could use *selective imitation*—choosing to imitate those behaviors they had watched another dog perform that had demonstrated the most likely success in obtaining a food reward.

A more commonly used form of imitation is called *social facilitation,* in which a dog watches another doing something and joins in. Your new dog learns to bark at people walking past the house by watching your original dog get aroused and vocal at passersby, and joins in the chorus. So if you have a dog who is already trained and you're trying to train your new puppy, social facilitation may work well for you. For example, your puppy may learn to come when called by following your older dog who comes to your whistle.

Luring. By using a piece of food as a lure or a target object that the dog has learned to touch, you can show her how to do the behavior you're asking for. You can lure a Down position, for instance, by holding a treat in front of the dog's nose, then moving it slowly toward the ground. The dog follows the treat and ends up lying down. You can also use a combination of luring and shaping to get the dog to offer you a complete Down, clicking her for heading in the right direction at first, even if she doesn't make it all the way down.

Lures should be *faded* (minimized, then eliminated) as quickly as possible, or both the dog and you may become dependent on the lure to get the behavior. You can fade the lure by replacing the food lure with body language (move your empty hand toward the ground to elicit a Down, then *click!* and get the treat from a pocket or a bowl on the table) or by waiting for the dog to offer a behavior after you have lured her several times.

Modeling. For a positive trainer, *modeling,* or physically assisting the dog into position, is the least desirable and least effective of these five training methods. The goal of positive training is to get your dog to be responsible for her own behavior. When you model her into position the way you would model clay, even if you do it gently, the dog doesn't have to think about what she is doing, and she may become dependent on your touch to make the behavior happen.

If you use lots of modeling, you may want to think more creatively in order to get your dog to offer desired behaviors. Train with your brain! If it is absolutely necessary to use physical assistance for a particular behavior, the assistance should be gentle—the minimum amount needed to get the behavior—and should be faded as quickly as possible.

Dogs who are trained purely by marking and rewarding offered behaviors can reach awe-inspiring heights of training accomplishment. They are generally the most fun, creative, confident, joyful, and clever of trained dogs, regardless of their breed. This kind of training may seem to take longer at first because you must wait for the dog to offer a behavior—or a small piece of it—so that you can capture or shape it. But it is worth the time and patience that it takes to realize your dog's greatest potential. You can often also train positively and efficiently by using lots of luring. Luring is a shortcut to getting a dog to offer the behavior. The dog doesn't have to think as hard when she is lured into a specific behavior. She may become dependent on the lure, however, and rely on you to help her when she gets stuck rather than think for herself. Still, luring can be a quick and effective way to get a behavior to happen. If your goal is simple obedience and quick results, be sure to include luring in your training tool kit.

MANAGEMENT VERSUS TRAINING

When you're training your dog, you may encounter situations or crises when you must do something that you would not normally do. For example, when friends of mine adopted Scooter, a forty-pound Golden Retriever-Chow mix, from the local animal shelter, I took Dusty, my eight-pound Pomeranian, to visit. We monitored the introduction and things went well, so we relaxed, chatting around the dining room table while the dogs played happily underneath.

Suddenly, however, Dusty was on his back screaming as Scooter had pinned him to the floor in a ferocious battle. Without stopping to think about positive techniques, I grabbed Scooter by the scruff of the neck, dragged her out from under the table, and screamed a loud "No!" in her face. Then I retrieved Dusty, who was shaken but otherwise unharmed. Lying on the carpet beneath the table was a rawhide chew—the coveted object that had triggered the fight.

At the moment that I dragged Scooter from under the table, I was managing the situation and doing crisis intervention, not training. As it turned out, we realized that Scooter had some issues with food/possession aggression that we needed to work on. Knowing this, we managed her behavior and prevented the problem from reoccurring by keeping food and highly valued toys picked up when there were other dogs or children around—until we could work on changing her aggressive guarding behavior.

Yet another, perhaps better management solution in this case would have been to not allow the two dogs to be together in the first place. Given their size disparity, there was significant potential risk that Scooter could have caused Dusty serious harm. Some dog care professionals warn strongly against keeping dogs together if their weight difference is greater than fifteen to twenty pounds, citing a phenomenon known as *predatory drift*. This behavior can occur when a larger dog is playing with a smaller one, and suddenly her brain perceives the smaller dog as a prey object instead of a canine playmate. She chases, grabs, and shakes the other dog as she might a bunny or squirrel. Although many small and large dogs live long and happy lives together, the risk is real, and these relationships bear close supervision.

Until training has taken place, there are many occasions when management is imperative. If your pup is not yet housetrained, you can manage her behavior by constantly supervising her, taking her outside frequently, and putting her in a crate or pen when you aren't home, when you are sleeping, and when you are otherwise too preoccupied to keep an eye on her. If your dog doesn't come when she is called, you can manage this behavior by not letting her off-leash in an open area until you have trained her to come on cue.

If your dog snaps at small children, you might crate her or otherwise stash her away in a safe place when children are visiting until you have desensitized her to the presence of children and she decides that they are good things to have around. If your dog begs at the dinner table when the family is eating, you can manage the behavior by putting her on a tether in the corner until you train her to stay on her own designated mat at mealtime.

Management does two very important things. First, it prevents your dog from practicing the inappropriate behavior. The more a dog is allowed to perform a behavior (and get rewarded for it), the more ingrained that behavior becomes and the harder it is to change it. An ounce of prevention truly is worth several pounds of cure. Plus, management keeps you from getting angry at your pup for urinating on the new carpet, chewing the mahogany coffee table leg, or snatching the steak off your plate.

Anger gets in the way of the relationship between you and your dog and impairs communication. The more you can prevent your dog from engaging in inappropriate behaviors and help her choose appropriate ones, the more solid the bond will be that grows between the two of you.

The lion may not lie down with the lamb yet,
but the dog can lie down with the horse in the
Peaceable Paws kingdom. (Photo by Paul Miller)

Chapter 8

Should You Ever Punish?

Sometimes when you're training, punishment (*positive punishment*—where the dog's behavior makes a bad thing happen) may be appropriate—but those times should be very few and far between. Since I started using positive reinforcement training, I have only had to use positive punishment with a dog on a rare occasion, and I considered those incidents a failure on my part because I was unable to devise a positive solution to a serious problem. In a crisis, I might explode with a deafening "No!" to interrupt a behavior that is risking someone's life or safety. But even though a loud "No!" is a verbal reprimand, it can very much be considered positive punishment, and therefore risks the same negative side effects that physical punishment does. I much prefer to use *negative punishment,* in which the dog's behavior makes a good thing go away, to change an unwelcome behavior.

The most notable example of my reluctant application of positive punishment involved a client's Pit Bull mix who was very dedicated to chasing horses. Happy's owners (an elderly couple) found him abandoned by the side of the road at the tender age of 5 weeks. They had briefly attended a traditional training class, but dog and owners were so offended by the forceful choke-chain methods used in the class that they dropped out. Three years later, Happy was totally out of control.

A series of private positive reinforcement lessons with dog and owners, however, quickly taught Happy his basic good manners. Before long, he was greeting visitors without bowling them over, sitting without even being asked, lying down on cue, waiting politely for his Frisbee to be tossed instead of grabbing it out of the thrower's hand, and coming when he was called (*most* of the time).

Happy loved to chase horses, though. About once a month, his desire to chase outweighed his response to the cue to come. He would duck under the electric fence and have a gay time terrorizing the occupants of the pasture. Not only was this stressful to the horses, but it was also dangerous to Happy, as flying horse heels whizzed past his head.

One day, I was at Happy's house, working with his owners on his training. It had been several weeks since Happy had chased a horse, and we were hopeful that we were making progress. But suddenly he took off after the herd and, sure enough, this time he got kicked squarely in the head. He fell to the ground, motionless, and I was sure he was dead. The three of us began running toward the pasture. Before we reached Happy he lifted his head, shook it, stood up, and began staggering toward us.

"Okay," I thought to myself. "He's not dead, but he has permanent brain damage."

Happy kept walking, and by the time he reached us, his stride was steadier. In ten minutes he was still a bit subdued but otherwise seemed fine. A trip to the vet confirmed that he had suffered a concussion but, by some incredible good fortune, nothing more serious.

What a relief! Certainly, getting knocked unconscious by a horse was perfectly timed and appropriate enough punishment to forestall any future horse-chasing ventures. Or so we thought. Several weeks went by without incident, and we were all sure that Happy had kicked the horse-chasing habit—until, on another of my visits, Happy went horse-hunting again.

We all agreed that we had to find a way to stop him. This was truly a life-saving intervention, not just the threat of an impatient owner who might dump his dog at the animal shelter if we didn't find a quick fix. Happy was going to get himself killed if he kept chasing horses.

It just so happened that Happy was gun-shy. A firing range was located a distance from Happy's house, and whenever someone was target-practicing, even though the gunshots were quite muffled, he would head lickety-split for the front porch. We decided to try using this to our advantage. I purchased a cap gun at a toy store, loaded it with caps, and waited for the moment.

True to form, several weeks later, Happy gave us the chance. As we were returning from a training session in a nearby field, he spotted the horses. His head went up, his eyes sparkled, he perked up his ears, and he took off like a bullet. I pulled out the cap gun and waited. Just as he ducked under the wire into the pasture, I fired. Happy wheeled in his tracks and dashed for the porch, where he sat glued to the floor until we joined him. It was the first time that we had succeeded in stopping him in mid-charge. We were hopeful.

Properly applied positive punishment should work within one or two applications. Anything more than that isn't doing the job and constitutes abuse. We didn't want to continuously use the cap gun to stop his charges after the horses. We wanted it to stop the behavior completely, quickly.

I left the gun with his owners, and we all crossed our fingers. They only had to use it one more time. Twice was enough to convince Happy to leave the horses alone forever. Mission accomplished.

Am I pleased that we found a way to keep Happy safe? Of course, I am. Do I wish I had found a way to do it without capitalizing on his noise phobia? Absolutely. To this day, I ask myself if there wasn't another, more positive way to accomplish our goal. I constantly bring Happy's case history up at trainer forums and on e-mail lists. I wonder if we could have succeeded with Leslie Nelson's "Really Reliable Recall." (See appendix IV, "Resources.") I am convinced that there was a positive way to do it—I just couldn't find it at the time.

There may be very rare occasions when some reasonable form of positive punishment is appropriate. But it should only be used after great deliberation, and only after all possible dog-friendly methods have been tried and ruled out. In the last two decades, a wealth of resources have become available to owners and dog-training professionals who are looking for positive solutions to training challenges, including Internet listserves, books, videos, DVDs, and training organizations and support groups. *Reasonable,* by the way, rules out the use of electric shock collars, hanging, helicoptering, and any other cruel technique that risks mental or physical damage to the dog. Appropriate occasions are few and far between, and they are, I believe, an admission of failure on the part of a positive trainer.

Having said that, let's get on with the rest of the book in which I offer positive reinforcement training methods and solutions (sprinkled lightly with gentle applications of benign negative punishment), and I studiously avoid any more discussion of the use of force.

PART II

The Trick Is in the Training: Basic Exercises

"Sit!" means sit anywhere, not just two feet in front of the refrigerator. (Photo by Paul Miller)

Chapter 9

It's All Tricks

In this chapter, I describe the mechanics of an effective training program. The subsequent chapters get down to the nuts and bolts of educating your dog. You are about to embark on an exciting adventure in mutual empowerment. It actually could be considered a foreign exchange program, because at the same time that you are learning about your dog's mind, behavior, and culture, she will be learning about yours. **Remember:** You are teaching her English as a second language, and you are about to become more fluent in hers.

Theoretically, each of the following six chapters represents one week's worth of training. However, because each dog (and trainer) is an individual, feel free to go more slowly if you'd like—or more quickly if your dog is an Einstein. When you and your dog have learned all of the exercises in the book, you will have completed the introduction to your dog's training career. The two of you will have an understanding of the behaviors and communication tools that will serve you both as you proceed on your journey through the rest of your lives together.

Your dog probably won't be able to perform all the behaviors perfectly by the end of the book; some of them will take several more weeks, or even months, to approach the level of reliability that you'd eventually like to see. For some dogs, a truly reliable recall—by my definition, 90 percent reliability or better in the face of serious distractions—can take years. But you *have* years. Training happens every day throughout your dog's entire life. Every time you interact with your dog is a training opportunity. Every time you and your dog are together, one of you is training the other. Wouldn't you rather be the trainer than the trainee?

The Core Exercises sections in the following chapters will lay a solid foundation for your dog's future. The Bonus Games sections are included to help remind you and your dog that training is supposed to be fun. After the instructions to the exercises, I also include training tips, where helpful, in the form of answers to common questions that arise when people begin to teach their dogs the core exercises. These should help encourage you and your dog to work through the rough patches you may encounter. You will want to do a thorough job of teaching your dog all the core exercises; they are the key to helping your dog develop her basic good manners. You will also need that solid foundation if you want to go on to more advanced training in any canine sport.

You can pick and choose from the bonus games based on your training goals, your dog's natural talents, and your own personal fancy. Including at least some of the bonus games in your training program is important. Because they are fun and sometimes frivolous, they will keep your training program enjoyable and help to strengthen the relationship between you and your canine partner.

People tend to be too serious when they teach their dogs the behaviors that they think are important, but they permit themselves to have fun when they are teaching behaviors that they call tricks. Rarely do you see someone punishing Queenie for not responding to a cue for a high-five. And rarely does Queenie not respond! It's a fun trick, and dog and owner both seem to enjoy showing off.

Positive trainers like to say, "It's all tricks!" Teaching Queenie to lie down on cue is no less a trick than teaching her to offer a paw. As soon as you get too serious about the Down cue, however, you're no longer having fun and neither is she. When you're not having fun, it's time to stop training—at least for that session. Pick up your tricks and treats again when you're in a more positive frame of mind.

CHOOSING YOUR CLASSROOM—WHERE SHOULD YOU TRAIN?

In the beginning, you will want to train in an environment that has few distractions. Wait until the toddler is down for a nap, then put the other dog in the garage, shut the cat in the back bedroom, and pick up the chew toys. You want to be the most interesting game in town so that your dog *wants* to pay attention to you. Indoors is infinitely better than outdoors, because you can't control the outdoor environment. Squirrels, rabbits, skateboards, and other dogs are just a few of a dog's favorite things that may outrank you in competition for her attention early in her training program.

If you consistently use the same room in the house to train, your dog will automatically start to focus on you when you set up to train. Use this room whenever you are going to teach something new. When Queenie seems to understand a new behavior, *then* you will want to take it on the road by practicing in different environments. It is critically important to do this if you want your dog to be well-behaved in public. Thousands of dogs are perfectly well-behaved in the luxury of their own homes when no visitors are around. But let Aunt Martha or the hot new boyfriend come over, or take Queenie for a walk to the park, and she turns into a maniac. This happens because your dog won't integrate distractions or generalize her training (be able to apply it to environments other than the one you trained in) well unless you help her.

If you always work in the kitchen and practice having Queenie sit two feet in front of the refrigerator, she will think that the cue Sit means "sit two feet in front of the refrigerator." The first time you take her into the living room and ask her to sit in front of the television set, she doesn't do it. She's thinking, "Are you nuts? How can I sit? There's no refrigerator here!"

Meanwhile, you are thinking that Queenie's being stubborn, obstinate, spiteful, or stupid because she knows darn well how to sit and she's ignoring your cue. Every time you move to a new environment or add distractions, you may need to back up a couple of steps in your dog's training to let her know that Sit means the same thing wherever she is, whether there's a refrigerator there or not. A group training class provides a perfect opportunity to train your dog in a distracting environment and to teach her this important lesson. You will need to find dozens more opportunities like this for her to understand that Sit happens *everywhere*.

Once she becomes more sophisticated about training and accustomed to working in different environments, Queenie will be able to learn new things despite reasonable distractions, and she will be able to generalize more quickly with each new behavior that you teach her.

THE BASIC TRAINING RECIPE

Training a new behavior follows a simple (although not always easy) six-step recipe. Just as good cooks add their own variations to a recipe, good trainers vary the training recipe when they decide that a particular training challenge needs a little more (or less) spice. When you have used the recipe enough to know it well, you can add your own spices as needed.

Six Steps for Teaching a New Behavior

1. Get the behavior.
2. Mark the behavior.
3. Reward the behavior.
4. Repeat the behavior until it happens easily at least 80 percent of the time.
5. Add the verbal cue just before the dog does the behavior to associate the word with the appropriate response.
6. Use the verbal cue to elicit the behavior.

You get the behavior by capturing, shaping, or luring it. You mark the behavior with the *click!* or some other reward marker that Queenie has already learned means that the reward is coming. Reward the behavior by following the *click!* or other reward marker with a yummy treat, favorite toy, or other desirable reward such as going outside.

Repeat the behavior until Queenie is offering it easily before you add the verbal cue, so that she will associate the word with the correct behavior response. For example, by saying "Sit!" just before she does it, you are telling her that the name of the behavior she is doing is Sit. If you ask her to do it before she's offering the behavior easily, you risk teaching her that the word *sit* means "stand there and look at me," or, worse, "sniff the ground and pull on the leash."

After Queenie has heard the word at least a half-dozen to two dozen times when you *know* she's about to perform the behavior—depending on how quickly she seems to learn—then you can say the word first to elicit the behavior. Be sure that her attention is focused on you so that she actually *hears* the word, and keep your body position the same as it was when you were getting the behavior before. If you had been doing the Sit while you were standing and you suddenly start asking for it while you are sitting, your dog won't understand that it's the same thing. It's the refrigerator phenomenon, remember?

Give her a few seconds to respond after you give the verbal cue, "Sit!" When she sits, *click!* and reward. If she doesn't sit, use the minimum amount of assistance necessary through body language (prompt) or a lure—*not* through physical assistance—to get the behavior. Then repeat the exercise. If you find that she will only respond if you help her, start to minimize (fade) the amount of help you give until she is sitting for the verbal cue without any assistance from you.

How Much Should You Train?

I remember when I used to go to old-fashioned training classes. The trainer would exhort us to put the choke chain and leash on our dogs and drill for forty-five to sixty minutes every day. In these busy times, few dog owners can find a solid hour of free training time every day. Fortunately, I won't ask you to. One of the many things I love about positive training is that it can happen any time, all the time. You don't need to get your dog "dressed" in special training equipment—she's ready whenever you are.

I suggest that you train in several five- to fifteen-minute sessions, for a total of thirty to forty-five minutes per day. This is easier than it sounds. Every time you interact with your dog, you have a golden training opportunity. By incorporating your practice sessions into your dog's daily routine, she learns that responding to your behavior cues earns her all the good things in life—it's not just something she does when you have a leash or a treat in your hand.

Keep in mind that *anytime* you are with your dog, one of you is training the other. Dog-human relationships are usually better if the human is the trainer more often than the dog. This means ideally that you are *always* aware of which of your dog's behaviors you are reinforcing—or not—to have the greatest impact on her future behavior, not just during formal training sessions.

Breakfast time? Hold Queenie's bowl up and have her do five puppy push-ups (see chapter 10, Core Exercise "1.5—Puppy Push-Ups"). Bingo—you just did a training session! Practice her Wait exercises a few times whenever she goes outside or comes back in. Do some "Stay" practice during TV commercials. Reinforce a polite greeting when you come home from work or from shopping. Before you know it, you will have easily exceeded your three to six sessions per day—and that's fine, too!

In any single training session, pick one or two exercises to focus on. Start with something that Queenie's good at, such as puppy push-ups, for example, to get her tuned in to you. There's nothing like success and rewards to get a dog excited about playing the training game! Then introduce something new or more challenging. At first, do enough repetitions so that your dog has an opportunity to figure out what you are asking her to do.

If your dog doesn't seem to be getting it, you may need to do more shaping by breaking the behavior down into smaller pieces and rewarding her more often for small bits of the desired goal behavior. For example, if Queenie won't lie down, you may need to *click!* and reward her at first just for looking toward the floor as you move your lure toward the ground. Keep marking and rewarding as she goes lower and lower, until she is all the way down (see chapter 10, Core Exercise "1.4—The Down"). If she quits playing the game with you, go back to the point where she was doing well and proceed more slowly, giving more clicks and rewards for smaller pieces of the goal behavior. If you sense that either or both of you are getting frustrated, it's time for a break. End the training session on a positive note by asking for a behavior that she loves to do—and only have her do it once or twice. Then take a recess.

When she has the hang of it, you can make the future practice sessions for that particular behavior shorter to prevent Queenie from getting bored. How long you train a particular behavior will depend on your dog's personality and level of training. Some dogs will quit after three or four repetitions, as if to say, "Okay, I did that already—can't we do something else now?"

Know your dog. If she gets bored after five reps, stop at three, while she is still fresh and enthusiastic. If you keep it interesting for her, you will be able to gradually build up her stamina and attention span. On the other hand, some dogs will happily repeat a behavior dozens of times because they love making the *click!* happen and earning the reward that goes with it. If you encourage this attitude, just performing the behavior itself can become the reward, because it has been so consistently associated with fun and play and other good stuff.

When Queenie starts to become *fluent* in a particular behavior—that is, when she seems to understand and perform the behavior on cue reliably in a wide variety of environments—then you no longer have to practice that behavior as often. In fact, some dogs will perform a behavior with more enthusiasm if you skip a couple of days between practice sessions.

USING YOUR TOOLS POSITIVELY

In chapter 6, I introduced the basic equipment and tools that positive trainers use. Before you get out in the field with your dog, however, I want to emphasize some of the finer points of using your equipment and tools to their best advantage.

Winning the Jackpot

Many trainers use the word *jackpot* as a cue to the dog that she has done something extra-special. This is usually a training breakthrough of some kind. For example, when Queenie *finally* lies all the way down after a challenging shaping session—or she starts to jump up as is her usual custom and, for the first time, you see her stop herself and make a conscious decision to sit instead—*click!* and give the verbal cue "Jackpot!" Say it in an excited tone of voice, followed by a handful of treat pieces delivered in rapid succession instead of just one tiny piece.

One jackpot theory is that the extra-large number of rewards makes an extra-big impression on the dog and greatly increases the likelihood of a repeat performance. Another theory is that it requires the trainer to take a breather and rewards the dog for the successful behavior by giving her a break. When your dog finally does something that has been difficult for her, it is human nature for us to say, "Wow, that was really cool—let's do it again!" If you ask her to do it again right away, she may feel punished, thinking, "Oh no, I have to do this hard thing *again?*" Giving her a jackpot and a break, however, gives her a big reward and also gives her time to process the behavior in her mind. This can have a definite training benefit.

I was convinced that a break helps our dogs process newly learned behavior early in my Peaceable Paws training career while working with a private client. The woman had just adopted Jessie, a lovely Australian Shepherd mix, from the shelter. I was doing the initial consultation. As is my customary practice, I played with Jessie while the owner filled out the questionnaire. During this time, I usually teach the dog that *click!* means "treat" and get her to offer sits for clicks. It takes about ten minutes to fill out the form and by the end of this time most dogs are usually eagerly throwing sits for me as fast as they can.

Well, dear little Jessie just wouldn't sit. She wouldn't offer a sit, and she wouldn't lure into a sit no matter what I tried. During this frustrating session, I held fast to my positive philosophies and refused to jerk or push her into a sit. Finally, just as the owner was finishing the form, Jessie sat, one time. I gave her a fast *click!* and a huge jackpot and left her to ponder the experience while I sat down with her owner to go over the questionnaire.

Normally, after I review the questionnaire, I return to the dog to show the owner how the dog already understands the clicker and the Sit. When I approached Jessie, I was prepared for another ten minutes of work to get a Sit. Not so. She got it. She sat immediately when I approached and happily offered sits as long as I kept cueing her to do so. Once again, I was reminded of the awesome power of positive training.

The Magic of the Clicker—It's All in the Timing

The secret of the clicker (or any other reward marker) is in the timing. The *click!* must happen the *instant* the dog does (or is doing) the behavior you want to reinforce. The offering of the treat is a separate step. Queenie sits. You immediately *click!* and pause—*then* move the treat forward and offer it to her. Novice clicker trainers tend to want to *click!* and treat at the same time, or even start to offer the treat before they click. When this happens, the dog is more interested in the approaching treat and doesn't hear or think about the *click!*

Have someone watch you while you train or, better yet, have that person videotape you so that you can watch yourself in action. If there is a distinct pause between the sound of the clicker and the offering of the treat, you've got it. If Queenie is already getting up before you *click!*, or the *click!* and the treat are happening together (or if you are clicking *before* fur meets floor), then you need to work on your timing.

The No-Reward Marker

Also called a *conditioned punisher*, the no-reward marker (NRM) tells Queenie that she has not earned a reward for the behavior offered. Some positive trainers use the NRM, others do not. It is perfectly possible to train without one, but many owners and trainers are more comfortable having some audible tool for marking a dog's behavior mistake.

The danger in using an NRM is that an owner steeped in the force-based tradition of training can easily overuse it and have it end up being a punisher, meaning "Bad dog!" rather than just giving an upbeat "Oops!," which means "You made a mistake, but let's try again." I do use NRMs, although very sparingly. I may use one when teaching the Stay cue to let a dog who is starting to move know that she is about to make a mistake. Then I quickly *click!* and reward when she settles back into place and stays for a second or two.

The NRM should be a lighthearted cue, and it should not be uttered in an angry voice. I prefer the verbal "Oops!" because it is hard to say in an angry or intimidating tone. Other trainers use "Too Bad!" or a medium-pitched throat-sound "Ank!" If you do choose to use an NRM, commit to keeping it positive and not intimidating.

Loose Leash—Try Saying *That* Ten Times in a Row!

Your dog's leash is an important management and training tool. It is a safety belt that keeps Queenie from either going too far away or getting into trouble. It is *not* a handle or a steering wheel. If you are training in a safe environment and Queenie is focused and staying with you, you don't even need the leash. If she is finding the environment more interesting than her trainer, however, the leash will restrict her access to environmental rewards. You can stand on the leash or tie it to your belt. This will keep you from being tempted to use it as a steering wheel by pulling Queenie into position (forcing the behavior to happen) when you should be figuring out how to get her to offer the behavior voluntarily.

If you do choose to hold the leash in your hand, it should almost always be loose (with a six-inch valley hanging down) unless you need to restrain her to prevent her access to an environmental reward such as jumping on someone, or a hazard such as running out into traffic. As soon as the restraint is no longer needed, the leash valley should reappear.

What kind of leash you choose to use isn't critical. Keep in mind that the bright designer-colored nylon leashes are hard on your hands if your dog is a puller. Avoid retractable leads for training; they are too bulky to hold along with clickers and treats, and they don't do a good job of restricting your dog's access to environmental rewards.

Most dog owners find that they are more committed to training if they have some structure in their training program. If you are this kind of trainer, you will find sample practice programs in appendix I, "Doggy Day-Planners." Feel free to copy and/or modify these practice programs to meet the needs of your own dog, increasing or decreasing the number of repetitions as her responses and learning speed dictate. Be sure to use a practice program as a guide, not as word of law. As a trainer, flexibility is an important skill for you to keep in your training kit.

Always remember that training is supposed to be fun. Find a way to end every training session on a positive note, with a behavior that your dog loves. Now, let's go do it!

Peaceable Paws client Jeanie Lewis and her pup Bear prove that Chows can be trained too! (Photo by Allen L. Lewis)

Chapter 10

The First Week—Sit Happens

CORE EXERCISES

1.1—Charging the Clicker

The *click!* of the clicker (or your verbal marker "Yes!") is the bridge, or reward marker, that allows you to communicate instantly to your dog that he has done the right thing—a rewardable behavior. You "turn on the *click!*" or "charge the clicker" to condition your dog to the reward marker as your very first exercise, because it is the equivalent of handing your dog a human/canine dictionary. When your dog knows the reward marker, he will be able to start making real sense of your very confusing human world, perhaps for the first time in his life.

This may well be the easiest exercise you ever do with your dog. I have never had a student flunk charging the clicker. Unlike most of the exercises in this book, once you've mastered charging the clicker, you will never have to practice it again. Every time you *click!* and reward for a behavior during training, you are reinforcing the connection between the *click!* and the treat. Your dog will know and love it forever.

Instructions

Have the clicker in one hand—either behind your back, wrapped in a scarf, or deep in a pocket. Some dogs are startled by the sharp sound of the clicker at first. Muffle the sound until you see how your dog reacts to it. *Click!* the clicker and pop a treat into your dog's mouth. He may look at the ground—some dogs think the *click!* is the sound of something dropping on the floor. If he doesn't appear frightened by the sound, repeat the *click!* and treat several times. Then bring the clicker out from behind your back or from your pocket or scarf and continue with clicks and treats.

Every *click!* gets a treat. You will know that your dog is "getting it" when his eyes light up at the sound of the clicker—he knows a treat is coming! This can take anywhere from a half-dozen to a couple of dozen repetitions. You won't be asking your dog to do anything to earn these clicks and treats—they are freebies. You do want to be sure, however, that he isn't doing a behavior you *don't* want to reinforce, such as jumping up. If he does jump, wait until he has all four on the floor, then *click!* and treat.

Training Tips

My dog is afraid of the clicker. If your dog is afraid of the clicker, you can do one of two things. You can use a different reward marker—a softer clicker, the click of a ballpoint pen, a mouth click, a finger snap, or a verbal marker such as "Yes!" Or you can desensitize your dog to the clicker by muffling the sound, either by wrapping it in soft cloth or by putting short strips of adhesive tape over the dot on the underside of the clicker box. The more strips you put on, the more the sound will be muffled. Keep putting strips on until you find the level of sound that doesn't frighten him, and work with it at this level until he decides that the clicker is wonderful.

Then, very gradually over a period of several weeks, remove one strip at a time until the clicker is working at full sound. If at anytime your dog appears frightened again, you have removed strips too quickly. Replace several strips and keep working. The muffled clicker works well with many dogs, but not all. If yours finds even the muffled clicker to be aversive rather than rewarding, switch to a different marker *before* he makes a negative association with the whole training game.

My dog isn't interested in eating the treats. You may need to use better treats or work in a location with fewer distractions. If you free-feed your dog (keep food in his bowl all the time), try feeding him regular meals instead. Then be sure to schedule his training sessions prior to mealtime—not after.

My dog is too interested in the treats—my fingers are bleeding. With some young puppies, you can yelp, saying "Ouch!" or "Yipe!" in a high-pitched voice. Then go away for a minute or two. This mimics what a puppy's litter-mates would do if he bit them too hard in play. Be sure to leave your puppy in a puppy-proofed place.

If that doesn't work, or if you are dealing with an older dog, you can toss the treats on the floor or spit them from your mouth, instead of feeding them from your hand. Or feed the dog like you would feed a horse, from the palm of your hand instead of from your fingers. Still another alternative is to use a food tube, available from camping supply outlets. Find a treat that is soft enough to easily squeeze through the tube opening. Use this to deliver treats, and your dog's teeth come nowhere near your fingers! The food tube doesn't, however, teach your dog to be soft with his mouth—an important skill for him to learn.

To get your dog to be softer with his mouth, put the treats in your closed fist and let him gnaw at your hand, only opening your hand to give him the treat when his bite softens. You can gradually reward only for softer and softer bites, until he learns not to put his teeth on your hand at all. Say "Gentle" *when* his bite softens, not before. If he's really a shark, do this with gloves on and use a low-value treat until he learns to be gentle. You can also use metal finger splints to protect your fingers from your dog's shark bite. Most dogs don't much care for the feel or taste of metal in their mouths.

1.2—The Name Game

Every dog needs to know his name, and not just so he doesn't have an identity crisis. You will use your dog's name to get his attention so that you can give him a behavior cue. His name means "look at me and wait for further instructions." For now it's okay if he comes when you say his name, but his name does not mean Come. This game is another one that's impossible to fail—it's almost as easy as Charging the Clicker.

Instructions

Clicker in hand, say your dog's name *one time*. If he looks at you, *click!* and feed him a treat. If he doesn't look at you, *don't say his name again*. Make a kissy noise (a very technical dog-training tool) or some other sound to get his attention. The instant he looks, *click!* and treat.

Even if your dog is looking at you already, you can say his name, *click!* and treat. You are just associating his name with good stuff, teaching him that his name is a very good thing—when he hears it and makes eye contact with you, he gets a reward. Repeat this game a dozen times, then test his response by waiting until he looks away. Say his name. His head should *snap* back toward you for a *click!* and treat. If it doesn't, keep playing the game.

Family Play Version: When Buddy starts to get the idea, you can play this game with two or more people. Have everyone sit in a semicircle. Everyone has treats and clickers. Take turns saying Buddy's name. When he looks in response, the speaker clicks and gives Buddy a treat. Then someone else says his name, clicks when Buddy looks, and treats.

Attention without Name Version: You also want Buddy to volunteer to focus his attention on you when you are training, without you having to ask for it. To teach him this important skill, put his leash on in a low-distraction environment. Any time he looks at you, *click!* and reward. If he keeps looking at you, keep clicking and rewarding, gradually increasing the length of time between clicks. You can add a Watch Me cue when he keeps his attention focused on you for several seconds.

When he keeps his attention on you for ten seconds or more without distractions, add small distractions at first, then bigger ones as he learns to give his attention to you no matter what is happening. Remember, the goal is to get him to *offer* his attention, not for you to have to beg for it. If he is distracted, just stand and wait until he looks in your direction. (He will, eventually.) Then *click!* and treat.

Training Tips

My dog doesn't look when I say his name. Make sure he knows that you have a tasty treat (see appendix II, "Delicious Treats and Delightful Rewards"). You might need to use better treats, find a location with fewer distractions, or schedule your practice session before his meals, instead of after. Squeak a squeaky toy or make other exciting sounds after you say his name. If he is really unresponsive to *all* sounds, have his hearing tested. Hearing-impaired dogs can be clicker trained by using a light beam or vibrating collar (*not* a shock collar) as the reward marker.

1.3—Sit Happens

Sit is one of the first behaviors taught in most training classes. In compulsion-based classes you are told to jerk or push your dog into a sit. Not here, though! Sit is one of the easiest behaviors to capture.

Instructions

Dogs sit a lot, so all you need to do is hang out with Buddy, clicker in hand, and wait for him to sit. *Click!* and treat. Now back up a few steps. Buddy will probably follow you and sit again. *Click!* and treat. Repeat this several times, and before you know it, Buddy will be *throwing* sits at you (that is, he will voluntarily, deliberately, and emphatically offer the behavior in hopes of being rewarded). As soon as Buddy is offering the behavior for you reliably 80 percent of the time, you can add the verbal Sit cue—first as he does the behavior, then later in order to elicit the sit.

Training Tips

My dog won't offer a sit. Experiment with different ways to lure a sit—use different body language or move the treat in different places. Hold it to his nose and lift it just over his head. If that doesn't work, try holding it higher or lower. If he backs up, back him into a corner and try again. You may be able to shape a sit by clicking a slight bend in the hind legs as you hold the treat above his nose, gradually clicking more bend in the hocks and knees until Buddy is sitting. You might need to try a tastier treat that he's willing to work harder for. Or, instead of actively trying to get him to sit, just hang out with him and wait for him to sit. He will sit eventually, especially if you do it after a rousing game of fetch when he's a little pooped. When he does, *click!* and treat. Then invite him to get up, and wait for the next sit.

My dog jumps up as soon as he sits. As long as your timing is good so that you *click!* the instant he sits, it's okay if he gets up again right away—you aren't asking him to stay yet. If he jumps up before you *click!*, wait until he sits again. He'll start slowing down when he realizes the *click!* has to happen before he gets the treat. If you gradually wait for him to stay sitting longer and longer before you *click!*, he will start waiting to hear the *click!* before he gets up. You can also keep clicking and treating as long as he keeps sitting, so he learns that staying in the sit position is also very rewarding.

Be careful how you deliver the treat if you want your dog to keep sitting. If you get it right to his nose quickly, he's more likely to stay in the sit position. If you're slow, or bring the treat in too high, you're actually luring him to jump up for it.

1.4—The Down

Down is an exceptionally useful behavior cue for your dog to know. It can be pretty annoying for your Great Pyrenees to pant in your visitors' faces and drool on their laps. Having him pant at their calves and drool on their shoes is much more acceptable. You can accomplish this when your dog knows how to lie down on cue.

Down is also probably the most misused verbal cue. Uneducated dog owners frequently use Down to mean "Don't jump on me," "Get off the sofa," and "soft feathers on a duck," as well as "Lie down." That's fine for us humans, who understand that one word can have several meanings, but it's very confusing for dogs. Does Down mean that you want him to lie down on the bed—or get off the bed? I use Down to mean "Lie down," and I use another word, like *off*, to mean "Get off of something," such as a person, the kitchen counter, or a piece of furniture.

Instructions

You can train a Down by capturing and rewarding the behavior when your dog lies down on his own. It may be faster, however, to lure and shape it, at least at first. Have a treat in one hand and your trusty clicker in the other. Ask your dog to sit. When he does, tell him he's a very good dog, but *don't click!* and *don't give him a treat.*

If you click and reward the sit, he might think he's done and you could lose his attention. Instead, because he's still waiting for his *click!* for sitting, he's paying attention to you, which is a great opportunity for you to ask him to do something else. Put the treat in front of his nose and move it slowly toward the floor, straight down. When he follows it with his nose and lies down (the moment his elbows touch the ground) *click!*, give him the treat, and tell him he's a wonderful boy! When you know he will lie down for you as you move the food toward the floor eight out of ten times, say "Down!" in a happy voice just before he lies down.

After a dozen or so repetitions, you are ready to ask for the Down. Stand straight, arms relaxed at your sides or behind your back. Say "Down!" in a pleasant voice and wait two or three seconds. If your dog lies down, *click!* and give him a jackpot. If he doesn't, move your hand to lure him into the Down, *click!*, and treat. Before long, he will realize that the lure motion follows the

To lure your dog into a down, start with a sit, and put a tasty treat in front of his nose. (Photo by Paul Miller)

Then move the treat toward the ground, straight down
between his paws. If he doesn't go all the way down
easily, *click!* and reward him for going partway down.
(Photo by Paul Miller)

As he gets comfortable going partway down, gradually move
the treat closer and closer toward the ground, clicking
and rewarding each try until he is all the way down.
(Photo by Paul Miller)

verbal cue, and he will start to anticipate by going down on the cue instead of waiting for the lure.

Many positive trainers use a combination of shaping and luring to teach the Down. By using a minimum amount of luring, however, you put more responsibility on the dog to think the problem through and offer the Down voluntarily. You are not just teaching your dog to lie down. You are teaching him how to solve training problems!

Training Tips

My dog stands up when I move the treat toward the floor. Start again from the sit position. Move the treat more slowly, and make sure you are moving it straight down. If you move it away from him as you lower it toward the floor, he will get up to follow it. You may need to shape the Down. When he lowers his head a few inches to follow the treat, but before he gets up, *click!* so he understands that moving his front end toward the floor *with his bottom on the floor* earns a reward. Then, gradually lower the treat, a few inches at a time, clicking and treating at each new increment until he is all the way down.

If he still has trouble with it, try folding him into a Down from a stand instead of a sit by moving the treat along the floor toward and underneath him, rather than away from him.

My dog won't lie down—he keeps sitting but he just stretches his neck down. You get to practice more shaping! The good news is that at least he's headed in the right direction. Start by giving him a *click!* and treat just for stretching down. Then, very slowly move the treat forward (away from him) just above the floor. *Click!* and reward any partial success (the dog bends down, moves one paw forward, and so on) until he creeps his way into a Down. Then say, "Jackpot!" As you repeat this process, his Downs will get easier.

I've tried shaping and he *still* won't go down. Get creative. Sit on the floor with one of your knees raised just high enough for him to crawl under. Have him sit next to you. Lure him under your knee with the treat so that he has to lie down to follow it. *Click!* and treat. A low stool or coffee table can serve the same purpose. Try getting him to lie down on a bed or sofa, where you can bring the treat below the surface he's on. If all else fails, capture the behavior. He has to lie down sometime! When he does, *click!* and treat. When he realizes that this behavior gets rewarded, he will start offering it to you.

He goes down for the lure just fine, but I can't get him to do it for just the verbal cue. Make sure you aren't holding the treat up at your chest. For many dogs, that's a body language cue for Sit, and dogs are much more fluent in body language than in words. If you give your dog conflicting signals, he will probably follow the body language. By this time, you should be fading the lure, with the treat out of sight in your pocket or behind your back, unless you are actually luring the behavior.

Now, are you pausing after you say the word *down?* You need to give your dog time to process the verbal cue in his brain and then respond. If it still isn't working, use your lure but start minimizing it. Instead of moving the treat all the way to the floor, see if he'll lie down if you move it four inches above the floor. Then six inches. Then eight. Then one foot. Gradually fade the lure completely, and he'll be responding to just the verbal cue!

1.5—Puppy Push-Ups

You can start practicing this fun exercise as soon as your dog will lie down easily for you with a lure. Have several treats in one hand and your clicker in the other. When your dog lies down, *click!* and treat, and then immediately hold another treat in front of his nose. Now raise the treat slowly, so that he rises back up into a sit. *Click!* and treat. Now say "Down!" and lure him down again, if necessary. When he lies down, *click!* and treat. Say "Sit!" and when he does as you've asked, *click!* and treat. At first you will *click!* and treat every position

When your dog lies down for you easily, you can do
puppy push-ups. Start with a Sit (then *click!* and treat).
(Photo by Allen L. Lewis)

Then lure him into a Down (then *click!* and treat).
(Photo by Allen L. Lewis)

Then back to a Sit (then *click!* and treat). When he's good at
doing Sits and Downs on just a verbal cue, you can eliminate
the luring and do puppy push-ups on verbal cues alone.
(Photo by Allen L. Lewis)

change. When your dog is doing it smoothly, you can start asking for two or three position changes in between clicks, then more. Vary it, so that he never knows how many he has to do to earn a *click!* When he is doing his Sits and Downs well on verbal cue, try puppy push-ups with just the words (Sit, Down, Sit, Down, Sit, Down . . .), without the lure.

Training Tips

After my dog lies down, I can't get him back up into a Sit. Aren't you lucky to have such a mellow dog? Some people would love to trade! Try luring with a tastier treat. If that doesn't work, get excited to encourage your dog to get up. Talk in a high, squeaky voice. Jump up and down. Clap your hands. Back up a step if your dog is facing you, or move forward a step if he is at your side. As soon as he starts to get up in response, *click!* before he stands up all the way, and then treat.

1.6—Stand By Me

The Stand is useful for home health checks, veterinary exams, grooming, and for showing off how handsome your dog is. It can also help prevent your pooch from sitting in a puddle on a rainy day!

Instructions

Have your dog sit in front of you. Take a couple of steps backward. If he gets up to follow you, *click!* and treat. If he doesn't, make a kissy noise or some other sound to invite him to get up. When he does, *click!* and treat. Or you can lure your dog to stand by putting a treat in front of his nose and slowly moving it away from him. To get him to stay standing longer, let him nibble at the treat in your hand instead of just giving him the whole thing. When you know that he will follow as you back up, say "Stand!" as you move. *Click!* and treat. After a half-dozen or so repetitions, give the cue first, then move. Gradually fade your body movement until your dog will stand on just the verbal cue.

Training Tips

My dog just sits there. Make yourself more exciting. Act silly. Jump up and down. Make squeaky noises. Pick up a favorite toy. Eat food. Do whatever you need to do to excite the dog into standing so that you can *click!* and treat.

BONUS GAME

1.1—Spin and Twirl

This game is fun and easy for most dogs. You can try free-shaping a Spin if you want—it's a great exercise to practice your shaping skills on. (*Click!* and reward for a head turn, then gradually *click!* and reward for greater and greater head and body turns, until your dog turns all the way around.) You can also lure it. I use *spin* when I mean "Make a counterclockwise circle," and *twirl* to mean "clockwise." You can make them mean whatever direction you want, or you can use entirely different words. Just be consistent. One of my students does musical freestyle with her Great Dane, Lucy. Kathy uses *doughnut* and *cheerio* because you can say those words without moving your lips and, ideally, in freestyle competitions, you don't want the judges to see your mouth move.

Instructions (Shaping Method)

Have your dog stand in front of you. Wait and watch. If he moves his head even a tiny bit in one direction, *click!* and treat. Now you've established the direction you are going to work on. Any time his head turns in this direction, *click!* and treat. After you capture a half-dozen to a couple of dozen head turns, you should notice that he is starting to turn his head deliberately in order to make the *click!* happen.

When you reach this point, start clicking and treating only the more obvious head turns. As you do this, your dog will start to offer more turns that are more obvious. Gradually, raise the criteria until he starts to turn his whole body in that direction. *Gradually* can mean all in one session or over several training sessions, depending on your dog. If your dog stays attentive and eager and continues working at it, keep going (just be sure to stop before he gets frustrated or bored). If your dog tends to get discouraged easily, it is better to raise the criteria over several shorter sessions. The biggest mistake that novice trainers make when shaping a behavior is raising the criteria too quickly. Make sure that your dog is confident and reliable at one level of performance before moving on to the next.

Instructions (Luring Method)

Have your dog stand in front of you. If he wants to keep sitting, back up while you ask him to spin. Have the treat in your right hand and let him see it. Lure him into a circle to your right (his left) by moving the treat at his nose level and in an arc toward his tail, then in an arc up the other side toward you to finish the circle.

Helpful Clicker Hints to Remember

1. Every *click!* means that a treat is coming. Every time. One *click!* = one treat.
2. At first, the treat needs to come immediately (a second or two) following the *click!* Later on in your training, there can be a short delay.
3. I use the term *clicker* to mean any reward marker. I encourage you to use the clicker, at least initially, to teach new behaviors because I believe it is the most effective reward marker (unless your dog is afraid of the clicker). If, however, you are using a different marker, just substitute your marker of choice every time I use the word *click!*
4. Although most dogs will alert to the sound of the clicker, remember that you are not using it to get attention or to cause a behavior to happen. You will be using it to mark a behavior, to communicate to your dog that whatever behavior he is doing (or just did) when he hears the *click!* has earned a reward.
5. As soon as you start clicking and rewarding specific behaviors, the timing of the clicker becomes critically important. Your dog will know that the behavior he is doing when he hears the *click!* is the one that gets rewarded. Hence, he will tend to repeat that behavior. If you consistently *click!* on time, your dog will learn quickly. If you consistently *click!* too early or too late, your dog will have a hard time figuring out which behavior is being rewarded and he will learn more slowly. Or worse, he may learn the wrong behavior very quickly!

When your dog completes the circle, *click!* and give him a treat. When he is doing the circle easily, start saying "Spin!"—first while he is turning, then just before. Gradually, minimize the hand motion and eventually eliminate the lure, until he spins on just the verbal cue or with a tiny motion of your hand or finger. For Twirl, do the same thing, only start with the treat in your left hand and go in the opposite direction.

Josie spins with glee in response to a hand signal
from the author. (Photo by Paul Miller)

Training Tips

My dog starts to turn but then gets confused and stops. You may need to use a combination of luring and shaping. If he turns his head 90 degrees and then stops, *click!* and reward when his head is turned about 80 degrees. Repeat this until he is confident with an 80-degree turn, then lure him a little farther. Repeat at each increased turn until he seems confident, then up the ante a little more. Your dog should soon be doing complete circles.

My dog spins one direction really easily but has a hard time spinning the other way. This is not unusual. Many dogs are left- or right-handed, just like us! Start with his easy side, and when he is good at that, work on his harder side using either the free-shaping or lure-and-shape methods previously described.

Click! Congratulations! You and your dog have completed the first week of training. You are well on your way to having a great dog and a loyal lifetime partner!

To do the spin, simply lure your dog in a circle. Some dogs
will do a full circle easily the first time. If your dog is hesitant, *click!* and reward just a quarter-turn until he is doing
that much with confidence. (Photo by Paul Miller)

Then go farther, bit by bit, clicking and rewarding
each time, until he's going all the way around in a full circle.
(Photo by Paul Miller)

Georgia dog trainer and Peaceable Paws client
Ethel Kaufman uses a target stick to get her
Golden Retriever, Sierra, to walk by her side.
(Photo by Lisa Rodier)

Chapter 11

The Second Week—On Target

CORE EXERCISES

2.1—Come

Come (also known as the *recall*) may well be the most important behavior you can teach your dog. A reliable recall allows you to give your dog the freedom of off-leash play, which gives her more opportunities to work off excess energy. A tired dog is a better-behaved dog! A dog who doesn't come when called is a nuisance to other dogs and to people, a threat to wildlife and livestock, and at a high risk for ending up at an animal shelter or, worse, being run over by a car, shot, poisoned, or stolen.

Never punish your dog for coming to you! You want your dog to think that coming to you is the best thing in the whole world. You want her to love to come running to you when you ask her to. To this end, you need to make sure that Come is always positive. No intimidation, anger, or punishment should ever be associated with the cue for Come. Say the word in an upbeat, happy tone of voice, and make sure good things always happen when the dog arrives. Think about this from the dog's point of view. If you call her to you when it's time to go home from the dog park or the beach, you actually punish her for coming to you by ending the fun. Use other strategies to invite her away from play when it's time to leave. Bounce a ball. Squeak a toy.

Run away and encourage her to chase you. If necessary, quietly walk up to where she is playing and gently take hold of her collar. Just don't use the word *come*, or she will learn to associate that all-important verbal cue with something negative, and then she may start avoiding you when you call her.

Instructions

Important Note: Do this exercise indoors at first, in a quiet location with no distractions around.

With your dog no more than a few feet from you, say, "Come!" and turn and run away. When she runs after you, *click!* and treat. If she doesn't follow you, or if she looks but doesn't move, make the kissy noise or squeak a small squeaky toy and run a few more steps, then *click!* and treat when she follows. Get excited and praise her so she gets excited too. You want her to be exuberant about coming to you. When she is running after you every time you say "Come!" and run away, you can gradually start decreasing your movement, until she is bounding to you while you stand still. The key to teaching the Come is to make yourself more interesting, exciting, and rewarding than the environment, at least until you have programmed a reliable Come response.

If your dog is more excited about play than threats, use her toys as a reward for coming. Come might earn a game of tug with her tug toy, or the opportunity to chase her ball.

You can also do a round robin version of Come: Add other family members, each in turn calling and rewarding your dog from various corners of the room, then from one room to another, until she dashes from one end of the house to the other in response to the Come cue. You will move the Come game outside in following weeks. Meanwhile, you can gradually add distractions indoors—the cat crossing the room, a bouncing ball, the refrigerator opening, a knock at the door, and so on.

Increase the distraction challenge of Come very gradually. Coming on cue in the dog park is exponentially more difficult for your dog than coming on cue in the privacy of your backyard. You may need several years of committed training in order for your dog to be reliable around *very* strong distractions. Be sure that she is always in a reasonably safe place when you let her off the leash, even if you are sure she will come when you call.

When your dog is coming eagerly on cue, start asking for the Sit when she reaches you. This reminds her that Come and Sit is better than Come and Jump Up. It also parks her when she gets to you and keeps her from dashing off again if you are trying to restrain her. Even if you're using play as a reward instead of treats, she can still sit first, then play, at least some of the time. Vary the amount of time you ask her to wait in the sit position before she gets rewarded. Remember that you want Come to be positive. If Sit is difficult for your dog, work on the Sit separately until she will do it quickly and happily, then add it to the end of the Come.

Training Tips

My dog comes when I call her at home, but not anywhere else. For now, don't let her off the leash away from home. She's not ready for that yet. Unless you are at least 80 percent sure she will come when you call her in any particular environment, don't use the Come cue there. If you have to get her to come to you, bounce a ball, make squeaky noises, run away from her . . . do something silly to get her attention and moving in your direction. *Then* say, "Come!" *Click!* the clicker when she is running toward you, and give her a treat reward when she arrives. You may need to go to her to collect her instead of calling her to you. (Don't do this if she runs away when you approach.) If it is safe—that is, if there isn't a lot of brush in the play area—you can let her drag a twenty- to thirty-foot light nylon cord from her collar while she is off-leash. Then all you need to do is approach within twenty to thirty feet of her, step on the cord, pick it up, and use it to restrain her until you can get her moving toward you. *Then* you can use your Come cue and reward her when she arrives. *Do not* use the cord to drag her in to you!

My dog has been punished for coming and runs away or plays keep-away when she hears the word *come.* Your dog has learned that *come* means "bad things happen" or that it's the cue for a game of let's play chase. Use a different word and start training the come exercise from the very beginning using the new word. Teach her a new word like *close* or *here* that means "great things happen."

2.2—On Target

Touch, or targeting, is teaching your dog to touch a target—your hand, or some other object—with her nose, on cue. Dogs love this game because it's easy for them and they get lots of rewards. The target is like a treat vending machine: They push the button, they get a treat. Cool! A lot of dogs will come to you in response to the Touch cue even when they won't respond to Come. It is also a very useful behavior that you can use later on to teach your dog to ring a bell to go outside, close doors, go bowling, play soccer, turn on the TV, do agility obstacles, and more. You can use a target to replace food as a lure. If nothing else, targeting is simply a very impressive behavior to show off to your friends.

I start the touch exercise by using my hand as the target. Dogs naturally want to sniff your hands, so it's easy to get the behavior that you want to reward. Plus, your hand is always with you, so you don't have to carry an extra piece of equipment.

Instructions

Stand in front of your dog with your clicker and treats in the same hand. Your empty hand is the target. Offer your empty palm to the dog, fingers pointed down. When she sniffs or licks your palm, *click!* and give her a treat. Remove your target hand, then offer it again. Repeat several times, clicking and treating each touch. When you know that she will touch your palm with her nose, say the word *touch* the instant before her nose touches. *Click!* and treat. Then start moving the target. If you back away from her, she will likely follow you and touch the target more emphatically. Put the target in different places at her nose level. When you know she's really confident about touching the target at nose level, try it closer to the ground, then higher, so she has to bend down or jump up to touch it.

Once she will target to your hand, you can easily teach her to target to a dowel, a pencil, a wooden spoon, or some other target object. To make a target stick, take a small dowel about three feet long and wrap a strip of electricians' tape around one end to identify the target area. Or stick a rubber pencil-topper on the end. Hold the stick vertically so the target end is near your dog's nose. If she sniffs the stick, *click!* and treat. Go ahead and *click!* even if she touches the stick but misses the designated target area at first. You can shape more precise touches later. If she is already targeting to your hand on cue, it will only take a few repetitions for her to understand that touching the stick is the same thing. As soon as she does, you can start using the verbal Touch cue for the target stick too.

If your dog is afraid of the stick, start by hiding it in your hand with just the tip sticking out. When she is comfortable touching the tip, gradually slide the stick down so the tip gets longer and longer, with many touch repetitions along the way, until she no longer feels threatened by it. When she has learned the target stick and promptly touches it on cue, you have a great tool for cueing behaviors higher, lower, or farther away than you can easily reach with your target hand.

Training Tips

My dog just stares at the hand with the treat in it. Hide your clicker or treat hand behind your back until she figures out that she has to touch the target first. If she still doesn't get it, rub a moist treat (like a piece of hot dog) on your target hand to entice her to sniff. Remember to fade the hot dog scent lure quickly so you don't become dependent on it.

I can't coordinate the clicking and treating. It does take practice! I hold the clicker between my thumb and forefinger in the same hand that holds the treats. It helps to have a clicker with a tab on it so you can hang it around your wrist, or a retractable clicker that zips itself back to the holder on a string if you let go of it. Retractable badge holders, available at office supply stores, work well for this. You can even put one on each side! Then you can drop it when you feed the treat if necessary, and pick it up again easily. You can also drop treats on the ground instead of putting them directly into your dog's mouth. If you drop a few extra from time to time, it's no big deal. It's also okay to have the treats in a bowl on a nearby shelf or table; once your dog clearly understands that the *click!* means a treat is coming, you can have a longer pause between the *click!* and the reward. If you're really having a difficult time coordinating clicker and treats, you may want to use a mouth click or a verbal "Yes!" marker instead of the clicker.

2.3—No-Jumping Zone

Dogs love to jump up. Lots of humans like dogs to jump up on them—except when the dog's paws are muddy. Jumping up is also a problem when the humans are dressed up, when the dog weighs 120 pounds and the human weighs eighty pounds or is 80 years old (or forty pounds and 4 years old), or when the human's arms are full of groceries. Unfortunately, because some people encourage dogs to jump up sometimes, those dogs may think it's okay to jump up whenever they feel like it.

Jumping up is a natural behavior for dogs. In the canine world they greet each other face-to-face, nose-to-nose. Plus, when they are cute, cuddly puppies, we often pick them up and cuddle them to our chest, so we reinforce their belief that "up" is a good place to be. When dogs grow up, they're not so cuddly anymore, however, and when they try to give us a polite doggy greeting or get to that nice "up" place, we get upset.

If you want to succeed in teaching your dog not to jump on people, the whole family has to agree not to reward her for jumping up. If Junior thinks it's cool and encourages Rambo to take a flying leap and bounce off his chest, Rambo's likely to do the same thing to your elderly Aunt Martha when she comes to visit. (You can read about the exception to this rule in chapter 12, Bonus Game "3.3—Jumpin' Jiminy.") You also need to manage the environment so that visitors and strangers don't reinforce Rambo's jumping-up behavior. This is generally easy to do with young puppies by teaching them to sit rather than jump up for attention. It is more challenging—but still possible—with an older dog who has a long history of being reinforced for jumping up. You can do several different exercises to help your dog learn not to jump on people. Some will require the presence of a helper.

In games 1 through 3, which follow, it is important that you wait for your dog to sit of her own volition—do not ask her to sit. You want a dog who chooses to sit without being asked, and the way to achieve that is to simply ignore the behavior you don't want, and reward the behavior you do want. This directive does not apply to "Jumping Game #4."

Instructions: Jumping Game #1—The On-Leash Jump with Strangers

Start with Rambo on-leash next to you. Have your helper approach and stop just out of leash range, holding a tasty treat high against his chest. Hold the leash and stand still. Now you wait. Rambo will eventually get frustrated that she can't jump on the helper, and she will sit to figure it out. The instant she sits, have your helper *click!* and pop the treat into Rambo's mouth. When she is sitting, relax the tension in the leash so she is holding the Sit herself, not being restrained by the leash. Keep repeating this exercise. It usually takes a half-dozen or fewer repetitions for Rambo to start sitting as the helper approaches. Now if she tries to leap up to get the treat when it is offered, have the helper whisk it out of reach and say "Oops!" in a cheerful voice. When she sits again, have the helper *click!* and offer the treat again. She will soon learn to sit tight in order to get the treat, instead of jump up for it.

In a variation of this exercise, *you* can *click!* and pop the treat in her mouth when she sits. If you do it this way, she will start looking at you and sitting when people approach, instead of looking at the people.

Repeat this exercise with as many different people as possible. When you are out walking and a stranger admires your dog and asks if he can pet her, toss him a treat and have him do the exercise. You will be amazed by how quickly Rambo will start sitting as he sees people approach him.

Instructions: Jumping Game #2—The On-Leash Jump with You

Okay, so you don't always have a friendly helper handy. You can still practice this exercise on your own by attaching Rambo's leash to a solid object (if she chews on her leash, use a *tether*, a four- to six-foot plastic-coated cable with snaps at both ends). Walk about ten feet away, then turn around and start walking back to your dog. As long as she is sitting, keep approaching. The instant she jumps up, stop. When she sits, move forward again. In this exercise, the reward for sitting is that you come closer.

Remember: You aren't *asking* her to sit; you want her to choose to sit without being asked. You can give Rambo a *click!* and a food treat when you reach her and she is still sitting, but you don't have to toss her one every time she sits. If you do, she's likely to jump up to get it rather than stay in the sit position. If you want to experiment with variations on this exercise, try turning your back on your dog or actually backing up a step when she gets up, and see if that gets her to sit even faster. The idea here is that not only does the reward (you) *stop* when the dog gets up, it (you) actually goes farther away! (Negative punishment, remember? The dog's behavior—getting up—makes something *good*—you!—go away.)

Instructions: Jumping Game #3—The Off-Leash Jump

You come home from work, walk in the front door, and see Rambo flying over the back of the sofa. You know an enthusiastic but brutal greeting is coming. There's no leash to restrain her. What should you do?

Turn your back on her! Watch her out of the corner of your eye and continue to turn away and step away as she tries to jump on you. Again, in a surprisingly short period of time, she will sit in frustration or puzzlement to figure out why she's not getting her ration of attention. The instant she sits, *click!*, feed her a treat, and pet her if she enjoys being petted (not all dogs do!). Yes, you have to have a treat with you when you walk in the door. I suggest keeping a jar of tasty biscuits on the front stoop. Or have cookies in your pockets all the time. If she starts to jump up again after she eats the treat, turn away and step away. Keep repeating this until she realizes that sitting gets the attention, not jumping. You want to be sure to give the *click!* marker when she is sitting.

Remember: The *click!* means "whatever behavior you are doing at the instant you hear this word has earned you a treat reward." Because all living things repeat behaviors that are rewarding to them, using the *click!* and reward

Your dog gets rewarded for jumping up
when you pay attention to her for doing so.
(Photo by Paul Miller)

Instead, turn your back and ignore her
until she sits. (Photo by Paul Miller)

for the Sit will increase the likelihood of your dog sitting when she greets people. If she is consistently rewarded for sitting, and ideally never rewarded for jumping up, she will quickly learn that jumping up is not a behavior worth continuing.

When you do this exercise, be sure you don't teach your dog a *behavior chain*—a series of behaviors that get connected, or "chained," together because the dog thinks the reward is dependent on the performance of *all* the behaviors, not just the last one. You can sometimes use behavior chains to your benefit. For example, a dog can learn to run an entire obstacle course for a reward at the very end without any direction from the owner, because the obstacles have been chained in a particular order. In the case of jumping up, if you're not careful, Rambo might learn the short behavior chain of jump up, sit, reward. The way to avoid this is to look for and frequently reward the times when Rambo sits *without* jumping up first. People have a tendency to ignore their dogs when they are being good, and pay attention to them when they are doing inappropriate behaviors. If you remember to look for opportunities to reward the good behavior of sitting, your dog won't think she has to jump up to get your attention first in order to get a reward for sitting.

Then give her the attention she wants (and a treat, too).
(Photo by Paul Miller)

Instructions: Jumping Game #4—Asking for an Incompatible Behavior

This game works if your dog responds really well to the verbal cue for Sit or Down. When your dog approaches you, say "Sit!" or "Down!" before she has a chance to jump up, and reward that behavior with a "Yes!" and a treat. With enough repetitions, she will learn that sitting or lying down gets rewarded, and she may start to offer them voluntarily.

Caution: This approach works only if your dog is immediately responsive to the cue for Sit or Down and does it the instant you ask. If you have to repeat the cue several times with Rambo jumping up on you all the while, you are paying attention to her (rewarding her) for jumping on you, thereby rewarding that behavior and teaching her to ignore your verbal cues Sit or Down at the same time. Oops!

2.4—Let's Walk

Walking politely on a leash is probably one of the most challenging behaviors we ask our dogs to learn. Dogs pull on the leash because we are slow and boring and because pulling seems to get them where they want to go. Dogs want to run around, sniff, chase things, eat things, and experience the endless variety of scents, sights, and sounds the environment has to offer. We plod along on the boring side-walk expecting them to plod quietly at our sides and ignore all the temptations around them. When you tolerate pulling, your dog learns that pulling gets her where she wants to go. In other words, pulling is rewarded! Remember the first part of the Concept 1 section of "Pat's Positive Training Principles." By the time most dogs get to a training class, pulling has been rewarded so much that it has become a deeply ingrained habit. The sooner you stop rewarding your dog for pulling, the easier it will be to teach her loose-leash walking.

Your dog does not, however, have to walk at your left side with her shoulder even with your leg, in the heel position. If you plan to show your dog in obedience competition, she'll have to learn this, but otherwise you can teach her to walk on your right side, or even in front of you, as long as she's not dragging you down the street. (If you want to get fancy, you can teach your dog different cues for walking in different positions. For now, just work on teaching her to walk without pulling.)

This 4-H member has taught her Sheltie to walk beautifully on a loose leash. (Photo by Angie Ford)

Management Tool: Tether/Time-out

While you are consistently teaching your dog that she only gets rewards and attention for *not* jumping up, you need to manage her behavior so she doesn't have the opportunity to jump on people who might inadvertently reward her because they don't know any better. Although you will want to prep as many people as possible *before* they arrive so they know how to ignore your dog's jumping up, you will undoubtedly have some unexpected visitors who have not been prepped. When that happens, or if Rambo insists on jumping on visitors despite their best efforts to ignore her, you can use a tether to manage her behavior. This strategy also works for those times when you want to be able to enjoy your visitors' company without having to deal with Rambo's rambunctious behavior.

You can secure one end of the tether around a heavy piece of furniture, or attach it to a strategically placed eye-bolt. Only use a leash as a tether if you know your dog won't chew on it—and watch her while she's tethered so she doesn't *learn* to chew on it.

For a while, you will need to think of walks with Wilma as training games rather than exercise or destination outings. Keep the sessions short at first, so you don't relent and let her pull just so you can get to the dog park. Until she is good at walking politely, drive her to her off-leash play areas or other destinations, practice polite walking between the car and the play yard or pet supply store, and let her get her exercise romping with her dog friends there. Meanwhile, if you need to take her for leash-walks so that she can relieve herself or work off excess energy before a training session, you might consider using a head halter so she doesn't keep getting reinforced for pulling.

Remember that excess energy is a primary cause of many unwanted dog behaviors. Practice leash-walking *after* Wilma has had a good hard play session in the backyard to take the edge off. If she is bursting with energy and excitement, she'll have a difficult time walking calmly with you.

Put a comfortable rug or bed and some chew toys at the tether locations. When Rambo is out-of-control and jumping on the company (or you!), she gets a cheerful, "Too bad, Rambo, time-out," and a few minutes on her tether. If you know in advance that she's going to maul Aunt Martha the instant she walks in the door, clip your dog to the tether *before* you open the door, and release her after she settles down. Ignore barking or whining; only release her when she is calm and quiet, so she doesn't learn that fussing gets her released.

The release part is important—dogs learn through repetition. If you just tether your dog and don't release her when she settles, she won't get the chance to learn that calm behavior wins freedom and out-of-control behavior wins another time-out. If you release her and she revs up again, you can always do another "Too bad, Rambo, time-out!" Remember, despite your frustration over her behavior, this is a cheerful interlude, not a forceful punishment. She will learn to control her own behavior in order to avoid time-outs, and you won't need to yell at her.

Note: The tether is intended to be a training tool and is not to be used for long-term restraint. You should be present whenever your dog is tethered.

Instructions

You can lay a good foundation for on-leash walking by starting without the leash. In a quiet place with few distractions, hang out with your dog. Walk around a bit. Every time your dog is walking near you, *click!* and treat. She will eventually decide that being near you is a great place to be! Then you can start using a verbal Let's Walk cue to let her know what the behavior is called. Gradually increase the distractions as you do this, until you decide you are ready to try it out in the real world.

Lots of unruly leash behavior starts before you even attach your dog's leash to her collar. You ask her if she wants to go for a walk, and she does doughnuts in the hallway. You pick up her leash, and she's springing off all four feet to look you in the eye. Putting the leash on is a struggle as she dances around you with glee.

Stop right there. As exciting as it is to go for a walk, Wilma needs to get control of herself. If she is doing doughnuts and paw springs, set your leash down on the hallway table and turn your back on her. If you've been doing your jumping-up exercises, she will understand this cue for Sit. As soon as she sits, pick up her leash. If she gets up, set her leash down again. (You can use a verbal Oops or Too Bad cue here to let her know she won't be getting a reward for *that* behavior. If you do use a no-reward marker, it should be in a lighthearted tone of voice. It is meant to give your dog information, not to intimidate.) Each time she sits, you pick up the leash. Each time she gets up, you set it down again. This is negative punishment—Wilma's behavior, getting up, makes a good thing go away (it stops the walk routine). Positive reinforcement (Wilma's behavior, sitting,) makes a good thing happen—it starts the walk routine again. In short order, Wilma will stay sitting when you pick up the leash. By the way, you don't need to *click!* and treat for calm sitting because you are giving her a *life reward*—a real-life reinforcement that, at this moment, is probably even better than a treat reward (in this case, the opportunity to go for a walk).

You can also take the thrill out of picking up the leash by doing it many times a day when you're *not* going for a walk with your dog. Pick up the leash and sit down to watch television. Pick it up and go to the bathroom. Pick it up and start cooking dinner. Right now, picking up the leash *always* means a walk. If more often than not it doesn't, your dog will calm down about it.

When she is sitting quietly, start to attach the leash to her collar. The same deal applies: If she gets revved up again, put the leash down. As soon as she settles, try again. Repeat until she sits quietly while you clip the leash to her collar. Now you can start your walk.

You will need a megasupply of treats and your clicker. This is a very treat-intensive exercise, at least at first. You don't want to run out of goodies a block from home. Open the door, say "Let's Walk!" and step outside. If your dog hits the end of her leash, stop. Don't jerk, just stand still and wait. Sooner or later she will look back at you as if to say, "Well, are we going or not?" The instant she looks back at you, *click!* and treat. Hold the treat in front of you or at your side so she has to come back to you to get it. Now that the leash is loose, take a step, say "Let's Walk!" and quickly *click!* before she has a chance to hit the end again. She should be alert to the sound of the *click!* and come back to you for her treat. If she has already reached the end of the leash, stop and wait again for her to look at you and put a little slack in the tight lead. *Click!* and treat again. Look for lots of opportunities to *click!* and reward before the leash tightens so she realizes that the object is to keep the leash loose, not tighten and then loosen it.

You can also do a lot of directional changes to keep your dog from getting bored with you. This also gives you more chances to *click!* and treat for a loose leash. If your dog is starting to get ahead of you, turn around and go the other way. Bingo! Now she is behind you and, as she turns to hurry and catch up, you have lots of clickable moments.

Caution: The intent here is *not* to jerk your dog off her feet when you go the other way. If she keeps going the wrong way, just restrain with gentle pressure until she realizes you've changed direction, then *click!* and treat when she turns to come with you.

The other important part of teaching your dog to walk on a loose leash is not allowing her to get rewarded by the environment for her pulling. This means you need to be one thought ahead of your dog. Does she always want to sniff the juniper patch at the corner? If she pulls as you approach the bushes, stand still and gently restrain her until she gives you slack in the lead. Then *click!*, treat, and point to the junipers. Tell her "Go Sniff!" and give her enough leash that she can reach the bush without pulling. In the future, keep her attention focused on you as you approach her favorite spots, ask her to sit next to you before she pulls, and then release her with the verbal cue Go Sniff.

The same rule applies if your dog tries to stop and sniff behind you. Keep moving forward, putting gentle pressure on the leash and using a cheerful voice to encourage her to move with you. As soon as she starts moving forward, *click!* and treat, and continue clicking and treating as she walks with you.

You can also use your target hand or target stick to help your dog understand that you want her to walk with you. Start with her at your side, preferably sitting. Place your target in front of her and say "Touch!" as you start to walk. After she has followed the target for several steps, let her touch it, then *click!* and treat. If you keep your target positioned next to you, she will have to stay near you to touch it. When she is walking well to the target, you will need to fade your use of it so she will eventually walk politely without it. Because your target hand is always with you, you can always use it in a pinch if she is distracted and needs a reminder of where you would like her to be.

Training Tips

My dog is too strong—I can't gently restrain her when she pulls. She drags me! You might benefit from trying one of the several brands of front-clip no-pull harnesses that are made and marketed especially for dogs. While most walking harnesses make it easier for the dog to pull, the front-clip models, by attaching at the dog's chest, turn her back toward you when she tries to pull. Be sure to *click!* and treat when she's no longer pulling! The most common front-clip model is the Easy Walk Harness, available at many pet supply stores. Other brands include the Sense-ation and Sense-ible harnesses, and the K9 Freedom Harness. A good safety measure is to attach your leash clip to the collar as well as the harness, in case your dog manages to step out of the harness.

My dog does the opposite—she doesn't want to come with me and pulls back on the leash! She may be fearful, in which case you need to build her confidence. Just stand and wait until she relaxes and moves toward you, even if it's just a lean forward. *Click!* and reward. You can coax her by offering treats—just be sure she actually moves forward for the treat. Work fairly quickly to get her going several steps, then wait for longer stretches in between clicks. Be sure to *click!* when she is moving, not when she stops. You don't want to teach her that she gets rewarded for stopping! If she is stopping to sniff or to eat something, then you need to keep going, putting gentle pressure on the leash, to prevent her from getting rewarded for stopping. As soon as she is moving forward again willingly, *click!* and treat.

My dog doesn't pay any attention to me or the clicker when we are walking. Your dog is overstimulated by the environment—she is either too distracted by all the great stuff, or else she is fearful and too stressed to think about eating treats. Try getting her attention focused back on you by doing simple exercises such as Puppy Push-Ups (see chapter 10, Core Exercise "1.5—Puppy Push-Ups") or Targeting (see this chapter, Core Exercise "2.2—On Target"), and then walk a few steps. If that doesn't work, you need to do four things:

1. Increase the value of the treat. Find something your dog would give her eyeteeth for, and save that treat *only* for walking on-leash in distracting environments.

2. Go back to working on "Let's Walk!" in a very quiet environment, and gradually add distractions until she is able to keep her attention focused on the exercise.

3. Be sure to walk her before meals, when she has a little edge to her appetite, not immediately after, when she is full.

4. Go to places where you can just sit on a bench and keep dropping treats. Sit for half an hour to an hour at a time, every day if possible (take a book along to read), and just keep feeding. Your dog needs to get out more so the excitement of "out" is less of a novelty. You want her to get a little bored. Take a rug or cushion along for her, so she has a place to lie down and settle when she decides that the world isn't that thrilling after all. Then you're ready to start playing her leash-walking game in public.

BONUS GAMES

2.1—Shake, Pardner

Instructions

You can teach your dog to "shake paw" in several different ways. Some dogs are naturally pawers. If your dog fits into this category, you can simply capture the behavior: *Click!* and treat your dog when she lifts her paw. When you see her deliberately offering her paw in order to win the reward, add the verbal cue Shake, then *click!* and treat. Hold out your own hand, palm up, as the signal for shake. When you have repeated the verbal cue often enough that you think she has made the association, try asking for the behavior with the word. Give her a couple of seconds, and if she doesn't offer her paw, offer your own hand to elicit the paw offer.

If your dog is not a natural shaker, you can shape the behavior by clicking and rewarding any tiny lift of the paw off the ground. When she is regularly lifting a paw slightly, start clicking only the more noticeable lifts. Gradually raise the criteria until she lifts a paw high enough for it to be considered a shake. Then add the verbal cue.

You may want to lure the lift. Your dog may paw at your hand if you hold a treat in front of her in your closed fist. *Click!* and treat! Other dogs need still more help. Try holding a treat just over your dog's head, then move it off to one side. Many dogs will lift a paw as they lean to follow the movement of the treat. *Click!* and reward.

If capturing, shaping, and luring don't work for you, try molding. Touch the back of your dog's leg. If she lifts, *click!* and treat. If a touch doesn't work, you can actually lift the paw, *click!*, and reward. Just remember that molding may teach your dog to wait for you to touch her before she will shake. The other methods are preferred because they encourage her to think for herself, which is ideally what you want.

2.2—Lefty/Righty

Instructions

This game is a variation of shake. When you teach your dog to shake her first paw, use the verbal cue Left (or Right) rather than Shake. Consistently work with that one paw until she gets it. Then work with her other paw, offering your other hand as the signal, and using the Right (or Left) cue. If she offers the left paw for the Right cue, just move your hand away, wait a few seconds, and ask again. She will soon learn to discriminate between the cues for left and right.

2.3—High-Five

Instructions

High-five is another easy variation of shake. For this one, instead of offering your hand with the palm facing up, do it with your palm facing your dog, fingers pointed toward the ceiling. At first, *click!* and reward any touching of her paw to your palm. You can switch immediately to the High-Five verbal cue as soon as she is lifting her paw for the new hand signal. When she is doing that easily, then start shaping for a more emphatic paw-to-palm slap by gradually rewarding increasingly vigorous responses.

2.4—Doin' the Wave

Instructions

Wave is yet another variation on shake. Your hand signal for this will be to present your hand, palm facing down, combined with a little wave of your fingers. Again, you can start with the verbal cue Shake, but switch to "Wave!" or "Bye-Bye!" as soon as your dog is responding to the hand signal by lifting her paw. Then shape the wave by waiting when she lifts her paw. At some point,

Long Beach trainer and APDT member
Terry Long's mixed-breed dog Buster
does an awesome wave.
(Photo by Terry Long)

she should get impatient or frustrated that you haven't clicked, and she will jerk her paw or lift it higher. *Click!* that motion and reward it. Repeat this until she easily and reliably waves once each time you ask. Then hold out for two waves, then more, until she waves several times for one cue.

Remember: When you are talking about shaping, you may shape a full behavior in one session, or your dog may need several sessions to reach the final behavior goal. Be patient and look for reward opportunities.

Tucker, the author's Cattle Dog mix, ignores a pile of tempting treats in the off exercise. (Photo by Paul Miller)

Chapter 12

The Third Week— Take It to the Limit

CORE EXERCISES

3.1—Wait

Wait means "Pause for a moment or two—don't follow me." It can literally be a lifesaver. I teach my dogs to wait every time I open the door to the outside, so that they don't think they can charge out whenever the door opens. I also use it in the car, so that an open car door is not an invitation to dash out onto the highway. In fact, I am so accustomed to having dogs in the van and reminding them to wait that I say the word even when there aren't any dogs in my van, just from habit. (Of course, crating or seat-belting your dog in your vehicle is even safer.)

Wait is also a frequent reminder to your dog to defer to you. Going through the door first is not so much about social status as it is about good manners. Because Wilbur probably goes in and out several times a day, this offers you lots of training opportunity moments to remind him that if he does what you ask (wait), good things happen (he gets to go in or out). When your dog knows the word *wait*, you can also use it to pause him if he is about to take off after the neighbor's cat or is just ranging a little too far ahead of you on an off-leash hike. Throughout the training thus far, you've been helping your dog learn to control his own behavior in order to make good things happen. The wait exercise builds on that foundation.

Instructions

Without the leash, invite Wilbur to a door that opens into a fenced yard or enclosed garage. Wait for him to sit, using sit body language, your hand at your chest, if necessary. If you must use a verbal cue, do so, but keep in mind that the goal is to get him to offer the Sit at the door without being asked. When he sits, say "Wait!" (You can also put your hand in front of his nose, palm facing him, as a hand signal to wait.) Reach for the doorknob. Before your hand touches the knob, straighten back up, *click!* him for not moving, and give a treat. If he moves before you *click!*, say "Oops!" and wait for him to sit again. Now reach only halfway to the door, or less if necessary, so you can *click!* and reward before he moves. Gradually increase your movement toward the doorknob until you can touch it, *click!* and give a treat without Wilbur getting up. Now repeat the cue Wait and jiggle the doorknob. *Click!* and treat. Open the door a crack, then close it. *Click!* and treat. Open it wider, then close it. *Click!* and treat. In gradual increments, open the door wider and wider, clicking and treating several times at each increment. If, at any time, he gets up, use your "Oops!" no-reward marker, have him sit again, and work with the door at that opening or less until he is steady, then open it wider. Then take a step through the doorway. *Click!* and treat. Step farther through the door with each increment, until you can walk through, turn, face him, and close the door. *Click!* and jackpot! (Don't forget that you have to open the door to give him his jackpot.)

Of course, letting Wilbur go out the door after a Wait is a life reward. Frequently when you practice this exercise, invite him through the door after he has waited, and play with him in the yard as his reward. Or take him for a walk or a ride in the car. If he knows that good things often happen when he waits, he will be eager to offer the wait behavior in hopes of winning an extra-special life reward.

When he is doing the Wait for you reliably at a safe door, you can try it at the front door, in the car, or even while you are out walking. When you try it at a door that leads to the real world, have Wilbur's leash on as an extra precaution in case he decides that the neighbor's kid clattering by on a skateboard is too tempting. Each time you change your location, you will need to back up several steps in the training process so he does it right.

You can also teach Wait using Wilbur's food bowl. At meal time, have him sit by you while you hold up his food bowl. Say "Wait!" and lower the bowl a few inches. If he stays sitting, *click!* raise the bowl back up, and feed him a treat from the bowl. If he gets up, say "Oops!" and raise the bowl back up without a click and treat. Repeat until he realizes he's not supposed to get up when you lower the bowl, then continue to repeat, gradually moving the bowl lower and lower until you can set it on the floor without him getting up. Do some repetitions with the bowl sitting on the floor, and finally give him permission to eat. Since you feed your dog at least once, probably twice, a day, this gives you two perfect built-in training opportunities!

Remember: The goal is to get your dog to succeed so you can reward him, not to challenge him into making a mistake. If he does make a mistake, or several in a row, it means that you, the trainer, have moved forward too fast. Back up, slow down, and help him win.

Training Tips

I'm doing the Wait off-leash, and my dog keeps wandering away. You aren't interesting enough to compete with the environment. Either make yourself more interesting with tastier and/or more frequent treats and a more exciting voice and body language, or make the environment less distracting by putting the cat in the other room, sending your kids outside to play, picking food scraps off the floor, and putting the dog toys away. If necessary, you can put a leash on your dog and use gentle restraint to keep him from wandering—but no tugs on his collar to try to force him to pay attention. When he is doing it well with the leash on, you can practice again without the leash.

3.2—Take It!

Take It is the beginning of teaching your dog to retrieve, and it's almost as easy as charging the clicker. It means "Take something into your mouth, either from my hand or from the ground." Your dog is already doing take it every time he picks something up in his mouth. You have endless opportunities to capture, mark, and reward the behavior without ever having to use force.

Instructions

Start with those ever-present tasty treats. Offer a treat from your hand and say "Take It!" (In this case, you can go ahead and use the verbal cue right away because you're 99 percent sure your dog is going to take the treat when you offer it.) As his mouth closes on the treat, *click!* the clicker. Repeat several times, holding the treat in different places so your dog has to work to get it—behind you, off to the side, between your legs. Get creative! Move it away as you say "Take It!" so he has to follow it. Make him work for it. *Click!* and give him the treat each time he responds to the Take It cue by reaching for the goodie.

Now pick up his favorite toy. Shake it, squeak it, tease him with it a little, get excited, and get him excited. When you can see that he really wants his toy, hold it out and say "Take It!" When he grabs it, *click!* and give him a treat. He will probably drop the toy when you *click!* in order to eat his treat. That's okay. You're only asking him to take it at this point, not to hold it. Holding it comes later. When he is easily taking the toy from your hand, try tossing it on the floor in front of you when you say "Take It!" He should pick it up. *Click!* and treat. Gradually increase the distance that you toss the toy and before you know it he will race across the yard to take the toy that you have thrown.

Keep your Take It sessions short—you want to stop the game before your dog gets tired or bored. Vary the items that you ask him to take, starting with easy things that he loves and working up to more challenging objects. When he is readily taking things on cue, you can start delaying the *click!* a second or two at first, then longer and longer until he is holding it as well as taking it.

Training Tips

My dog takes food easily, but nothing else. Some dogs are natural retrievers and will pick up anything. Others are fussier and seem not to be very interested in toys. Often this is because their natural instincts to hold things in their mouths were stifled as puppies, when they got yelled at every time they picked something up. Some dogs, like retrievers, spaniels, and herding dogs, have been genetically selected for strong retrieving instincts. Others like the Basenji and Chow have not. Still, they all pick things up in their mouths sometimes, especially as puppies. Most dogs, even those who are not natural retrievers, can be taught to retrieve. The instant your dog picks something up on his own, capture it with a *click!* and treat to encourage the behavior (assuming it's not a forbidden object like your jogging shoe). Practice this game at a time of day when he is really full of energy and more likely to play. Try high-value foodlike items like a Kong stuffed with cream cheese or a toy that's been rubbed all over with a meat treat.

You can also shape your dog to take it. **Remember:** Take small steps toward the final behavior goal. Steps for shaping might look like this:

1. Place the Take It object on the ground or on a chair. When your dog looks at it, *click!* and reward. Every time he looks at it, *click!* and reward. If he won't look directly at it, *click!* and reward him just for looking in the general direction.

2. When he realizes he's getting clicked for looking at the object, he will probably occasionally bump it with his nose, especially if he has already learned about targeting (see chapter 11, Core Exercise "2.2—On Target"). Be sure to *click!* and treat him for this. As the nose bumps get more frequent, stop clicking for looks and only *click!* and treat for actual nose bumps.

3. As the nose bumps get more consistent, he will probably open his mouth occasionally as he makes contact. Give him a jackpot the first time this happens, and celebrate! Then try again. As open-mouth contact becomes more frequent, stop clicking for bumps and only *click!* and treat the open-mouth contacts.

4. As he does more open-mouth contacts, he will eventually bite down on the object, maybe even pick it up. Congratulations! This is a major breakthrough and another occasion for a jackpot and a celebration. At this point, you are well on your way to teaching a reliable Take It.

My dog will take it from my hand but not off the ground. Practice Take It from your hand by gradually lowering your hand until it is resting on the ground. Then hold your hand next to the object. Gradually move your hand farther and farther away from the object until your dog is taking it off the ground.

3.3—Leave It!

This exercise is one of my favorites! *Leave It* means "Whatever you are looking at, I want you to leave it alone." It's a fun game because you really get to see the light bulb go on in your dog's brain when he gets it. Plus it's an extremely useful exercise; you can use it when you set the hors d'oeuvres on the coffee table, when your toddler is waving a cracker in front of Vacuum's nose, when your four-footed carpet sweeper finds a chicken carcass in the gutter, when he's about to pounce on the sofa with mud-drenched paws, or when he's enthusiastically greeting your 93-year-old Aunt Martha at the front door.

Instructions

Stand in front of Vacuum with a solid, nonsquishable, medium- to high-value treat in your hand. (Freeze-dried liver cubes work well for this.) Hold your other hand behind your back, with your clicker and a reservoir of treats. Say "Leave It!," *one time*, place the treat under the ball of your foot. Let him sniff, lick, nibble, claw, and gnaw at your foot. **Note:** Don't wear sandals or shoes that could be easily damaged by your dog's efforts to get the treat. At the *split second* he stops sniffing, licking, and so on, or when he looks away, even if it is by accident, *click!* and give him a treat. Keep repeating until he backs up or turns his head away at the Leave It cue. Over time, increase the length of delay between the turning away and the *click!* so Vacuum learns to *stay away* from the treat for longer and longer periods. *Click!* and treat *several* times when he's looking away from your foot so he learns that he gets rewarded for *staying away* from the forbidden object, not just for moving away from it, and not for repeatedly looking at it and looking away.

When he's leaving your foot alone for at least several seconds at a time, pivot your foot so the treat's uncovered but so you can easily cover it with your foot again if necessary. If Vacuum dives for the exposed treat on the floor, just cover it again with your foot to prevent him from getting it. *Do not say "No!"*

or give him any other correction. Just hide the food by moving your foot over it, and wait. *Click!* and reward when he looks away. Keep repeating this step until you can leave the treat uncovered and he doesn't try to eat it. Now continue to practice placing the treat on the floor after your Leave It cue until you don't have to cover it with your foot at all.

Remember: Each time you change the rules, you need to lower the criteria, thus making it easier for your dog to succeed. Dogs pretty much think anything that falls on the floor belongs to them, so they try to get the forbidden object when you put it on the ground. Always keep your foot close enough to cover the food on the floor until you are sure Vacuum is reliable. When you start actually moving away from the treat, be prepared to block it with your body if he dives for it. If you've ever watched one dog guarding a bone that another one covets, you'll recognize that this exercise very much mimics the way a dog hovers over the possession, guarding a valuable resource, sending very clear ownership messages.

How quickly you move through these three steps of the Leave It game depends on you and your dog. If the trainer's timing is good, some dogs can accomplish all three steps in one fifteen- to twenty-minute session. Ironically, the more your dog likes food, the quicker he will learn leave it. Dogs who are very food motivated figure out quickly that the fastest way to get the reward is to ignore the forbidden treat offered so temptingly on the floor. Louie, a Border Collie client of mine in Santa Cruz, learned Leave It in just three repetitions. Of course, Border Collies are known for being fast learners, and Louie was very food motivated.

Training Tips

My dog won't stop sniffing and licking. Be patient. Be sure to look for, *click!*, and reward even very brief lapses of attention. They will eventually happen.

My dog licks the treat under the edge of the shoe. Tip your foot to block him from being able to reach the treat with his tongue. As long as he can lick it, he's being reinforced, and he won't learn the Leave It behavior.

BONUS GAMES

3.1—Ring My Bell

This game expands on the touch behavior (see chapter 11, Core Exercise "2.2—On Target"). Now that your dog knows how to target, you can start asking him to touch a variety of different objects. You can teach him to roll a ball, close a door, turn on a TV, or ring a bell on a string by the door to let you know he has to go out.

Instructions

Find a bell that you can attach to a string. Hold the bell in the palm of your hand and ask Chimes to "Touch!" He will try to touch your palm as you taught him in week 1, but the bell is in the way, so he will touch it instead. After several repetitions, start using the verbal cue Ring It. Remember to *click!* and treat each successful touch. Now hold the bell by the top and say "Ring It!" Hold it in such a way that Chimes will touch the bell even if he is still aiming for your hand. Gradually move your hand farther and farther up the string until you are holding the end of the string and he is touching the bell dangling at the bottom. Now start moving the bell around—out to your side, up in the air, next to the TV, next to the back door, and so on.

Gabriel rings the bell to go outside.
(Photo by Virginia Broitman)

Don't worry at this point if Chimes isn't touching hard enough to ring the bell. When he is promptly touching the bell in response to your verbal cue, you can shape him to touch it harder by only clicking the more emphatic touches. You can still praise him for softer touches, but he only earns a *click!* and reward for increasingly harder touches until he is ringing the bell every time.

Now put a hook by the door and hang the bell on it. Every time you want to take Chimes out for a bathroom break, get him a little revved up, ask him if he wants to go out, and then tell him "Ring It!" When he does, substitute a life reward for the *click!* and treat by opening the door and taking him out to his bathroom spot. After he does his business, give him a *click!* and treat, play for a few moments, and take him back inside. Over time, stand farther and farther away from the bell when you give him the Ring It cue. At some point he will try ringing the bell on his own to get you to take him out. Be sure to listen for this moment and respond when he does. If you want him to ring the bell only for bathroom breaks, make sure you go out with him to his bathroom spot each time at first, and reward him for eliminating. If you want him to ring the bell anytime he wants to go out, you can let him out into a safely fenced yard without going with him.

3.2—Sitting Pretty

This behavior is also often called Sit Up or Beg. I don't happen to like the negative connotation of begging, so I call it Sit Up. You, of course, can call it anything you want!

Note: Dogs with bad backs or hips should not be asked to do this behavior.

Instructions

Start with your dog sitting facing you. Hold a treat over his nose so he has to stretch his head up to sniff it. Some dogs will lift themselves into a Sit Up the very first time. *Click!* and reward. Some dogs are not as well balanced, and you will need to shape the Sit Up gradually by clicking slight attempts to lift the front paws off the ground. When the paws are coming off the ground with each attempt, then *click!* and reward only the higher paw lifts until your dog is doing a complete Sit Up. Then add the verbal clue.

Remember: In order to get the behavior on a verbal cue, say the cue just before you lure your dog into the Sit Up, wait a few seconds, and then lure. Gradually fade the lure until he'll sit up for just the verbal cue. In order to get the Sit Up on an unobtrusive hand signal, such as the movement of your index finger, gradually minimize the lure motion until it becomes the finger cue.

4-H photographer Angie Ford's
sister teaches her Sheltie to sit pretty.
(Photo by Angie Ford)

3.3—Jumpin' Jiminy

I recommend this game only when someone in the family really likes having Jiminy jump on them. You can teach Jiminy to jump up on a particular cue such as the word *hugs* (*not* patting your chest, because too many well-meaning strangers and children will invite the behavior without realizing it), and teach him that the *only* time he can jump on someone is when he is given the cue. This means that he only gets rewarded when he has been invited to jump up, and never gets rewarded for jumping on a person without an invitation.

Instructions

Decide on a cue for the Jump Up that is not likely to be offered accidentally by friends, guests, or strangers. My terrier mix, Josie, would put her paws on my shoulders only when I got on my knees, patted my shoulders, and said "Hugs!" Not many of my acquaintances did this to her in normal conversation! Because you have spent a considerable amount of time rewarding Jiminy for *not* jumping, it may take some coaxing to get him to offer the behavior now that you want it—or it may not. If Jiminy immediately jumps up on you when you invite him, you're home free . . . almost. *Click!* and reward. Then decide if you want to be more specific about how he jumps. If his paw smacked you in the face, you might want to shape his behavior so that his paws land on your shoulders.

If Jiminy doesn't jump up when you invite him, you will need to convince him that jumping up *on invitation* is now an acceptable behavior. Get more excited when you ask him up, and shape the jump up in small increments by clicking and rewarding for small paw lifts, like you just did for the Sit Up, until he is putting his paws on you in the manner that you want.

Note: Now that you have taught Jiminy that it is okay to jump up sometimes, you have to be very careful not to reward him for jumping up without an invitation or you will undo all the hard work that went into teaching him not to jump up. I don't recommend teaching this behavior if you have family members who have difficulty with consistency.

Peaceable Paws client Golden Retriever Cayenne,
owned by Tom and Cynthia Hanson, goes to his spot
on cue. (Photo by Tom Hanson)

Chapter 13

The Fourth Week—Everyone Needs Her Own Spot

CORE EXERCISES

4.1—Go to Your Spot

Every dog needs her own spot—a place you can send her to when you need a break from her undying devotion, or when she's begging at the dinner table. You can have just one spot, you can have several that all work with the same verbal cue, or you can have a different cue for each location. "Place!" could mean the mat in the corner of the dining room, "There!" is the one in the kitchen, and "Settle!" means the one next to the television in the living room. Spot's "place" mat is portable. You can take it with you to the beach to keep Spot from sharing the picnic blanket with her sandy paws, or bring it with you when you have breakfast at your favorite outdoor cafe and have Spot settle quietly at your feet. Because her mat is familiar to her, a little piece of home that she can take with her anywhere she goes, it will help her feel comfortable in strange places.

One Peaceable Paws client was concerned because her spaniel mix, Bess, had a tendency to greet people rather exuberantly at the door. We used this exercise to teach Bess that the doorbell was the cue to go lie down on her rug in the front hall, where she learned to wait politely until company entered and came over to greet and reward her.

Instructions (Shaping Method)

My preference is to train the go-to-your-spot behavior as a shaping exercise. It lends itself beautifully to shaping—and I recognize that not all dog owners are as nuts about shaping as I am, so if this doesn't excite you, try the luring method described next. But if you want to fully engage your dog's brain and help her be a better problem solver, read on and try your hand (and clicker) at shaping!

When you shape, you simply set up the environment to allow your dog to do the desired behavior, then *click!* and treat for very tiny steps in the right direction until you have shaped the entire behavior. You are building it in pieces. It's a fun game; it teaches your dog to think and learn, and encourages her to figure out what you want her to do and to offer desired behaviors.

Start by having someone place a rug or mat on the floor four to six feet away from you and your dog. She can be on-leash or off-leash if she will stay with you and play the game. Watch her closely. *Click!* and treat for any behavior associated with the rug. If she looks at it when your friend places it on the floor (or any time after that), *click!* and treat. You can *click!* and treat if she even looks in the general direction of the rug. *Click!* and treat if she leans toward the rug or takes a step toward it.

When she starts moving toward the rug, *click!* and then toss the treat on the floor behind you. This will enable her to return to you—"reset" herself—after each move, so she can do it again. Watch for her movements to start becoming very deliberate—when she *knows* if she moves toward the rug she can make you *click!* This is the sign that she's starting to understand. When she is moving to the rug routinely, start shaping her to sit, then lie down on it. Then practice from all different sides of the rug, and from varying distances.

With shaping, you add the verbal cue when your dog is consistently offering the entire behavior. When your dog lies down on her rug without any prompting from you, you can add a verbal cue such as "Place!" or "Mat!" or anything that makes sense to you.

This exercise takes *patience*. You have to appreciate the value of teaching your dog how to learn. It's tempting to want to help her by moving your body or luring her, but the more you do this, the less she learns how to learn, and the more she will always rely on you to show her what to do. Try to restrict any help you give to simply looking at the rug (she'll tend to look where you're looking), and hide your treats and clicker behind your back so she doesn't just stare at them.

Instructions (Luring Method)

Select a throw rug or easily portable dog bed as Spot's mat. Stand about two feet away from the mat with Spot next to you. With a treat in your hand, point to the rug, say "Place!" or whatever cue you plan to use, lure her onto it with the treat, and ask her to give you a Sit. *Click!* and treat. You can use the verbal cue right from the start with this exercise because you are at least 80 percent sure Spot will do it for you the first time you lure her to the rug. After several repetitions, start asking for a Down instead of a Sit when she gets to the mat.

Ultimately you want *place* to mean "Go lie down on the mat." You can also frequently ask Spot to wait when she is lying on the mat so she doesn't get into the habit of jumping up as soon as she gets there. Then reward her several times for staying in place. If you reward her occasionally just for lying there, she will decide that lying on the mat is a very wonderful place to be.

You set the standard for how much of Spot's body has to actually be on the mat to qualify for a *click!* Some of my clients require every last hair to be on the mat, others accept a little spillover onto the floor, and still others are happy achieving token mat contact with a paw or a tail. I personally would accept a little spillover.

When you think Spot is starting to get the idea, say "Place!" and then wait a few seconds to see if she starts to move toward the rug. If she does, be sure to be right behind her to *click!* and jackpot when she gets there.

Gradually start moving farther and farther from her place, until you can send her to it from different corners of the room. If she needs a little extra help to really get the concept, you can sometimes *bait* the rug by putting a couple of treats on it when she's not looking so she finds a pleasant surprise when she gets there. This can greatly increase her eagerness to go to her place when you ask her to.

4.2—Relax

You've probably noticed that when your dog is really relaxed, she stretches out on her side, rests her head on the floor, closes her eyes, and goes to sleep. It's an interesting phenomenon that body language can often elicit the mental state that goes along with it. When you're happy, you smile. If you aren't particularly happy but you make an effort to smile, you may find yourself feeling happier. Try it! Similarly, if you ask your dog to lie in a position of relaxation, you can often actually help her to relax. Relax is simply getting Bounce to lie quietly on her side on cue. It's also the beginning of teaching her to play possum or roll over. (See chapter 14, Bonus Games "5.1—Playing Possum" and "5.2—Roll Over, Beethoven.")

Instructions

Ask your dog to lie down. When she does, praise her but don't *click!* or give her a treat. Observe her down position. If she is lying on one hip with her hind legs out to one side, you're ready to start Relax. If she's perfectly square, lying in the sphinx position, you need to get her to rock onto one hip first. To rock her onto one hip, let her see a treat in your hand, then move the treat in a semicircle hip curl from the tip of her nose toward a point on her spine between her shoulder and her hip. As she follows it with her nose, she should rock onto one hip. *Click!*

and treat. Now continue to move the treat over the top of her spine until she starts to roll onto her side. As she rolls, move the treat up her spine toward her head to a point on the floor just in front of her nose. (This will get her to put her head on the floor.) As soon as she is flat, say "Relax!" *click!* and treat.

To teach Relax, start with your dog in the down position, with a tasty treat in front of her nose. If she's not already rocked onto one hip, start moving the treat in an arc toward a point on her ribs between her shoulder and her hip. When she rocks onto her hip, click! and reward. (Photo by Paul Miller)

Keep moving the treat toward that point on her spine so she curls her body into the shape of a C. Click! and treat as often as necessary to keep her interested in playing the game. (Photo by Paul Miller)

Start moving the treat up toward her spine, to curl her into an even tighter C.
(Photo by Paul Miller)

When she is tightly curled, make a right-angle turn with the treat,
moving it past her shoulder and face to get her to roll onto her side.
(Photo by Paul Miller)

Then move the treat to the ground to get her to lie completely flat in the relax position. (Photo by Paul Miller)

This is also a great time to practice gently handling your dog all over so she will accept grooming and veterinary exams. Don't worry if she jumps up when you *click!*—you can work on getting her to stay there longer, later. When she is staying in the relax position for several seconds or more, you can also give her a soothing tummy rub or do some massage techniques as a life reward.

Repeat this sequence until she is luring into the relax position easily for you each time. Then start giving the verbal Relax cue first and then minimizing the lure until she relaxes onto her side for you on just the verbal cue. You can also minimize the lure into a tiny hand or finger cue. One Peaceable Paws student taught Skippy, her Jack Russell Terrier, to relax on a very slight tilt of her head.

Training Tips

My dog is very tense. She won't rock onto one hip—she turns her head a few inches and then jumps up. You will need to lure-shape this behavior. If your dog turns her head four inches and jumps up, start giving her a *click!* and treat for a three-inch head turn. When she does that easily, ask for a four-inch turn. Then five inches until she turns her head far enough to rock onto one hip. You may need to continue on from there in increments also, rather than get the Relax behavior all at once. You can also pet her calmly (long, slow strokes, not pats) and massage her when she is lying down to help her relax.

4.3—Stay Just a Little Bit Longer

Stay is very different from the wait exercise that you did in chapter 12, Core Exercise "3.1—Wait." While *wait* just means "Pause," *stay* means "Stay in the position I left you in until I *tell* you to get up." When you leave the house to go to work in the morning, you ask for a Wait as you go out the door because you don't want Stanley to follow you through the door. If you say "Stay!" technically Stanley should spend the next eight hours immobile at the door until you come home from work and tell him he can move again. Even *my* dogs would not do that, and they're pretty well trained!

Stay has three elements, or, as trainers often refer to them, the three Ds: duration, distraction, and distance. *Duration* is the length of time the dog stays; *distraction* is the reliability of the dog's Stay in the presence of distractions; and *distance* is the distance you can move away from the dog. **Note:** It is critically important to work on the length of time and distractions *before* you work on distance. If Stella won't do a reliable stay with distractions when you are standing in front of her, you can't expect her to do it when you're across the room. The most common mistake people make in teaching stay is trying to ask for too much too soon. You ask Stella for too much, she makes a mistake, and you are sorely tempted to correct her for "breaking" the Stay. Remember that you want her to succeed so you can reward her for doing the right thing. Positive training is a win-win game. You can use negative punishment here if necessary (the dog's behavior makes a good thing go away), but creating positive opportunities to *click!* and treat is better.

Instructions

Start by asking Stella to sit. Tell her she's a good dog, then hold up a treat. After one second, *click!* and feed her the treat calmly, so she doesn't jump up, then use a release word and encourage her to get up. You can praise her for getting up but don't *click!* the release because it's the Stay behavior that you're really reinforcing and rewarding. When she is staying for several seconds at a time, you can add the verbal Stay cue in a pleasant tone of voice *while she is staying*. Owners tend to want to say "Stay!" harshly, as an order. Remember that you aren't trying to intimidate Stella into staying; you're just using the word as information, a cue for a behavior.

There is an art to positioning the treat for the stay. You need to either hold it directly under your dog's nose so she can nibble on it—essentially luring the stay—or hold it far enough away that she realizes it's not worth trying to lunge for it. If you hold it in the danger zone—usually about six to twenty-four inches in front of her nose—she will probably get up to eat it, either because she thinks you are trying to lure her into a Stand, or because the treat is close enough that the temptation is too great.

A release word is the cue that means "Get up now, the Stay is over." Lots of people use the word *okay*, and the only problem with that is that it's a word people use a lot in conversation. Because I use Okay as my release word, I have to be really careful. If my dogs are on a Down-Stay at the beach and I turn to my husband and say, "Okay, let's go to the movies tonight," whoops . . . there go our dogs! They *listen* for that release word!

Other words you can use for the release are *all done, you're free, break time, get up, release, free dog, at ease*—actually, you can use just about any word or phrase you want. You could even use *peanut butter* if you'd like. **Remember:** Your words mean nothing to your dog until you give them a meaning.

When Stella is staying for one second in the Sit-Stay, extend the time to two seconds. Then increase the stay to four, then seven seconds. Then ten. If you're not good at estimating time by counting one-one thousands in your head, you can use a stop watch or have someone else count for you. Don't use a timer—the dog will start releasing herself when she hears the ding.

A Peaceable Paws class does a group stay. (Photo by Pat Miller)

As the stays get longer, you can *click!* and reward Stella *during* the stay, then remind her again not to move with another verbal Stay cue. Reward with clicks and treats several times during the stay, then release her *before* she decides to get up on her own. You want her to succeed. If Stella does get up before you release her, whisk the treat behind your back. (This is the negative punishment part: Stella's behavior—getting up—makes the good thing—the treat—go away.) When she sits again, the treat comes back out, and she gets it after she stays again, for at least a second at first, then longer as she gets better at stay. (This is the positive reinforcement part: Stella's behavior—sitting and staying—makes a good thing—the reward—happen.)

The process for Down-Stay is exactly the same, except Stanley is in the down position instead of the sit position.

As the Stays get longer, you can start fading the treat so you don't have to always hold it in front of your dog's nose to get her to stay. Over a series of Stay repetitions, gradually relax your arm until your treat hand is at your side. During this process you can still whisk the treat away if your dog gets up. As she gets more confident about the stay, you can start asking for the behavior without a treat in your hand at all. *Click!* when she stays for you, and get the treat out of your pocket or off a table or shelf. She will soon be staying without the visible treat as the incentive.

When Stella will stay for ten to twenty seconds, you are ready to add small distractions. Ask her to stay, and take one small step to the side. Then step in front of her again. *Click!*, reward, and release. Do another Stay and take a hop on one foot. *Click!*, reward, and release. Gradually build the distractions until Stella will stay as you hop up and down without stopping, do jumping jacks, clap your hands, sit or lie down on the ground in front of her, spin in circles, bounce a ball, have someone go by on a skateboard—whatever creative distractions you can invent. Taking it gradually is the key here. You want Stella to succeed. If you go directly from one hop to the skateboard, you're probably going to lose her. Gradually is also subjective, depending on your dog. Bailey the Bloodhound may progress to a twenty-second Stay in the first session, while Chili Pepper the Chihuahua may excel at three seconds. Some dogs will achieve a solid Stay at a distance with distractions within a few weeks, others will take longer.

When Stella is doing twenty- to thirty-second stays *with distractions*, you are ready to start working on distance. Now you lower your expectations for the other two elements: you shorten the time and remove the distractions. Ask Stella to stay, and take one step away. *Click!*, return, reward, and release. Gradually increase the distance, remembering that you want to add distance slowly so Stella will succeed. *Always return to Stella to reward and release her.*

You want the Stay to be rock solid. If you start calling Stella to you from the Stay, she may start breaking the Stay in anticipation of the joy of being near you—and the reward that ends the Stay. If she thinks the Stay is *never* over until you return to her, the Stay will become solid as granite. Only in higher training levels do you start *occasionally* calling a dog from a Stay. Even then, you return and release ten times for every one time you call her.

When Stella will stay at a distance, you can combine all the elements. Again, lower the bar by adding distractions when you are one step, then three steps, then five steps away from Stella, always returning to her to reward and release. At this point, you can even start leaving the room while she is on a Stay, *briefly* at first. Take one step out, step back in, *click!* return, reward, and release. Gradually increase the length of time you stay out of sight. You can set up a mirror in the doorway if you want to keep an eye on Stella, always remembering that you want to return *before* she moves out of her Stay position. You want her to succeed. If she makes several mistakes in a row and you return each time to try the Stay again, she is learning that the "mistake" of breaking the Stay makes you return to the room. Any time she starts making mistakes, return to an easier version of the exercise and get several successes in a row before you raise the bar again.

4.4—Give

Give is an everyday, useful behavior for playing canine games and for rescuing forbidden objects. It is also part of a formal retrieve. Because puppies are so good at picking things up in their mouths, the sooner they learn Give, the better. You want, at all costs, to avoid teaching your dog the chase-me game when they pick up a forbidden object. You can avoid this by teaching her to give on cue, willingly and voluntarily.

Instructions

Hold Chomp's favorite toy in one hand. Get her excited by shaking, squeaking, or bouncing the toy. Then offer it to her or drop it on the ground so she can grab it. When she has it in her mouth, say "Give!" and hold out your hand with a tasty treat in your fingers. What a grand coincidence: As she opens her mouth to take the treat, the toy falls to the ground! *Click!* but hold onto the treat, letting her nibble at it. As she nibbles the treat in your hand, reach down and pick up the toy *with your other hand*, then give her the whole treat. Now she gets a life reward too—you're going to toss the toy again!

When Chomp is giving up her toys easily, start practicing with a real (but safe!) forbidden object. Many dogs love to grab tissues, paper towels, or socks. Walk past Chomp and drop one "by accident." When she grabs it, play the Give game with a treat and a *click!* You can practice this with any other forbidden but harmless object that she loves to play with. Be sure that you don't actually encourage her to play with a forbidden object—just "inadvertently" drop it near her.

When Chomp has learned to give, your challenge will be to react appropriately when she has a truly forbidden object, especially one that is potentially harmful to her. Your natural instinct will be to try to grab it from her. Resist that instinct, go into the Give game mode, and she will give up the antique doll or box of rat poison as happily as she gives up the paper towel.

Remember to keep playing Give with toys and life rewards by tossing the toy back to her after she gives it up. If you only do Give with forbidden objects that she never gets back, she will learn that Give ends the game, and she won't want to play.

Caution: *Do* **not** *do this exercise if your dog is a resource guarder—that is, if she tenses, growls, snaps, or tries to bite if you approach or touch her when she has toys or food (see chapter 22). If your dog is aggressive when she has high-value objects, seek the assistance of a qualified positive behavior professional. Do not punish her for resource-guarding behavior—punishment is likely to make her aggressive behavior worse.*

Training Tips

My dog won't give up a toy or forbidden object, even for a treat. Try using tastier treats. If that doesn't work, drop several treats on the ground. Treats on the ground are usually more tempting than treats in your hand. When your dog is eating the treats on the ground, move slowly and gently to pick up the object she has dropped. If you make a sudden move for it, she will likely grab it again. If necessary, make a little *Hansel and Gretel* trail of treats to move her away from the object so you can get to it and pick it up.

BONUS GAMES

4.1—Weave

This game has no real useful application, but it's a lot of fun and a very impressive trick to show off to your friends. It is a move commonly used in canine freestyle (dancing with your dog)—a new and exciting canine sport.

The author uses targeting to teach Josie to weave. (Photo by Paul Miller)

Instructions

Start with your dog on your left side. Step forward with your right foot. Place your target (hand or stick) behind and below your right knee so your dog can see it from the front, and say "Touch!" As she moves to touch the target, move it back and out to the side so she has to walk between your legs to touch it. *Click!* and treat. Now step forward with your left foot and repeat the move with your left hand behind your left knee. Repeat until she is weaving between your legs with ease. Then gradually reduce the frequency of the *click!* and reward until she can weave a whole line with just one *click!* and treat at the very end.

Remember: When your dog is comfortable with the weaving, you can fade the use of the target until she is weaving on verbal cue alone or with just a very subtle hand signal.

Training Tips

My dog is afraid to walk between my legs. This fear is common. You just need to shape the behavior instead of expecting to get it all at once. Hold your target behind your knee and ask her to touch. Don't move the target away. *Click!*

and treat her for just touching the target between your legs. If she's afraid to even do that, push the target forward so it is actually in front of you but between your legs. Find the point where she is willing to touch it, and keep doing repetitions there until she is confident, then move it very slightly back between your legs. ("Very slightly" will vary from one dog to the next. Some dogs can handle six-inch increments, others can only advance an inch at a time.)

You can also lure with a treat rather than ask her to touch. She may be willing to follow a real live tasty piece of freeze-dried liver between your legs. If she'll move between your legs at all, try tossing the treat a couple of feet behind you so she runs through your legs to get it.

4.2—Score!

This is another game that makes use of targeting. It's just for fun, but it can keep your 4-year-old toddler and your obsessive Border Collie occupied together for hours.

Instructions

First, teach Bumper to target to a large ball by holding the ball in your hand and asking her to touch, like you did with the bell (see chapter 12, Bonus Game "3.1—Ring My Bell"). The ball needs to be large enough that she can't hold it in her mouth. When she tries to touch your target hand, she will touch the ball instead because it is in the way. Gradually lower the ball to the ground, asking her to touch as it gets lower and lower. As you do this, gradually change your verbal cue from Touch to Touch—Score and then to Score. When the ball is sitting on the ground, gradually move your hand away until Bumper is touching the ball on "Score!" without your hand near it. Some dogs will get to this point in the exercise in one session. Others may need several sessions.

You will notice that when the ball is sitting on the ground and Bumper touches it, sometimes she will touch it hard enough to make it move. Now you are going to start shaping for the harder touches by only giving her a *click!* and treat when the ball actually moves, then eventually when the ball only moves a significant distance. (Again, "significant" will depend on your dog, but will probably be farther for Larry the Lab than for Chili the Chihuahua.)

When Bumper is pushing the ball a decent distance, set up your goal posts (or orange cones, or whatever works for you) close enough that a solid push will send the ball through them. Now shape the score by only clicking and rewarding when the ball actually goes through the goal. If she pushes the ball but it doesn't go though, tell her she's a good dog and ask her to try again.

If you have your toddler sit on the floor with his feet spread apart to make a V, his shoes can be the goal posts. When Bumper rolls the ball to him, he can roll it back, and they can play and baby-sit each other until one of them gets bored.

You can also set up plastic bowling pins and teach Bumper to bowl using the same technique. Junior can make a great pin setter.

4.3—Let Us Pray

This is another fun game without a serious practical application. Have Theresa sit in front of a chair or stool that comes about to her mid-chest level. Ask her to sit up (see chapter 12, Bonus Game "3.2—Sitting Pretty") and then encourage her to rest her feet on the stool. You may need to *click!* and reward for very short paw rests at first, or for just one paw on the stool, until she leaves her paws on the chair for longer and longer periods. When she is sitting confidently with her paws resting on the chair for extended periods, lure her nose between her paws with a treat so she is looking down at the floor. *Click!* and

The author's dog Josie learns how to say her prayers.
(Photo by Paul Miller)

treat. When you know she will look between her legs without taking her paws off the stool, start using your verbal cue Say Your Prayers or Meditate or whatever word or phrase you want to use. Gradually fade your use of obvious cues until your dog will run over to the stool, prop up her feet, and "say her prayers" with just a verbal cue or hand signal.

Training Tips

My dog moves her paws off the chair as soon as I try to lure her nose down. Slow down and shape the nose drop instead of trying to get it all at once. When your dog is sitting with her paws on the stool, move your treat hand toward her, *click!* before she has a chance to move her paws, and reward. (If she moves her paws off the stool after the *click!* that's okay. As long as the *click!* happened while her paws were on the stool, she knows that is what she is getting rewarded for.) Gradually move your hand (and her treat) closer and closer to her before you *click!* until you can move it under her front legs without her moving.

No matter what I do, my dog is afraid to put her paws on the chair. Try using something else for her to prop her paws on—a stool, a wooden box or platform, or even your lap. Try sitting on the stool yourself and have her put her paws up on your leg, then work on the prayers part. For smaller dogs, you can sit on the floor with your legs crossed and have them put their paws up on your knees.

Association of Pet Dog Trainers (APDT) member trainer Ann Dresselhaus's dog Luna retrieves a dumbbell over a jump. (Photo by Ann Dresselhaus)

Chapter 14

The Fifth Week— Up and Over!

CORE EXERCISES

5.1—Swing Your Partner

By now you have taught your dog to sit in front of you when you call him in order to park his doggie rear and so that you can put a hand on his collar if you need to restrain him (see chapter 11, Core Exercise "2.1—Come"). The swing exercise moves him back to your side facing the same direction you are, so if you want to walk forward, he is in a good walking position. Swing is used in obedience and rally competitions, but it also has a practical application because it gets your dog out of your way and into an approximate heel position, allowing you to walk forward together. The instructions for this exercise will be to move your dog to your left side, since that is the show ring side for heeling. If you want your dog on the right side, reverse the instructions. If you want to be able to move your dog to either side, teach one side first, then the other, using a different verbal cue for the second side. I like the swing—it's like a dance step. Athletic dogs can even learn to leap up in the air, turn in mid-leap, and land sitting next to your side.

Instructions

Start with Stanley sitting directly in front of and facing you, close enough that you can pat him on the head. Have the clicker in your left hand and the treats in your right. If you are doing this exercise on-leash, have the leash in your left hand also. Remember that the leash is just to keep a dog from leaving—it is not used to pull or guide him into position.

Take a long step *straight back* with your left foot. Lure Stanley to your left and back with the treat, turn him *toward you* with the lure, and bring him up along your left side. Now lift the treat over his head to get him to sit, *click!* and treat. Use the verbal Sit cue if necessary to ask him to sit. He is now sitting next to you, and you are both ready to walk forward without tripping over each other. **Remember:** If you want Stanley to end up on your right side, reverse these instructions.

Notice you haven't used the verbal Swing cue yet. The mechanics of this move can be a little confusing at first. You want the dance step to be smooth before you introduce the verbal cue so that Stanley doesn't associate the word with the wrong behavior. When he seems to have caught on and is moving easily back and into the sit position for you, add the verbal cue Swing.

To teach the swing, start with your dog sitting in front of you, a treat in front of his nose. (Photo by Paul Miller)

Take a big step back on your left foot, and lure him way
back. (Your right foot doesn't move.) (Photo by Paul Miller)

Then turn him in toward you with the lure, and bring your
left foot back up into position next to your right foot . . .
(Photo by Paul Miller)

... and have him sit next to you. If you plan to show in obedience, you can work on getting a perfectly straight Sit after he gets the idea of Swing.
(Photo by Paul Miller)

Training Tips

When I lure my dog forward and into the sit position, he turns and faces me rather than facing forward. This usually happens because you are holding the treat in front of you. Try holding the treat off to the side, in front of your dog. Put the treat where you want his nose to be. You probably won't get a perfectly straight sit at first, but you can start shaping straighter sits by only giving a *click!* and treat for increasingly better ones. The show ring is the only place where "perfect" Sits really matter. If you don't plan to show your dog, you can set whatever standard you want for "straight enough."

5.2—Leave It—Temptation Alley

Temptation alley is an exercise you do to reinforce and expand on the Leave It exercise you learned in week three (see chapter 12, Core Exercise "3.3—Leave It!"). Vacuum has already learned not to eat a treat in your hand or on the ground in front of you when you say "Leave It!" in an upbeat tone of voice. Now he's going to learn to leave things alone that he discovers on the ground during your walks.

Instructions

Set up a temptation alley exercise on a nongrassy outdoor area by making several piles of mildly interesting treats such as dog kibble or dry dog cookies. (Nongrassy is important. You need to be able to see the piles before Vacuum sniffs them out and inhales them.) The piles should be at least ten feet apart. Take Vacuum outside on his leash and walk him for five to ten minutes to settle him a little. Then approach the first pile. The *instant* his eyes fall on the pile, say "Leave it!" in a happy voice and stop moving. Do not jerk him back with the leash, but do restrain him so he can't eat the goodies. (You need to plan ahead here; be sure you stop soon enough or have the leash short enough that you can gently prevent your dog from reaching the pile when you stop.) Now wait. Do not repeat the Leave It cue and don't pull him back. Sooner or later he will look away from the pile. The instant he does, *click!* and give him a treat that is *much better* than the kibble or cookies on the ground. Now proceed to the next pile. Continue this exercise at each pile until you can walk him past them and he looks away from the pile and back at you on the verbal Leave It cue without any leash restraint.

Next time, put the piles in different places. Practice in different locations. When your dog is responding readily and reliably to Leave It with relatively boring treat piles, up the ante by putting better treats in the piles and adding some piles of his favorite toys. Continue to have a higher-value treat to give him as a reward for the Leave It. When he has the idea, experiment with using Leave It in real life, such as when you are walking around the block and he finds a fast-food wrapper in the gutter or a tipped-over garbage can.

When he is responding reliably at least 80 percent of the time on-leash, try the exercise off-leash. Go back to your quiet, nongrassy area and boring treat piles to start, then gradually up the ante again until he will leave the tastiest rotting squirrel carcass at your gentle request to leave it. If he "oopses" (makes a mistake) off-leash and grabs a forbidden treat pile or object, go back to more on-leash work.

5.3—Up and Over

Now that you've worked really hard to teach Bounce not to jump up on you, you're going to teach him to jump on and over *objects*, which is an entirely different thing.

Note: Puppies under the age of 1 year and dogs with physical disabilities should not be asked to overexert themselves with jumping games. Check with your veterinarian for recommendations on how high and how much your dog should be allowed to jump.

Most dogs love to jump. It's a great game for using excess energy because they have to exert themselves strenuously to jump on and over things. When I was a kid, I used to put brooms and mops across chairs all through the house and have my Collie leap over the hurdles. It is soul-satisfying to see your dog fly gracefully through the air, and it can make hikes through the park easier and more fun if Bounce can bound over fallen logs and other woodsy obstacles. Jumping is also an important skill for a dog to learn if you have an interest in competitive dog sports.

Instructions (Over)

Although jumping is a very natural behavior for dogs, being asked to jump over something may be a new experience for Bounce, so you want to start slow and easy. Lay a dowel or broomstick on the ground with one end against a wall or fence and walk him over it. (Some dogs are wary of a stick in your hand, so be sure not to frighten your dog with it.) As he steps over, say, "Over!" in an excited tone of voice and give him a *click!* and a treat as he reaches the other side. Repeat this several times until you are sure he has no hesitation about walking over the stick. Now lift it a couple of inches. You can rest each end of the stick on a book. Stand at the end that is away from the wall and ask Bounce to wait on one side of the stick. Say "Over!" and toss a treat on the other side. As he steps over the stick to get the treat, *click!* and praise him. Continue to repeat the game at slowly increasing heights until he is freely jumping over the stick. Remember to gradually fade the use of the treat as a lure so he will eventually jump on just the verbal cue, followed by the *click!* and a reward. (You can also use a life reward of a ball or a toy to encourage Bounce over the jump, as long as you can get it back afterward so you can play over again!)

Instructions (Up)

The key here, too, is to start small. If you want Bounce to jump in the back of your SUV, you may need to lower your sights at first. Even big dogs can be intimidated by such a leap! Find or build a low, flat, *solid* surface to practice on.

Nothing puts off a cautious dog more than having the surface he lands on jiggle under his feet. A cast-off exercise stepper from a yard sale is a perfect choice for a small- to medium-sized dog.

Set your platform on flat ground and encourage Bounce to get on it. Place your hand or a target stick over the platform and ask him to touch. If he jumps on it right away to touch the target (as lots of dogs will), bingo! *Click!* and treat. You've captured the behavior in one fell swoop. You can start using your verbal Up cue and keep repeating the exercise until he will do it reliably on request. Then transfer it to different surfaces: the fallen tree trunk in the backyard, the boulder by the creek, the bed or sofa (if he's allowed on the furniture), and, yes, the SUV.

If he doesn't give you the whole behavior all at once, shape it. Give him a *click!* for one foot on the platform. When he does one foot easily, go for two, then three, then all four. When he is willing to have all four feet on the platform, start using the Up cue. (If you want to get cute, use a different verbal cue for each step up and work with him until he will put the stated number of feet on the platform on cue.) When he is willing to put all four feet on the platform, work on excitement and enthusiasm until he happily jumps on the platform for the Up cue. Now you can start working on different surfaces. You may get the Up on cue with each new surface, or you may need to reshape the Up with each new scary thing.

BONUS GAMES
5.1—Playing Possum

Possum is an amusing extension of the relax exercise and is halfway to roll over. I like to teach possum before roll over because when your dog learns to roll all the way over, you may have a hard time getting him to stop halfway in the belly-up possum position. Possum is also a good exercise because it teaches your dog to voluntarily go into a subordinate position without using any of the forceful (and often dangerous) alpha roll exercises that some traditional trainers teach. I strongly caution you against ever attempting to *force* a dog onto her back. Some dogs appropriately see this as a threat and try to defend themselves, which could result in a serious bite. When your dog trusts that you are not a threat, he will happily and willingly go belly-up for you, and you can easily search for fleas, ticks, lumps, and bumps, and groom those hard-to-reach spots underneath.

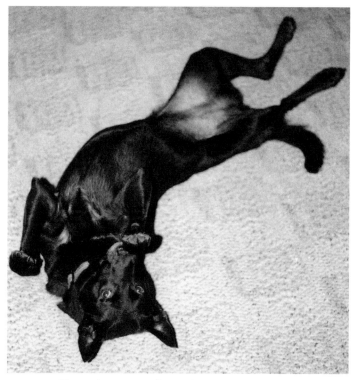

The author's Australian Kelpie, Katie, shows off her possum technique. (Photo by Paul Miller)

Instructions

Ask your dog to relax on a soft, flat dog bed or carpeted surface (see chapter 13, Core Exercise "4.2—Relax"). When he is in the relax position, encourage your dog to turn tummy side up by using a treat as a lure. Put the treat by his nose, then move it up in an arc toward his spine so his head turns as he follows it with his nose. As soon as he shifts so his legs lift off the floor ever so slightly, *click!* and treat. Gradually increase the amount of the arc until he is turning onto his back. When he is able to turn onto his back, add the verbal Possum cue and continue to repeat the exercise, encouraging him to hold the position longer and longer before you *click!* and reward. To get the behavior on a verbal cue or hand signal, use the word first, and start to minimize luring.

Caution: Some dogs, especially those with narrow backs and deep chests such as Greyhounds, Afghans, and Salukis, find this exercise very difficult, if not impossible, to perform. Always be aware of your dog's physical limitations, and never ask him to do anything that may be harmful to him or that he is physically incapable of doing.

5.2—Roll Over, Beethoven

When your dog can do Possum, Roll Over is a snap! Even dogs who physically can't hold the possum position can often roll all the way over.

Instructions

For most dogs, this exercise is almost too easy for words. Start the Possum exercise, then just keep on going! When the dog passes the point of equilibrium, gravity takes over and the roll just happens. When your dog is doing one roll easily, try two in a row. Then more, until you can get him to do a whole series of roll overs.

Many dogs are *one-sided*, meaning they'll roll easily in one direction but not the other. If your dog is having trouble with this game, try having him roll the other way. Then, when he has the easy direction figured out, make him "ambipawstrous" and shape the roll the other way as well. If you *really* want to impress people, get him to roll over while you roll over at the same time.

Starting with Relax, Peaceable Paws client Marianne
O'Connell teaches her Jack Russell Terrier, Skippy,
to roll over. (Photo by Tom O'Connell)

From Relax, she lures Skippy into Possum . . .
(Photo by Tom O'Connell)

. . . and finishes by luring him all the way over!
(Photo by Tom O'Connell)

5.3—Tug

Some trainers tell you not to play tug of war with your dog because they say it teaches him to be aggressive and dominant. I believe that if you play tug with rules, not only is it a great energy diffuser for your dog, it also teaches him to control himself and to defer to you. Men and boys, more than women and girls, seem to like to play rough physical games with their dogs. Tug is a way to direct that rough play into appropriate channels. Your dog should know the Give exercise (see chapter 13, Core Exercise "4.4—Give") before you start playing Tug.

Instructions

Knotted rope toys are perfect for tug games; the longer the better because the length keeps Yankee's teeth away from your skin. The ropes with plastic handles make it easier for you to hold on (an important point because *you* will need to win the tug game). Dogs seem to like the ones with three or four rope branches to choose from.

Here are the rules for playing tug:

- The tug toy is *only* for playing tug. It is not left lying around. When the game is over, put it away someplace where Yankee can't get to it.

- *You* decide when it is time to play tug. If Yankee stands next to the drawer where the tug toy lives and barks demandingly, do not get out the toy and play tug. Wait until he goes away. *Then* you can get it out and invite him to play.

- At least nine times out of ten, *you* win the game, not Yankee. That means you end up with the toy and he doesn't. If he will give it back to you when you ask him to, you can let him win very occasionally. If he won't give it back, you and Yankee need to do more work on Give before you try to play Tug. *If* Yankee is very timid or nonassertive, you can let him win more often to help boost his confidence—as much as one-half to three-quarters of the time. You still need to win sometimes, though!

- If Yankee's teeth even so much as graze your skin or your clothes, the game is over. Say "Oops!" turn your back on him, and put the toy away. Wait a few minutes before you play again.

- Yankee gets to grab and tug the toy only when you give him the verbal cue Tug. If he lunges for the toy before you give him the cue, say "Oops!" and hide it behind your back. Give the Tug cue only when he is standing (or better yet, sitting!) quietly in front of you, with all four paws on the floor.

- Play growling is okay. Serious growling (accompanied by snapping or a refusal to release the toy on your Give cue) ends the game. Put the toy away for at least ten minutes.

- If you have more than one dog, and your dogs tend to get aggressive with each other when they are excited and competing for toys or attention, do this game with Yankee only when the other dogs are sequestered in another room.

- Small children should not play this game with dogs. They aren't strong enough to win the game, and they can't be depended on to follow the rules consistently.

Now that you know the rules, you can teach Yankee the game. Bring out the tug toy, shake it a little, and see if he will grab it. If he does, pull gently back on it to encourage him to resist. When he does, tell him "Good boy, tug!" As he gets enthusiastic about tugging, keep telling him "Good boy, tug!" and get more energetic with your tugging in response. After five to ten seconds of tugging, stop moving. Still holding on to your end of the tug toy, stand still, and in a calm but happy voice say "Yankee, give!" **Remember:** You are not intimidating him into giving you the toy—you're just giving him information and asking him to respond with the appropriate behavior. Because you have

Skippy plays tug with his Labrador Retriever pal Scooter.
(Photo by Tom O'Connell)

already trained him to give, he will let go of the toy. *Click!* and give him a treat. Eventually, you can give him a life reward of reengaging in the tug game, but at first you don't want to encourage him to lunge for the toy after he releases it. This is one exercise where you may find the verbal marker "Yes!" easier to use than the clicker, because your hands are busy with tug toy and treats.

If he doesn't give up the toy easily on your request, don't argue with him, but don't let him win, either. Trade him for a treat. If necessary, drop the treat on the ground (or drop several treats) until he is tempted enough to drop the toy and eat the treats. Now try the tug game again, but for a shorter period, and don't encourage him to get so excited. If he continues to choose not to give when you ask him to, put the tug toy away for a few more weeks while you work on the Give. When you feel he is more reliable with Give, you can try Tug again.

As soon as Yankee is easily letting go of the tug toy on cue, you can occasionally use the toy itself as a life reward. When he lets go of the toy, tell him "Good boy!" Wait a second, then offer him the toy and say "Tug!" again. As with the Give, many dogs are more willing to let go of the toy if they know they are going to get it back for another round of tug. Now you can sometimes reward with a treat and sometimes use a life reward. Remember to use negative punishment (the dog's behavior makes a good thing go away) if Yankee starts getting grabby for the tug toy before you give him the cue, or if his teeth touch your clothes or skin.

And remember to put the toy away when you're done.

Josie backs away from her mom in response to the Excuse Me verbal cue and hand signal. (Photo by Paul Miller)

Chapter 15

The Sixth Week— Well, Excuse Me!

CORE EXERCISES

6.1—Well, Excuse Me!

If you've ever tried to walk though a doorway with your arms full of groceries, a laundry basket, or a newborn baby only to find your path blocked by Roadblock, a furry, four-footed barrier, you will appreciate the value of this exercise. With a simple verbal cue, Roadblock willingly backs out of your way and politely allows you to proceed.

Instructions

Start with Roadblock standing and facing you. Hold a treat just below her nose level and let her nibble at it. Move the treat toward her chest and take a step toward her. As she takes *just one step* back, *click!* and reward. Repeat this several times, clicking and rewarding for just one or two steps, until she is doing that easily. Then try several repetitions at three steps, then four. Remember to increase the challenge slowly. You want her to succeed until she is confident at each level of difficulty before making it harder for her; otherwise, she may give up. If that happens, you'll know that you asked for too much too soon, and you'll need to go back to an easier point. Once Roadblock is smoothly backing up four to six steps, add the verbal cue Excuse Me as she is backing up. After a dozen or so repetitions, start using the verbal cue first, give her a few seconds to respond, then help her back up by moving toward her if she hasn't started back. When you start using the verbal cue first, be sure to *click!* and reward Roadblock's smallest attempt to move backward. **Remember:** When she takes a hesitant step back, it is as if she is saying, "Is this right?" If you *click!* and reward that attempt, you are answering her with a "Yes, that's it!" You will immediately boost her confidence, and she will get it very quickly. Then you can work back up to the four- to six-step level (and beyond!) that she was doing with the hand cue.

Training Tips

My dog backs up, but she backs crooked. You are probably asking her to do too much too soon. Go back to just one or two steps, and only *click!* and reward the straightest ones. Shape for straighter and straighter steps until she is doing two straight ones. Then add the third. If she goes crooked on the third, only *click!* and reward the straightest ones until she realizes that only straight steps get clicked. Each time you add a step, only *click!* and reward straight ones. If you are still having trouble, you can practice next to a wall to help her stay straight, then gradually move farther and farther away from the wall.

My dog sits instead of backing up. If your dog sits in front of you instead of stands, take a couple of steps back and start the Excuse Me exercise when she stands up to follow you. If she is standing, but she sits as you try to get her to back up, try holding the treat lower and move it between her front legs. Be sure to *click!* and reward the tiniest step back with even *one* foot so she gets a chance to understand what you are asking her to do.

6.2—Long-Distance Down

Along with Come, this exercise may be one of the most useful ones you teach your dog. When you can get your dog to drop on a dime at a distance, you have achieved superb control of her motion and activity. My first Australian Kelpie, Keli, was a Type A, workaholic control freak. (I affectionately describe Kelpies as Border Collies on caffeine.) When something was, in her perception, the least bit out of place, she thought it was her job to put it right. Out of place in Keli's dictionary included strange dogs and people wearing odd clothing. Because we worked at an animal shelter in California, strange dogs and odd clothing were daily fare—so you can see the problem we faced. A herding dog controls things by charging them and trying to herd them, a move that can easily be perceived as aggression by other dogs and humans. Although I knew the likelihood of Keli actually biting someone was low, it was always very reassuring to the person she was charging that I could calmly ask Keli to lie down and she would drop to the ground from a full charge, even at a distance of one hundred feet.

In that same scenario, if I asked Keli to come, there's a good chance she would not have responded. When you ask a dog in an aroused charge to come, you are asking her to stop moving forward, take her eyes off of her prey (or the perceived threat), turn around, and come back to you. That's a lot to ask. When you ask for a Down, all you are asking her to do is to stop the forward motion and drop to the ground. She can still keep her eyes on her target, and she doesn't have to move away from it. When you have her in a Down position, her level of arousal starts to subside and it is easier, after several seconds, to then get her attention focused on you and ask her to come back.

Instructions

You've been practicing a verbal Down since week one (see chapter 10, Core Exercise "1.4—The Down"), so Charger should be pretty good at it by now. If you have a friend who can help you, have your assistant hold the leash with Charger sitting by her side with three or four inches of slack in the leash. If you don't have a friend to help, tether Charger to a solid object.

Stand in front of Charger, facing her. She should be at the end of her leash so she can't move forward toward you. Take one step back. Now give the verbal Down cue. Remember that the verbal cue is spoken in a happy, upbeat tone of voice. You are giving Charger information, not trying to frighten or intimidate her into lying down. When Charger lies down, *click!* step forward, give her a treat, and tell her what a brilliant dog she is! Then ask her to sit, and repeat the exercise several times at a distance of one step.

You will need to put some variety into this exercise. Sometimes when you step back just *click!* and return to feed her a treat without asking her to lie down. Sometimes ask her to sit after you step back. If you have her lie down every time you step away, she will soon learn that you stepping away is the cue for the Down, and she'll start anticipating your verbal cue.

When she is doing the distance down easily at one step, do it at two steps, then three. Gradually increase the distance between you and Charger until she will lie down promptly on your verbal cue from across the room. Then start adding distractions. **Remember:** Every time you change the criteria in one arena, you need to make it easier for your dog in another. In this case, reduce the distance—go back to one or two steps while you add distractions such as a child skipping by, someone bouncing a ball, a cat walking through the room, another dog running by. When she is doing the distance down with distractions while you are near her, start gradually increasing the distance again. When she is responding promptly at least 80 percent of the time, try it without the tether. Once again, start close to her without distractions, then gradually increase distance and distraction levels.

Now start looking for opportunities to ask Charger to lie down while she is in motion. Try it while you are walking her on-leash, first with no distractions, then as other dogs or people pass by. Practice when she wanders aimlessly through your living room, then in your fenced yard when she is strolling around sniffing bushes. Then up the ante by asking for the Down when she is moving faster—first trotting, then eventually when she is romping. Be sure to use a happy tone of voice and to give her treats and lots of praise when she does it. You can use a rousing game of tug or chase the ball as a life reward after a distance down to get her really enthused about dropping for you at a distance.

Training Tips

My dog gets up and tries to come to me when I ask her to lie down from a distance. This is because you have taught her that *down* means "lie down in front of me or next to me." She thinks she is doing the right thing! This is why you attach the leash to something solid or have a friend hold the leash to restrain the dog. Have enough slack in the leash so that your dog is comfortable—but not enough that she can reach you. The friend should just restrain your dog, not jerk back on the leash. You may need to start a little closer to your dog when you first ask for the Down, and increase the distance very slowly.

My dog doesn't get up, but she doesn't lie down either—she just sits there when I ask her to lie down from a distance. She may be a little confused because you are changing the rules of the Down game. She knows that *down* means that she is supposed to lie down close to you. She might think she can't do the Down because she can't *get* close to you. Make sure you are no more than one step away from her. Ask for the Down and pause for two to three seconds. If she doesn't do it, step forward and help her by luring her down. *Click!* and treat. If she doesn't get it after several repetitions of this, you may need to go back to working on your verbal Down cue and try the distance down again later, when she is better at responding to the verbal Down.

6.3—Dropped Leave It

Here is yet another practical application of the Leave It exercise you learned in week three (see chapter 12, Core Exercise "3.3—Leave It!"). You are in the kitchen slicing the Thanksgiving turkey (or for some of us, the Tofurkey) when the knife slips, sending the entire plate crashing to the floor. Vacuum, who has been lurking by the refrigerator just waiting for the right opportunity to knock, darts forward. You calmly and clearly say, "Vacuum, leave it!" and she reluctantly but promptly backs away while you bend over and salvage dinner. You do, of course, tell her "Yes!" or *click!* your clicker if it's handy, and slice a small piece off the main course to give her as a reward for her exemplary behavior.

Instructions

Have Vacuum sit in front of you. Say "Leave It!" and carefully drop a treat so it falls slightly behind you and off to the side a bit. If she moves to get it, step in front of the treat and body block her so she can't reach it. When she looks away from the treat on the floor, *click!* and reward her with a treat from your hand. Repeat until she no longer tries to get it when you give the Leave It cue and drop the treat. Gradually start dropping the treat in less-protected places until she'll leave it no matter where it's dropped.

Now turn it around a little. Drop the treat *first* and say "Leave It!" an instant *after* the treat hits the floor. This more closely approximates real life, where you're likely to drop something accidentally—like your medication—and have to remember to quickly give your dog the Leave It cue before she swallows your blood pressure pill. Again, be prepared to body block if necessary until she understands this new version of the Leave It game.

For an even more advanced version of the dropped leave it, have Vacuum on a leash with just a few inches of slack. Position an accomplice at a distance of about twenty feet. Give him a bowl of slightly boring treats. Tell him that you are going to walk toward him and that when you nod your head, he should drop several of the treats close to his own feet. Now stroll toward him with Vacuum walking politely on her leash at your side. When you are about ten feet from your accomplice, nod your head. As the treats fall, give the cue Leave It. Stop moving, and restrain Vacuum so she can't get to the treats. Only give the Leave It cue one time. Just wait, as you did in your other Leave It exercises until Vacuum turns her attention back to you (see chapter 12, Core Exercise "3.3—Leave It!"; chapter 14, Core Exercise "5.2—Leave It—Temptation Alley"). Then *click!* and reward with a truly scrumptious treat. Repeat until she is turning to you immediately on the Leave It cue without you having to put any pressure on the leash. Practice in different locations with different kinds of treats until you feel she is at least 80 percent reliable. Finally, as you did with the temptation alley exercise, try it off-leash, starting with boring treats as the drop and eventually moving up to more tempting targets.

BONUS GAMES

6.1—Cross Your Paws Like a Lady

Cross paws puts a classy touch on your dog's Down and will draw admiring comments from your friends. It's also simple to teach through luring and shaping.

Instructions

Ask Lassie to lie down, and when she does, tell her that she's a good girl. Experiment with your treat lure by moving it slowly in front of her nose from left to right. As she follows it with her nose, watch to see if she moves one foot toward the other to keep her balance. *Click!* and treat if she does. Repeat the lure, *click!* and treat until you see that she is deliberately moving one foot toward the other. Now start clicking and rewarding only the attempts that bring Lassie's moving leg closer to the stationary one. As the frequency of the closer attempts increases, raise the criteria by only clicking the ones that actually touch the other leg. Keep upping the ante until the moving leg is crossing over and resting on the stationary one. Now you are ready to add a verbal cue, such as Cross Paws, or "Be a Lady," as Lassie does the leg movement. Now she can lie down with her legs crossed like a proper lady, and you have a very classy Lassie!

6.2—Crawl on Your Belly Like a Reptile

Instructions

Ask Python to lie down facing you and hold a treat in front of his nose. Keeping the treat just an inch or two above the ground, back up a step and *very slowly* move the treat toward you. As Python strains to follow the treat, she should drag herself forward a tiny bit. *Click!* and reward. Keep repeating the

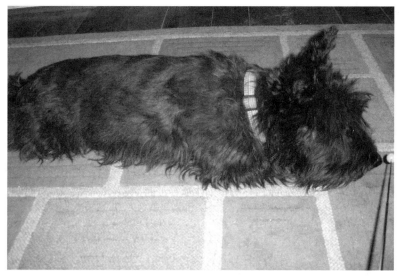

Here's another easy behavior for most dogs, and one that many seem to enjoy. It works best if you do it on carpet or grass—lots of dogs won't crawl on a hard or rough surface. (Photo by Pat Miller)

sequence until she creeps farther and farther forward. If she jumps up to follow the treat, you may have moved it too far or too fast. Slow down, and remember to *click!* and reward tiny bits of the crawl so Python can figure out how to do the right thing. The biggest mistake most people make when training their dogs is trying to go too fast—asking for too much too soon. Ask for small behaviors so your dog can win. As long as she keeps winning, she will be more willing to keep trying.

When Python is confidently crawling longer distances, you can fade the lure and minimize the hand motion. Put the behavior on a verbal Crawl cue or a barely noticeable hand signal.

6.3—Bravo

You can end your routine with a flourish when you and Buddy take a bow together. This is another impressive behavior that is usually easy to teach.

Instructions

Have Buddy stand in front of you or at your side. Put a treat in front of her nose and move it toward her chest, down toward the floor. Here's the tricky part. If you have taught her to lie down by moving a treat toward the ground, she may try to lie down here. Watch her very closely. When she has a slight bend in her elbows, *click!* and raise the treat so she stands up again. Then reward. If you are slow, she will probably lie down. (Don't *click!* the Down.) The quicker she is at

Josie takes a bow. Bravo! (Photo by Paul Miller)

lying down for you, the quicker you will need to be at clicking the elbow bend and raising the treat up before she goes down.

If you are really having difficulty with this, you can try slipping your hand or a small box under Buddy's tummy to keep her from going down. This works for some dogs; others find it very disturbing and distracting. Gradually encourage Buddy to dip lower and lower until she can bow with her elbows touching the ground and her rear end high in the air. When you are sure you can get a half-bow or better without having Buddy go all the way into a Down, you can start using the verbal cue. I suggest using a word other than *bow*, since it sounds a lot like *down*, and you are already risking confusion because of the similarity of the luring motion. One of my students uses the word *bravo*, which I like a lot; another uses *curtsey*. Others use *take a bow*, with the emphasis on the word *take* rather than *bow*. As you have done with all the other behaviors you have taught Buddy, you want to start fading the lure as soon as she is giving you the bow easily, working toward getting it on a verbal cue or small hand signal. When she will do a full bow, you can ask her to stay in the bow position and you can bow (or curtsey) next to her. Or tell her to stay, step away, and let her accept all the accolades herself!

Strike up the band and wave the flags—
you've completed the Peaceable Paws basic
training program! (Photo by Paul Miller)

Chapter 16

Click! and Jackpot!

You have now finished the Peaceable Paws basic training program. Congratulations, and a super *click!* and jackpot to both of you. If you have followed the program, you and your dog should now have a relationship based on communication, trust, respect, and understanding. You have laid a solid foundation for whatever you plan to do with your dog in the future. The two of you can look forward to a life of joy and companionship together. As Karen Carpenter sang in the 1970s, however, "We've Only Just Begun."

In part III, I will explain how you can use the principles and skills you and your dog have learned to prevent, manage, and modify common behavior challenges. The simple Peaceable Paws formula for modifying unwanted behavior is in the Concept 4 section of "Pat's Positive Training Principles" at the beginning of the book. Think in terms of what you want your dog *to do*, not what you want him *not to do*. When you are thinking about your dog in this manner, problem solving becomes simple:

1. Visualize the behavior you want your dog to do. Have a clear picture in your mind of the behavior you're trying to achieve with your dog.

2. Figure out how to prevent your dog from being rewarded for the behavior you *don't* want.

3. Reward him consistently and generously for the behavior you *do* want.

But before you begin tackling behavior issues, let your dog and yourself bask in the light of your training success thus far by thinking about some of the fun activities the two of you can do by using the training tools you have learned. The door is now open for you to pursue a canine career in agility, freestyle, tracking, animal-assisted therapy, obedience, flyball, Frisbee, rally obedience—or just take relaxing hikes in the woods with your dog, if that is your goal (and a perfectly fine goal it is).

If you haven't already, take some time to figure out what you and your dog enjoy the most. If you have a bold, active dog, agility, flyball, or Frisbee might appeal to you.

Agility involves teaching your dog to negotiate a series of obstacles, including jumps, tunnels, and teeter-totters, as well as weaving in and out of a series of poles. Although active and agile dogs such as Border Collies excel in this sport, any healthy dog can enjoy the agility challenge.

Flyball is another great sport for the very active dog. In this activity, the dog speeds over a series of hurdles, touches a trigger on a box that shoots out a tennis ball, catches the ball, and speeds back over the hurdles to the owner. This is a team sport, done as a relay race. The fastest team—whose dogs all bring the ball back—wins. Jack Russell Terriers seem to love this sport. Border Collies also do exceptionally well, but, again, any dog who can fetch a ball and jump a low hurdle can have fun with flyball. The excitement of team competition is a great motivator for canines and humans alike.

Canine Frisbee is such a popular sport that it's hard to find a dog owner who has never seen a dog catch a flying disc. It is on television, at football games, in the local park—dogs and owners never seem to tire of the game. Once again, the herding breeds—Border Collies, Australian Shepherds, Cattle Dogs, and the like—seem to excel at making those spectacular flying leaps. But dogs who have any athletic ability at all can master the art of disc catching. Owners sometimes get discouraged when their dogs don't fly through the air on the first attempt, but remember the technique I've used throughout this book to teach a complex behavior. Break it down into smaller pieces and work on a small piece at a time. You may need to teach your dog to retrieve the Frisbee first and do short tosses directly to your dog—or even roll it on the ground—until he can grab it from a foot or two away. Then gradually toss it farther and farther until he's ready to chase a Frisbee with the best of them.

If your dog likes to sniff, he might love to do tracking. If he's bold and likes to follow scent, and you have an altruistic and adventurous streak, search-and-rescue might be in your future.

Tracking consists of teaching your dog to follow a scent that you have laid down for him until he reaches the end and finds a reward there. Although tracking is fun as an activity by itself, you can also enter competitions and win titles for tracking. Search-and-rescue makes use of a dog's tracking abilities to find humans who are lost. Many kidnap victims, earthquake and avalanche survivors, and people who have gotten lost hiking in the woods owe their lives to search-and-rescue dogs. Dogs have even been trained to search for missing pets! Scenthounds such as Bloodhounds and Beagles are naturally suited to tracking work, but *all* dogs have very sensitive noses, and many different breeds and mixed breeds are well suited to do tracking and search-and-rescue work.

Canine freestyle calls for creativity. Perfectionists might prefer traditional obedience competition, while those who like their obedience faster and freer might go for the new sport of rally obedience.

Be joyful together. (Photo by Pat Miller)

Canine freestyle is also called dancing with dogs. It's sort of like pairs figure skating, only you do it with your dog, and you don't do it on ice. You select your own music and choreograph your own routine, starting with the basic obedience exercises and embellishing them with all kinds of creative moves such as spins and twirls, and having your dog weave between your legs, jump through your arms, and run around you in circles. If your dog can do it, you can probably include it in a freestyle routine!

Traditional obedience competitions are offered by many different organizations, including the American Kennel Club (AKC), the United Kennel Club, and several mixed-breed organizations. In an obedience competition, your dog must heel precisely at your left side and respond instantly to a single cue. Other exercises include come and stay, and in more advanced levels, jump and retrieve. You and your dog can win titles in obedience and even compete in national championships if you're good enough.

Rally obedience is offered by the Association of Pet Dog Trainers (APDT) and the AKC. The intent of rally is to make obedience more fun. Instead of being very structured and formal like traditional obedience, you are encouraged to interact with your dog on a rally course. Instead of following a judge's instructions, you follow signs on a preset course, praising and talking to your dog throughout the run.

Sighthounds might love lure coursing, while the terrier breeds might take to earthdog trials. If you lean more toward quiet adventure, animal-assisted therapy might appeal to you. The opportunities are endless, and they are just waiting for you to find them.

In appendix III, "Canine Activity Contact Information" at the end of this book, you will find contact information for many of the canine activities that are available to you and your dog. Appendix IV, "Resources," contains a list of resources—books, magazines, and videos—that can help you follow the positive path to your training goals. Remember that every time you interact with your dog, one of you is training the other. Even if you never do an organized canine sport, you are training your dog for the rest of his life. Or he is training you. Or perhaps both.

Training is much more than teaching your dog how to behave. It is a way of being with your dog. Be fair. Be kind. Be positive. Be as loyal and honest with him as he is with you. And most of all, be joyful together.

PART III

Ain't Misbehavin':
Addressing Behavior
Challenges

Always make "Come!" fun and rewarding for your dog.
Don't poison your cue! (Photo by Pat Miller)

Chapter 17

The Poisoned Cue (And Other Important Training Concepts)

Now that you and your dog are well on your way with your basic Good Manners training program, it's time to give the two of you some additional food for training thought. In this chapter you find some more advanced concepts and training methods that help you hone your training skills, improve your dog's reliability and responsiveness, and enhance your relationship with your canine best friend.

HABITUATION/LEARNED IRRELEVANCE/ THE POISONED CUE

Habituation occurs when your dog learns to ignore an environmental stimulus—a sound, for example, like the ringing of the doorbell, or a disturbing sight, like a full-sized poster of Santa Claus. A dog who has lived all her life in the country or suburbs may discover many disturbing stimuli if she moves to the city.

Dubhy, our Scottish Terrier, was an adolescent when we found him as a stray and brought him home to join our pack. He had lived all his life outdoors, and the first time he saw his reflection in a full-length mirror he spent several minutes, on several occasions, peering behind the door to try to find the other dog. Eventually he habituated to the elusive Scottie and stopped looking. Habituation is useful for training because dogs can adapt to stimuli that are initially quite startling and distracting.

Sometimes *sensitization* occurs instead. Rather than habituating to a sound such as the doorbell, a dog may become more and more reactive each time the stimulus occurs. Thunder sensitivity is a perfect example of this. Force-based trainers (not us!) make use of sensitization in training in situations involving avoidance conditioning (booby traps) and aversive counter conditioning. Positive trainers rarely do. I have not resorted to doing this since the early days of Peaceable Paws (more than ten years ago) when I used it once. (See chapter 8, "Should You Ever Punish?")

Learned irrelevance is similar to habituation. It applies to a dog who has learned to ignore a specific *cue*, rather than become accustomed to a startling stimulus. This is not deliberate willfulness on the dog's part, but rather her lack of response to a cue that has failed to have consistent and sufficiently strong significance attached to it. The cue becomes meaningless if it doesn't have a consequence.

Come is a commonly used cue that has attained learned irrelevance for far too may dogs. Lots of dog owners use this word to call their dogs long before they ever take the time to actually *train* their dogs to come on cue. By the time they try to teach the cue, the dog has already learned that the word is meaningless—she has learned to ignore it. You always want *wonderful* things to happen when your dog comes to your call—the meaning of the word "Come" should be, "Hurry over here—there's really, really good stuff happening!" She should have, as consistently as possible, a totally positive association with the Come cue so she always wants to come when you call her, and so the cue doesn't become irrelevant—or worse.

On the extreme end of the cue/association continuum lies the ominous-sounding "poisoned cue." A cue becomes poisoned when it sometimes has a negative consequence instead of a positive one. Again, Come is a perfect example. Your dog dashes out the front door when you open it to accept a UPS package. You charge after, calling Dash at the top of your lungs. She zips across the street, almost getting hit by a car. Now panicked, you scream "Come!" in your most intimidating tone. Hearing the fear and anger in your voice, Dash runs away even faster. When you finally catch up to her in a neighbor's yard and she meekly creeps to your stern command to come, your adrenalin has fueled your emotions to a peak. You fiercely tell Dash what a bad girl she's been, march her back home and shove her into her crate for a timeout. Even though you usually try to make good stuff happen when you call Dash to come, she's now learned that sometimes bad stuff happens when you call her. Oops. You've just poisoned your Come cue.

Poisoning isn't even always caused by harsh punishment—it can just be a repeated association with something the dog finds mildly aversive. Perhaps Dash doesn't like to have you reach for her collar. In fact, that's one of the reasons she's hard to catch when she dashes out the door. But frequently when you call her and she comes to you, you take hold of her collar to put her in her crate (which she's also not fond of), clip her nails (another distasteful activity), or give her a bath. She has *lots* of negative associations with his Come cue—it was poisoned even before you yelled at her in the neighbor's yard and marched her home.

The insidious thing about cue poisoning is that once it has taken place, it can be very difficult to reinstall a positive association. If your dog has learned that the word *come* means there might be a good consequence but there might be a bad one, it will be easier for you to train her to come with a new cue than to try to make the association consistently positive. I have heard owners and trainers use words such as *close*, *let's go*, and *here* in place of a poisoned Come.

Once you've trained a new Come cue, you have to remember not to poison that one too. If you have to do something to your dog that she's not fond of, do something wonderful when she gets to you, and a few minutes later end the fun and do the not-so-nice thing. Or go get her instead of calling her to you.

Meanwhile, make it a point to change her association with the things she doesn't like. Teach her that a hand moving toward her collar makes yummy treats happen. Then touching her collar. Then grasping her collar. Teach her that a hand moving toward her paw makes yummy treats happen. Then touching her paw. Then holding her paw. Then touching her paw with nail clippers. This process of *counterconditioning and desensitization*—changing the association with a stimulus—can be applied in countless training and behavior modification situations. It works best when done gradually with numerous repetitions at each step, and not moving on until the dog is obviously happy about the process at each step.

The fewer things a dog must do in her world (or have done to her) that she doesn't like, the less likely you are to poison her Come cue!

SALIENCE

When we say something is *salient* to a dog, we mean it has noticeable significance to her. Your dog learns to sit even in the face of distractions because the hotdog you are holding in front of her face is very salient. When we associate the hotdog with the verbal cue Sit, the cue itself becomes significant. The salient stimuli in the environment—you, your hotdogs, and the Sit cue—are more significant than the distractions. They *overshadow* the dog barking across the street, the skateboarder whizzing by on the road, the slamming of a car door down the block. If your dog is too distracted to respond to the Sit cue, then the distractions are more salient than you and your hotdogs. You either need to move your training to a less distracting environment, or find a way to make you, your treats, and your cues more significant to your dog.

BLOCKING

Blocking is a phenomenon that occurs when the use of a known cue overrides the dog's ability to learn a new cue for the same behavior. Keep in mind that while dogs can only learn one response to a particular cue (*sit* must always mean "sit," it can't sometimes mean lie down), they *can* learn several cues that all mean the same behavior. Dubhy, our Scottie, can lie down in response to the Down cue in English, French, Spanish, German, and two different hand signals. This happened as a result of his role as a demo dog in some of my classes.

I use the Down exercise to introduce my students to the importance of teaching their dogs to respond to verbal cues without body language assistance. I start by having the handlers lure the Down. As soon as the dog will lie down easily by following the lure (treat), I introduce the verbal cue and explain that any new cue being taught must always *precede* the known cue. I use a demo dog to show them that the dog doesn't initially understand or respond to the word *down* until we associate it with the luring motion that means "down" to the dog. The motion is *salient* to the dog—the word is not.

I explain to my students that in order for the dog to hear the word and learn that it also has significance, they must say the word *first*, then lure the dog down. If they give the verbal cue at the same time or after they lure, the lure *blocks* the dog's ability to learn the new cue.

With enough repetitions of the sequence—verbal cue, followed by lure (and *click!* and treat when the dog performs the behavior)—the dog will learn that the verbal cue also has salience, and you will no longer need to lure her down—she will lie down when you give her the verbal cue.

Oh—Dubhy's multilingual talents? As soon as he learned a new verbal cue for down, I could no longer use that cue to show my students what to do when the dog hadn't yet learned the word—Dubhy would go down too quickly. I had to keep switching to new verbal cues in order to show them how to avoid blocking when adding a new cue for a known behavior.

FADING THE LURE

One of the biggest complaints you'll hear about positive training is that you always have to have food in your hand to get your dog to do what you ask. This is true *only if* you don't make the effort to fade your lures—that is, to get your dog to respond to your cues when there's no treat in sight. If you don't fade lures fairly early in your training program, you and your dog can *both* become dependent on the presence of food to get behaviors to happen.

The good news is it's easy to fade lures; you just have to remember to follow the steps to do it. Let's take Down as our example:

1. **Lure the behavior:** Move your treat toward the floor, clicking your dog for following, giving a nibble of treat with each *click!*

2. **Add the cue:** When she lures down easily every time, say the Down cue each time just before you lure her down. Repeat a half-dozen times. Remember to *click!* and treat each time.

3. **Pause before luring:** Now say "Down!" and pause. Wait for several seconds, then lure her down. *Click!* Treat. By following the word with the lure, you are translating, telling her that the word *down* means exactly the same thing as moving the treat toward the floor. Repeat several times.

4. **Add a little body language:** As you say "Down!" or immediately thereafter, bend forward just a tiny bit from the waist. Since you probably bend forward when you lure, this little body language hint might jump-start your dog's brain into moving down. If not, wait a few seconds and then lure.

5. **Watch for clues:** Sometimes your dog will make small movements that tell you she's starting to make the connection between the cue and the behavior. When you give the Down cue, she may look at the floor or lower her shoulders a little bit and then look at you as if to say, "Is this right? Is this what you mean?" If you catch these clues with a *click!* and quickly lure her the rest of the way, you've answered her question and she'll probably understand and respond to the cue more quickly.

EXTINCTION

Extinction means taking a behavior that has been reinforced and making it go away by removing all reinforcement. You can deliberately extinguish an unwelcome behavior by taking away any reinforcement your dog might be getting for it. We extinguish the behavior of jumping up by making sure no one pets, talks to, or looks at the dog when she jumps, and by stepping away so she doesn't even have the pleasure of making contact with her paws.

You can also *accidentally* extinguish a *desired* behavior by forgetting to reinforce it or by not reinforcing it enough. Reinforcement isn't always treats—it's anything your dog likes: toys, play, eye contact, praise, pets, runs . . .

When you use extinction to make a behavior go away, be aware that there is often an *extinction burst*—the behavior gets worse before it gets better because the dog is trying really hard to get reinforcement for a behavior that paid off in the past. You want to be sure *not* to reinforce the dog during an extinction burst, or you've just taught her that *trying harder* gets reinforced. Don't give in (unless the dog is in danger of injuring herself); comfort yourself with the knowledge that the extinction burst usually means you're close to success.

Another extinction-related phenomenon is *spontaneous recovery*. Days, weeks, or even months after you extinguished a behavior, it suddenly rears its ugly head again, probably because the right set of circumstances occurred to refire the same old neuron pathway. The good news is, assuming you make sure the behavior isn't reinforced, it should go away again quickly, and much more easily than the first time.

Premack

Since we have the Premack principle, one of my interns, tongue in cheek, wondered in a recent academy if there are mack or postmack principles. The answer is no. Premack is the surname of a scientist (first name David) who in the mid-1960s articulated the concept that you can use a *more* rewarding behavior as the reinforcer for a *less* rewarding behavior, thereby improving the performance of the lesser behavior. For example, if your dog would rather chase a bunny than come when you call her, you can use the Premack principle to teach her that she will get to chase a bunny—sometimes—if she comes to you first. You start by using Premack indoors in a controlled environment to teach her how it works, and when she's doing well there, move her outside.

Leave your dog on a sit/stay and walk across the room. Your helper, with a plate of tasty treats, stands halfway between you and your dog, slightly off to one side. Your helper should also have a bowl to cover the treats when your dog tries to eat them.

Now call your dog. If she stops to investigate the plate of treats, the helper covers the plate and doesn't let her have a taste. You keep calling your dog cheerfully and enthusiastically. When she finally comes to you, gently grasp her collar, say "Good girl!" then release her collar and say "Go get it!" Race with your dog back to the treats, now uncovered, and let her have a couple of bites. Then cover the plate and try it again. Eventually—sometimes surprisingly quickly—she will realize that she gets the treats *sooner* if she comes to you *first* and she will fly past the uncovered plate as fast as she can.

This principle is also sometimes called Grandma's Law, expressed as "You have to eat your vegetables before you can eat your dessert."

There are a couple of drawbacks to using Premack in real life: (1) If the vegetables are too unpalatable, dessert may also lose its appeal; and (2) you can't control the bunnies.

GENERALIZATION

You may have heard your trainer say that dogs don't "generalize" well. This means that just because Sweetpea learns to sit beautifully in front of the refrigerator in your kitchen, she may not necessarily sit when you ask her to at the reception counter of your dog's veterinary clinic. She thinks *sit* means "sit in front of the refrigerator." You think she's being stubborn because she "knows" how to sit, when in fact she really only knows how to sit on cue at home, in the kitchen, in front of the refrigerator—she hasn't learned to generalize the behavior.

The statement that "dogs don't generalize well" is actually only a half-truth. Most dog owners can tell stories of "one-trial" learning—where a single experience taught a dog to fear small children, or to chase bunnies that run, or programmed some other high-arousal, strong behavioral response.

Behaviors that are slow to generalize are most often those that involve *operant conditioning*, where the dog acts on the environment. Fido has to *learn* that she can make good things happen by sitting. Then she has to learn that the same "sitting" behavior makes good things happen in lots of places. Behaviors that involve a strong emotional response such as fear, or the chase instinct, are quite often learned in a single incident—a child tripped over her and startled her, or a rabbit jumped out in front of her, tantalizingly close, and she gave adrenaline-pumping chase. In these cases of *classical conditioning*, where the environment acts on the dog, Fido doesn't have to *learn* the emotional response, it just happens. It's easy for the response to happen the next time she sees a child, or a rabbit, even if the child doesn't trip over her or the bunny doesn't jump up and run.

So how do you help your dog learn to generalize operant behaviors? By doing exactly what your trainer probably told you to do—practice with her in as many different places as possible. In line at the pet supply store. At the veterinary clinic. On your walks around the block. In the waiting room at the groomer. In the aisles of the home improvement store. In addition, if a dog has truly generalized her Sit cue, she will sit if you whisper it, yell it, if you're standing next to her, sitting on a chair, or lying on the floor across the room.

The more behaviors you help her generalize, the easier it becomes for her to generalize each new behavior. Before long, you'll have a dog who is as well behaved in public as she is in the comfort of her own home.

CHAINING AND BACKCHAINING

These are vitally important concepts that come into play when teaching a complex sequence of behaviors. The behaviors are linked together so that each behavior is the signal for the next behavior in the chain, and the opportunity to perform the next behavior becomes the reinforcer for the previous one. When a talented musician learns to play a piece by memory, he is *chaining*—each note or chord draws him forward to the next note or chord in the piece. He doesn't have to stop and think about what comes next. His reward at the end of the piece is the satisfaction of a job well done, the praise of his music teacher, and the audience's applause when he performs the piece flawlessly at the next recital.

The obedience retrieve is an example of chaining. With his dog sitting at heel, the handler tosses the dumbbell, then gives the cue to take it. Without any further instructions, the dog runs out to the dumbbell, picks it up, returns to her handler and sits perfectly straight in front of him, still holding the dumbbell in her mouth, until the handler gives the cue to release it and return to heel position. The retrieve over high jump is a similar chain, except the dog sails over the jump *in both directions*, going out and coming back, again without further cues from the handler.

Backchaining begins with the last behavior in the chain. Each step is added in reverse order, until the dog is performing the complete behavior. The theory is that when you teach the last thing first, your dog is always moving toward what she knows best, so she gains confidence as she learns the new links in the chain. The theory works. I wish I had known about this technique when I played piano as a child—I *hated* those recitals!

In the last years of Dusty's life, his hind legs weakened, and he could no longer navigate the steps to our back deck. We placed a ramp over the three steps down to our back yard so the aging Pomeranian could go up and down more easily. Dusty was afraid of the ramp. I tried luring him up, but he refused to set more than his front two feet on the surface. So we backchained. I set him on the top of the ramp, one body length from the deck, and lured him up to safety. He did that easily, and after several repetitions I placed him a little farther down the ramp and lured him up to the deck. It took less than ten minutes to get him confidently running up the ramp. Then we reversed it, and in just a few minutes he was running down the ramp as easily as he was running up.

The song "The Twelve Days of Christmas" is a classic example of backchaining. You may forget how many lords-a-leaping there are or how many maids a-milking, but I'd bet you get faster and more confident in your singing once you get to the five golden rings, and you *never* forget that partridge in a pear tree!

THE PRINCIPLE OF PARSIMONY

This is one of my favorite scientific principles of behavior and learning. Like most behavior principles, it applies to situations far beyond dog behavior and training, but it's very applicable here too.

It says unless there is evidence to the contrary, you must account for a phenomenon with the simplest explanation available. Or, as a favorite radio personality of mine likes to say, "When you hear hoofbeats, think horses, not zebras."

If your adult dog declines to go outside to the back yard when you ask her to, the simplest behavioral explanation is that she prefers to be indoors, and/or that she has no need to eliminate at the moment. Fear of the back yard and physical difficulty traversing the back porch steps are lower down the list, and "defiance" doesn't even count. The appropriate response is to make "going outside" as fun and rewarding as being indoors with you. If she continues to decline the invitation, then a more complex behavioral or medical cause would be suspect.

If your dog constantly pulls on the leash, the simple behavioral explanation is that she wants to go somewhere faster than you do. Dominance and defiance aren't even in the picture. If she normally walks politely on-leash but suddenly starts pulling, simple explanations would be that something frightened her and she's trying to get away from it, or something very enticing is in front of her and she's trying to get to it. Again, dominance and other complex motives are unlikely.

As you can see, training can be a little more complicated than the basic sit, *click!* and treat. The more you learn about the workings of your dog's brain, the better you'll understand how and why she does what she does, and the better prepared you will be to respond appropriately. And the more you'll want to know! It can only enhance your already wonderful relationship with your best friend.

The ideal housetraining subject—a brand-new puppy.
(Photo by Pat Miller)

Chapter 18

Pees on Earth: Happy Housetraining!

Nothing is more frustrating than a housetraining challenge. Just when you think you've got a handle on it, you look in the spare bedroom and find the spot that Spot has been using for a toilet ever since that day three weeks ago when you caught him in the act in the living room and let him know in no uncertain terms what a bad puppy he was.

When you communicate with your dog, you are sometimes teaching him something very different from what you intend. You thought you were teaching Spot that it was bad to go to the bathroom in the house. But he learned that going to the bathroom in front of you is a bad thing. So for three weeks now, he's been running off to the back bedroom when he had to go. Because no one yelled at him *there*, he's sure that he's doing the right thing. Well, at least the *safe* thing. You could take a long time, get very frustrated, and ruin a lot of carpets trying to teach Spot all the places that he's *not* supposed to use as a bathroom. But teaching him where he *is* supposed to go is much quicker and far more effective. Remember, think in terms of what you want him **to** do.

Like so many other training challenges, in the case of housetraining, an ounce of prevention is worth many pounds of cure. If you're just embarking on your housetraining journey with a new puppy, great! You've got all the advantages of starting with a clean slate. If you're tearing your hair out because your current housetraining program has been unsuccessful with your pup, or you have an adult dog with a housetraining problem, that's okay too—you just need to back up and start over again—and do it the right way this time. Yes, it will be more difficult, especially if your dog now has a well-established pattern of eliminating in inappropriate places, not to mention a fear of eliminating in front of humans. But housetraining is hardly ever impossible.

HOUSETRAINING IS SIMPLE

Dogs are naturally clean animals. They have an innate desire to keep their dens unsoiled. If you take early advantage of this, housetraining is usually simple.

When you first bring Spot home, whether he's a youngster or a grown-up dog, your goal is *never* to allow him to have an accident in the house. The formula for this is simple, but not always easy—it takes commitment and follow-through.

In the beginning, Spot will *always* be on a leash, in a crate or pen, or under the direct supervision of a responsible adult or older teen. You will give him lots of opportunities to do the right thing (go to the bathroom outdoors) and manage his behavior so that he doesn't have the opportunity to do the wrong thing (go in the house). Here's how this might look on Spot's first day home.

Developing Spot's Routine

Dad pulls into the driveway with puppy Spot in a crate in the back of the mini-van. He takes Spot out of the crate, puts the leash on, and walks him directly into the fenced backyard to the potty spot that the family has previously agreed upon. Spot can sniff around, but he doesn't get to go play yet. Dad waits patiently at the potty spot, resisting Spot's nearly irresistible attempts to engage him in play. After thirty seconds of restricted exploring, Spot squats and pees. "Yes!" says Dad, and gives Spot a tasty bit of dog cookie. "Good dog, Spot!" Now Dad takes the leash off and motions to the rest of the family that they can come out and greet the pup. Twelve-year-old Sissy and fifteen-year-old Junior walk out the back door, controlling their excitement. They calmly greet Spot, rewarding him with attention, treats, and praise when he sits, and turning their backs if he tries to jump up.

After several minutes of play, Dad suggests that they take Spot indoors. It's almost the pup's lunchtime, and Dad wants him to calm down before his meal. Spot's puppy pen is all set up and waiting in the middle of the living room. This was Junior's project. He first laid down a tarp, covered the tarp with a thick layer of newspapers, then set up the wire pen (often referred to as an *exercise pen*, or *ex-pen* for short) on the papers so that it pinned the edges down as much as possible. He put a Spot-sized crate in the pen (see chapter 6, "A New Leash on Life" for instructions on crate sizing and training) with soft bedding inside, placed a durable rug on the papers in the middle of the pen, and scattered several toys on top of it. Finally, he set a heavy crock water dish in one corner, away from the pen gate, and a couple of puppy pee pads in another. Now all the puppy pen needs is a puppy!

Dad walks into the living room with Spot on a leash so that the little guy can't dart off and initiate a game of chase the puppy. Dad walks into the pen with Spot and sits on the floor with him for a few minutes, encouraging the pup to play with his toys. While he plays, Mom fixes a bowl of puppy food in the kitchen. When the food is ready, Dad exits the pen, leaving Spot inside. Mom stands by the pen, and when Spot sits and looks up at her, she says, "Yes!" and sets the bowl inside the pen.

Spot devours his lunch, then looks around for something to do. The family is sitting around the coffee table eating their lunch. A little unhappy at being left out of the party, Spot whines for attention. The family ignores him. Realizing that he is *very* tired, the pup whines a few more times, then curls up on his rug. Mom says "Yes!" gets up, walks over to the pen, and hands Spot a small piece of cookie. Spot can barely finish chewing and swallowing before he is deep in doggy dreamland. While he sleeps, his brain processes three lessons he has begun to learn:

- That funny "Yes!" sound means I'm going to get a cookie.
- After I peed I got a "Yes!" and a cookie and then I got to have fun.
- Whining didn't get me anything. Quiet got me a "Yes!" and a cookie.

Junior and Sissy know that when Spot wakes up in twenty minutes or so, he will need to go to the bathroom. They stay in the living room, reading a book, and keep half an eye on their new puppy. As soon as he wakes up, they put him on his leash and take him outside to his designated bathroom place. Like their dad, they wait patiently at the spot until he pees. Sissy says "Yes!" and feeds him a cookie, then wants to play with him. Junior tells her they have to wait. Because Spot just ate lunch, Junior knows he's probably not quite done yet. Sure enough, in another minute Spot leaves a pile in his bathroom area. Junior says "Yes!" and Sissy feeds him a cookie; then they take him back inside to play.

Sissy wants to take the leash off. The kids take Spot to the den and close the doors. They don't want the pup to leave the room and get into trouble out of their sight—they know they are supposed to supervise him closely! The three youngsters play together for thirty minutes. Then Sissy remembers that she has schoolwork to do, and Junior has softball practice. They put Spot's leash back on, walk him to his pen, and leave him inside with a kibble-and-cream-cheese-stuffed Kong toy to keep him happy. Dad is cooking in the kitchen. He makes a note of the time so that he can take Spot out in another half-hour or so. For the rest of the day, while Mom does yard work and the kids are busy, Dad takes Spot out to the toilet area every hour on the hour. In the evening, Sissy and Junior take over Spot duty until their bedtime. Mom takes the little guy out for a last bathroom call at midnight.

Spot spends the night in his crate in Mom and Dad's bedroom. He fusses a bit before going to sleep, but when fussing doesn't pay off with attention from his humans, he gives up and goes to sleep. At 3:00 AM he wakes up, aware of a very uncomfortable sensation in his abdomen. His bladder is full—he has to pee. He looks around his crate for a suitable spot, but it's too small—he does not want to pee in his own bed. He tries holding it for a while, but he really has to go! He whimpers in discomfort. Then he starts to cry loudly. This is really serious! Finally Mom hears him. She jumps out of bed, opens Spot's crate, snaps his leash on his collar and carries him out to his bathroom place. She knows that his bladder is so full that she can't risk walking him through the house. Spot pees as soon as she sets him on the ground, and she gives him his "Yes!" and a treat. She waits a few more minutes, in case he has to poop too, but when nothing more is forthcoming she walks him inside, puts him back in his crate, feeds him another treat, and goes back to bed. Spot wants to play, but Mom knows that if she plays with him, he may start expecting "Romper Room" at 3:00 AM, so she ignores his crying. In a few minutes Spot settles down and everyone goes back to sleep.

Reinforce the Routine

This will be Spot's basic routine, with gradual modifications, for the next several months. The Yes will be replaced with the clicker, and starting on day two, all family members will start using the phrase Do It when he starts to eliminate. This will teach him to go to the bathroom on cue—a very useful thing when it is pouring rain or below zero outside! Spot can also be on-leash in the house near one of his humans rather than in his pen, perhaps keeping Mom company while she works in her home office, or lying on the rug next to Junior while he does his homework. The frequency of his outdoor excursions will gradually diminish as his ability to control his bladder and bowels improves. The length of his supervised, off-leash, indoor playtimes after he potties can gradually increase as he matures. When he starts leading his humans directly to his bathroom spot, he can start going out off-leash (assuming the yard is fenced), but someone still goes with him to reward him for his superb bathroom behavior. This is important—if he goes out alone and gets a cookie when he comes in the house, he is only being rewarded for coming back in, and he may forget to poop and pee outside in his excitement to come back in for his treat. Plus, if you don't know whether he went to the bathroom, you don't know if it's safe to give him some supervised free playtime. Don't get lazy!

Spot will probably be able to sleep through the night within a couple of weeks. He will always be confined, on a leash or under direct supervision when loose, however, until there is no doubt in everyone's mind that he is fully housetrained. If he is consistently rewarded for going to the bathroom outdoors and prevented from going indoors through proper management, he'll be housetrained before you know it!

WHEN HOUSETRAINING ISN'T SIMPLE

There are a few complications that can make housetraining more difficult. The first is medical. It is impossible to housetrain Spot if he has a urinary tract infection or loose stools. If Spot is going to the bathroom frequently, even in his crate, there's a good chance he has an infection or digestive upset. Have him checked out immediately. The sooner you take care of the medical problem, the sooner he can get back on the housetraining track. The longer he has accidents in the house, the more difficult your housetraining task will be.

Dogs and puppies who have been raised in an unclean environment can be devilishly difficult to housetrain. A dog who has been forced to live in his own filth may lose his natural inhibitions against soiling his own den—a soiled den is all he has ever known. This is one of the many insidious pitfalls of purchasing puppy-mill puppies from pet stores and disreputable backyard breeders. Clean cages in a pet store don't tell you anything about where or how the pup spent the first six to eight weeks of his life. This is also why it is a horribly bad idea to leave a puppy crated for too long. If he is forced to eliminate in his crate because you left him there for four hours, it's *your* fault. You will pay the price of losing the crate as a valuable housetraining tool if you destroy his den-soiling inhibitions.

As long as the basic inhibitions are intact, the housetraining program described in this chapter will work for adult dogs as well as for puppies. Prevent the accidents with good management, and reward and reinforce appropriate bathroom behaviors.

If the training program isn't working, or if you have an inhibitions problem, you need to get even more dedicated about preventing accidents. If Spot is soiling his crate at night, you may need to set your alarm every two hours and take him out—assuming there's no medical cause for his incontinence. Be sure the problem is a housetraining challenge and not submissive, excitement, or marking urination. Those are dog behavior challenges of a different color!

If you have followed a solid housetraining program and have ruled out medical and other types of behavior problems but Spot is *still* having accidents, it's probably time to call in a competent positive dog trainer or behavior consultant to help you find the key to Spot's bowels and bladder. Better to do this sooner rather than later—remember that the longer the problem continues, the harder it can be to resolve. In the meantime, you can take advantage of my favorite use for a rolled-up newspaper as a training tool: Every time Spot has an accident you can take the rolled-up newspaper and hit yourself in the head with it three times, while repeating, "I *will* supervise Spot more closely. I *will* supervise Spot more closely. I *will* supervise Spot more closely!"

Bart and Walt in happier times. (Photo by Pat Miller)

Chapter 19

Canine Social Misfits

Bart started out with all the advantages that a dog could want in life. His breeder was active on the show circuit and Bart, a handsome tricolor Australian Shepherd, was earmarked for the show ring. He should have lived the life of a pampered prince, touring the West Coast and maybe someday doing Madison Square Garden. But somewhere along the line, something went wrong. Maybe his nose was a little too long, or his stifles a little too straight. Whatever the reason, Bart's breeder decided he wasn't show quality and, at age 10 months, he was in the market for a new home.

Young adult, purebred Australian Shepherds should normally have no problems finding a pet home; they are intelligent, attractive, and easily trainable. And the *Babe*-generated (the film) popularity of the Border Collie has spilled over onto other herding breeds, Aussies included. Unfortunately, Bart wasn't normal. His breeder had overlooked a critical part of his early education. She lived in a remote area outside of Las Vegas, and Bart had not been exposed to enough other people or to the sights and sounds of the real world. He was unsocialized.

Bart's breeder had the audacity to list herself on the Internet under breed rescue for Australian Shepherds in order to seek a home for Bart. Perhaps she didn't see the irony. Most likely, she knew that it was a good way to find someone with a kind heart who would take her homegrown problem off her hands. At least she didn't have the nerve to charge an adoption fee when Walt, a kindly retired gentleman from Carmel Valley, California, contacted her about a possible adoption. When Walt met Bart, he knew the timid young dog would be a challenge. Taken by the dog's striking good looks and sensitive personality, however, Walt agreed to the adoption.

Meanwhile, across the country in Chattanooga, Tennessee, a female Chow—long gone feral after being abandoned by her owners—was scavenging in a dumpster at a county maintenance yard, trying to find enough nourishment to feed the puppies growing within her body. She and her three feral packmates were fed regularly by Missy, a soft-hearted resident who lived nearby, and irregularly by several county workers. Still, life was difficult for the pregnant feral dog. Her pups, soon to be born in a drainage pipe near the maintenance yard, would open their eyes in a few weeks to bleak prospects. Unless someone intervened, they would grow up wild, if they even survived, to face the same meager existence as their mother.

THEY'VE GOT TO BE CAREFULLY TAUGHT

Dogs aren't born full-fledged "man's best friends." As with all baby animals, there is a period in their lives when they must learn about the world in order to survive. This critical period is a window of opportunity for socialization—a time when puppies learn what is safe and good and what is not. Opinions differ as to how long the window is open, but it falls somewhere in the period between 4 and 16 weeks. After the window closes, anything not previously identified as safe will automatically fall into the unsafe category. Dogs must be socialized to the human world during this time or they will forever be fearful of new people, sights, and sounds.

Dogs who are well socialized receive lots of gentle human contact and handling from the time their eyes open. As they get older (8 to 16 weeks), they are given careful exposure to other stimuli—visits to the vet hospital and groomer; walks in town; rides on elevators and escalators; sounds of cars, motorcycles, and skateboards; people of different ages, sexes, and ethnic backgrounds; people who dress, talk, and move in strange ways; and people with umbrellas, crutches, wheelchairs, and facial hair. The more positive exposures a dog has to a wide variety of experiences during this period, the more confident and well adjusted she will be throughout her life, and the more easily she will accept new experiences, even without prior exposure. Guide Dogs for the Blind and other service dog organizations send their puppies to live with 4-H families, because the 4-H participants try to take their service puppies with them everywhere they go.

It is inexcusable that Bart's breeder, who should have known better, would allow him to grow up without the necessary social skills. And it is tragic that the Chow's puppies were born into a society that holds life in such low esteem that dogs are dumped by their owners to breed and produce feral puppies.

To a lesser degree than these two cases, there are many poorly socialized dogs around us—the dog who snaps at children; the one who shakes uncontrollably in the car; the pup raised in the country and then moved to the city, where she now overreacts to the bustle of urban life and the apartment dwellers next door complain about her incessant barking. An unsocialized dog is a canine social misfit—the doggy equivalent of the socially inept human who hides in corners at parties because he never learned how to relate to others. There are a lot of canine misfits out there hiding in the corners of life.

An Ounce of Prevention

The easiest way to avoid this problem, as with most serious dog behavior challenges, is through prevention. Although your veterinarian, concerned about diseases, may caution you against exposing your new puppy to the real world, failure to do so can result in a poorly socialized adult dog. The answer to this dilemma is to expose a properly vaccinated young Bart to a controlled social environment. Take him to a well-run puppy class, where he can meet lots of different people and lots of healthy puppies. Invite friends of all ages and races over and have them dress up in odd clothes, hats, umbrellas, and sunglasses. Invite children over to play gently with Bart and to feed him treats. The more positive encounters he experiences while his socialization window is open, the more adjusted, confident, and gregarious he will be as an adult. As long as you are careful to only expose your dog to other healthy dogs and puppies, your veterinarian's fears are not likely to be realized. In the long term, lack of socialization can be a bigger threat to your puppy's well-being than the risk of disease.

A Positive Pound of Cure

If you are the owner of a canine social misfit, don't despair. The good news is that you can take steps to make the world a less terrifying place for your unsocialized dog. The quality of her life can be improved with desensitization training that gives her confidence and helps her make sense of the world around her. Desensitization takes a lot of work and a patient owner, but it can be done.

It should come as no surprise that the methods used to rehabilitate an unsocialized dog must be positive ones. The poor pooch is already terrified of the world. Progress is slow in the best of circumstances, and when she starts taking tentative steps to emerge from her shell, the tiniest correction can send her scurrying back to safety. Each dog will progress at her own pace—some progress far more quickly than others. You must be patient. Pushing an unsocialized dog too quickly can destroy weeks, even months, of painstaking progress.

Here are the steps to take to foster courage in an unsocialized canine:

1. **Teach your dog a reward marker.** Review chapter 10, Core Exercise "1.1—Charging the Clicker," for more information.

2. **Reward-mark his entire meal.** If the dog is extremely unsocialized— fearful even of you—let this be the *only* way she gets to eat: by being in your company and, eventually when she's brave enough, by eating out of your hand. She needs to learn that *you* are the source of all good things. Reward-marking won't work well for a free-roaming feral

dog—she will have access to other food sources and won't have to tolerate your presence to find food.

Note: I *absolutely do not* advocate starving a dog in order to get her to take food from you. You will need to find an environment where she feels comfortable eating in your presence—if necessary, do this at first in a room or yard that's large enough where she can be fairly far away from you while she picks treats up off the ground and gets reward-marked for it.

3. **Reward-mark her for calm behavior around others.** When the dog knows that the bridge means treat you can *click!* and treat *any time she is being brave*. If she is normally afraid of children and she sits quietly next to you on a park bench while a child walks by, *click!* and reward. Look for very small, rewardable behaviors. If she glances at a child and doesn't react, *click!* and reward.

4. **Make a list of her fear triggers.** You probably have a good idea of what frightens the dog. These are her *triggers*. Make a list, and include *everything* you can think of. Ask other family members to help. Then prioritize your list. Now decide which trigger you want to start with in her desensitization program. Start with something achievable. For your dog's sake *and* for yours, it's important to have small successes throughout the process. You might need to take a big trigger and figure out how to break it down into smaller pieces.

   For example, if her number-one trigger is tall men with beards and cowboy hats, you might start with tall men. Using the process described in the next step, step 5, work on desensitizing her to clean-shaven tall men without cowboy hats. Meanwhile, start leaving cowboy hats around the house in conspicuous places, and occasionally put one on yourself. Other family members and people who are well liked by the dog can do the same. When she accepts tall men, you can advance to clean-shaven tall men with cowboy hats. Meanwhile, work at desensitizing her to short men with beards. Then try tall men with beards *without* cowboy hats. When you have desensitized her to all of the pieces, then you can finally put them together as tall men with beards wearing cowboy hats.

   Remember: This takes time and patience. If you skip steps, you may undo all of your painstaking training progress and have to start over again.

5. **Use counterconditioning and desensitization.** *Desensitization* is the process of gradually acclimating the dog to the things she is afraid of. *Counterconditioning* means replacing her involuntary undesirable reaction—fear—with a more desirable one that is incompatible with fear, such as the eager anticipation of a tasty treat.

Let's say the dog is afraid of strangers. Because you can't control a stranger's behavior, you need to create a stranger who will work with you. Get a friend (one the dog hasn't met) to act as your stranger and brief her ahead of time. Set up a system of simple hand signals so you can let her know if you want her to stay where she is, come closer, go farther away, or move to the side. If your dog's fear threshold is thirty feet—that is, if she starts acting stressed when strangers are thirty feet away—start with your stranger at thirty-two feet.

You should be sitting comfortably with the dog on a leash next to you in a controlled environment. You don't want some real stranger to wander through and destroy your carefully staged training session! While your dog is calm about the stranger's presence just beyond her threshold, feed her *lots* of tasty teats. Handfuls! Feed a few treats at a time, but keep them coming constantly. Then have your stranger walk by at a distance of thirty-two feet, gradually—very gradually—moving closer, a few inches at a time, if necessary, with each pass. (Of course, your stranger must be talented. She has to act natural, not be furtive or suspicious, and she can't make eye contact with the dog. A direct stare is a threat in dog language and is especially threatening to a dog who is already stressed.)

Keep feeding treats the whole time the stranger/friend is passing by. You want the dog to believe that the presence of strangers causes treats to rain from the heavens! If she starts to get nervous at twenty-nine feet, signal the stranger to stop. Feed the dog more treats until she relaxes, then end the session. Have the stranger walk away (another *huge* reward for the dog's good behavior; calm, brave behavior makes the scary thing go away!).

Schedule another session for the next day. (I *told* you this could take a long time!) If you made it to twenty-five feet during the first session, then for the second session you might have your stranger start at a distance of twenty-nine feet—if you think the dog is ready for that. If she seems stressed as you begin the second session, start again at thirty-two feet. If the dog continues to stay relaxed as the stranger moves around and approaches, give her lots of rewards and stop the session at a reasonable distance *before* she gets stressed. Don't push it. Success in slow increments is the key. Slow success is *far* more important than fast progress. You want the dog to know that the presence of strangers makes *good things* (lots of treats) happen.

Caution: Avoid Coddling!

As tempting as it may be, do not allow yourself to coddle your bashful dog. You will be adding to his stress and exacerbating his timid behavior, not giving him confidence, like you might think. If *you* act concerned, he will be even more convinced that there is something to be afraid of. You'll do better to act matter-of-fact, reassure him cheerfully, use calming touch and massage, and let him know that everything's okay. The target stick works really well in place of coddling.

It's important to always remember that your unsocialized dog is not acting out because of spite or malice. He is truly afraid, even terrified, of the things that he reacts to. Don't blame him. It's not his fault. Be patient and help him to slowly learn that the world is not such a frightening place after all.

In order for desensitization and counterconditioning to work, you need to be very good at recognizing your dog's signs of stress. The DVD *The Language of Dogs* by Sarah Kalnajs is an excellent resource for learning how to read your dog's body language signals.

6. **Reward-mark while others feed treats.** If your dog is more tolerant of people than in the scenario described in step 2, you can have other people feed her treats when you reward-mark, or they can reward-mark and treat. The ultimate goal is to have the dog believe that people are safe and good, not scary and dangerous. The more she will accept treats from others, the more she can associate the treats with good things, not just you.

7. **Teach her to target.** (Review chapter 11, Core Exercise "2.2—On Target.") Dogs love this exercise. It's like a treat vending machine—they push the button, they get a treat. By placing the target, which they love, near something that they are wary of, you can get them to approach the scary object. When they get clicked and treated for touching the target near the object, they soon decide that the scary thing isn't so bad after all.

OUTCOMES

Let's revisit the lives of Bart and the Chow-mix puppies. What became of them?

Walt engaged my services, and Bart progressed beautifully. He bonded to Walt immediately and with a few exceptions—most notably Walt's housekeeper—started to accept the world around him. In fact, he progressed so well that Walt often walked him off-leash around his peaceful gated community, and Bart made many friends. He even helped Walt host a pool party of more than one hundred people. Sadly, Bart died at a relatively young age, but he lived a happy life, thanks in no small part to Walt's commitment to positive training.

The drainage-ditch puppies fared even better. Missy found their den when they were 4 weeks old, took them home, and hand-raised them. By the time they were 8 weeks, they were well started on their socialization lessons, greeting visitors with welcoming yips and wagging tails. Missy placed them into carefully screened homes with caring families who were willing to commit to giving them lifelong loving homes, spaying and neutering them, and continuing their education so they could grow up to be normal dogs, leading normal doggy lives.

Dogs will be dogs; it's up to you to show them
how to be dogs around people. (Photo by Mary Bloom)

Chapter 20

Don't Worry, Be Happy

One dark and cold California winter evening, I noticed that our four normally well-integrated dogs were getting extremely cranky with each other. It was a particularly wet El Niño winter, and aside from brief potty excursions, the dogs had been shut indoors for several days. I eventually realized that they were suffering from cabin fever and needed to engage in some typical dog behavior. So I went to the dog supply cupboard and hauled out a few of their favorite things. In seconds, peace returned to the living room as our pack gnawed contentedly on their Chew Hooves and stuffed Kongs.

Healthy dogs chew. They also bark, dig, and run around. These behaviors are natural and necessary for them. As much as some of these behaviors may irritate us, trying to stop them is as futile—and potentially harmful—as trying to prevent our dogs from urinating and defecating. You don't try to stop your dog from going to the bathroom—you know that would be useless. Instead, you teach him to go to the bathroom at appropriate times, in appropriate places. You will be far more successful in dealing with the challenges of chewing, digging, and barking if you address these natural behaviors the same way.

CHOOSE YOUR CHEWS

Most dog owners realize that puppies need to chew. They chew to exercise their jaws, to ease the pain of teething, to explore their environment, and to relieve stress. Accordingly, most owners also provide their baby dogs with a flood of toys into which the pups can sink their needle-sharp teeth. The smart owner selects chew toys wisely, recognizing that she is laying the foundation for her dog's lifetime chew habits. Stuffed Kong toys, marrow bones, and other indestructible but inviting chew objects are better choices than items that resemble our valued human possessions. Discarded socks and old tennis shoes teach a pup to head for the closet floor and the laundry basket when the chewing urge is strong. It's not Jaws's fault that he can't tell which socks are his and which ones you are still using! Carrots, apples, and other hard raw fruits and

Tucker works on a Goodie Ship stuffed with liver treats.
(Photo by Pat Miller)

vegetables are also ideal puppy chews—satisfying to crunch, tasty to eat, and healthful all at the same time.

Chewing is also a good stress reliever, which is why dogs who are anxious about being left alone at home often become destructive. Your dog is *not* chewing your good sofa cushions out of spite or to get even with you for leaving. Rather, he is trying to ease the crushing panic he feels about being left alone. **Remember:** Dogs are pack animals. In the wild, being left alone can be a very serious threat to survival. To avoid anxiety-related destructive behavior, puppies should gradually be conditioned to being left alone so they can overcome their very strong and natural instinct to always be in the company of their pack. Providing your dog with a desirable and appropriate chew object prior to your calm departure can often help prevent separation anxiety from becoming a problem.

Safety First

You will need to use good judgment when choosing your dog's chews. Not all chew items offered for sale commercially are safe for all dogs. Dogs have been known to choke on rawhide, which can get soft and slimy when chewed, sliding down a dog's throat and blocking the airway. Rope toys can shred, and if swallowed, the pieces of string can become entangled in a dog's intestines—a life-threatening situation. Plastic eyes, noses, and squeakers from plush toys also pose a hazard to your dog's well-being. If your dog is a gentle chewer, then you have many more chew-toy options to offer him. If his nickname is Shredder, stick to the sturdiest toys you can find—the black rubber Kong toys are among the toughest—and even then, supervise to make sure he isn't whittling those down to a size he could swallow.

Oldies but Goodies

Sometimes we forget that adult dogs need to chew, too. As Jaws matures, you pick up his clutter of puppy toys and expect him to lie quietly on the hearth rug. In the wild, however, Jaws would still be chewing through the bones and muscles of the pack's latest kill. Because most of us feed commercially processed dog foods and our dogs don't get to exercise their important jaw muscles and teeth by gnawing on caribou legs, we have to make a conscious effort to provide our dogs with caribou-leg substitutes. If you feed your dog a raw diet rather than commercial foods, you can regularly give your dog chicken and turkey wings and necks. **Note:** These are fed *raw*, not cooked, as part of a complete diet plan. If you are interested in exploring a more natural, raw diet for your dog, research carefully and consult with animal care professionals who are knowledgeable in the field. *The Whole Dog Journal* is a good resource for information on feeding a natural, healthy diet, as are books by Dr. Ian Billinghurst. (See appendix IV, "Resources," for more information.)

You can teach good chew habits, like so many other behaviors, by managing your pup's behavior to prevent the behaviors that you don't want. If Jaws never learns in his youth that it feels good to chew on the leg of the antique mahogany coffee table, he's not likely to take up the hobby when he's grown. If he consistently relieves his urge to chew by chomping on a hard rubber Kong that tastes like cream cheese or peanut butter, guess what he's going to look for when the urge to chew happens? This means that Jaws, and the adult dog who already has inappropriate chew habits, must be kept in a chew-proof environment like a crate or an exercise pen while he is being programmed to chew on the right stuff. When not in the pen, he should be

supervised so that any intent to chew can be interrupted before tooth contact happens and redirected appropriately.

Punishing Jaws *after* you take a forbidden object away from him does no
good—he is likely to think that the last thing he did (giving up the object) is
what he's being punished for. Jaws can learn very quickly that chewing on an
item of high value to humans is a good thing to do because it will initiate a
rousing game of chase the puppy. If you punish him after you catch him, you
won't teach him not to play the game; you'll just teach him to run faster next
time! Don't let him suck you into his game—use management and supervision
to interrupt and redirect him *before* he is doing doughnuts around the dining
room table with your $150 running shoe in his mouth.

CAN YOU DIG IT?

Digging is a natural behavior for dogs, although one not quite as universally
strong as chewing. Dogs dig to bury valuable objects like bones; they dig to root
out burrowing animals; they dig to make dens and create cool resting spots on
hot days; and sometimes they dig just for the sheer fun of it. My Bull Terrier,
Clown's Caper, loved to dig, and I encouraged her to do so, in appropriate
places. One day while we were out hiking on the levee, she started digging with
unusual enthusiasm, even for her. I egged her on, and we were both having a
grand time—until she raised her head up from the hole with a big grin on her
face and a burrowing owl (a threatened species) in her mouth. I was aghast.
Fortunately, she acquiesced immediately to my Drop It cue, and the owl flew
off, apparently none the worse for wear.

Dogs who are most likely to engage in inappropriate digging are those who
are left to their own devices in the backyard for long periods. The obvious solution is to bring them into the house, where, in my philosophy of dog-human
relationships, they belong anyway. Dogs are *companion* animals, and they serve
that function best when they share our homes (dens) with us. Dogs who are
exiled to a pen or to the backyard are often excruciatingly bored and/or lonely, which gives rise to a long list of behavior problems, including barking, digging, escaping, hyperactivity, poor socialization, and aggression.

The Miller dogs spend a good twenty-three hours a day indoors. They are
always inside when we *aren't* home, and they go out several times a day for
potty and play breaks when we *are* home. They have very little opportunity to
dig destructively. Tucker, our Cattle Dog mix, would, on a hot day, dig a moist,
cool scrape in the shade of a hickory tree. Josie, our terrier mix, loved to dig for
gophers. If we had left them outside unsupervised for more than short periods,
the yard would certainly have suffered for it.

If you must leave your dog outdoors frequently for long periods, you can minimize yard damage in several ways. You can physically fence off the parts of the yard that you want to protect from Dozer's attentions. Keep your expensive landscaping in the safely protected portion, and resign yourself to hardy grasses and sturdy trees in Dozer's part. Good rodent-control measures that keep moles and gophers out of your yard will reduce the digging motivation for dogs like Josie who hearken back to their ancestral hunting drives. Some of the cooling pad products now on the market can eliminate your dog's need to dig up a cool resting place. These pads release moisture over a period of several days through the cooling process of evaporation.

If you want, you can even *encourage* your dog to dig—in the right place. Just as you teach your dog when and where it's okay to go to the bathroom, you can teach Dozer when and where it's okay for him to dig. You can build a wooden digging box frame—spacious enough to accommodate Dozer's size with room to spare—and set it where you want him to dig. Dig up the dirt within the framed area so it is soft and inviting. If your dirt is hard clay, add sand and

Keeping your dog cool can eliminate one cause of destructive digging. Here, Josie stays on a cooling pad that is soaked in water and cools the dog as the water evaporates. (Photo by Pat Miller)

potting soil to break up the soil and keep it soft. Now invite Dozer to dig in his box by burying a toy or bone just beneath the surface of the soil. Get excited and tell Dozer to go dig. Then help him dig up the toy. Repeat this game often, until he will run to his box and start digging from anywhere in the yard when you tell him to go dig. You can bury toys and bones in the box when he's not looking so that he never knows what he'll find in there. If you do see him starting to dig where he shouldn't, say "Oops! Go dig!" to interrupt and invite him back to the box. If he doesn't have lots of unsupervised time to reward himself for digging in the wrong places, he will eventually confine his digging to his box. An additional benefit to teaching him the Go Dig cue is that you can use it anytime you are in a place where digging is allowed—like the beach, where digging in the sand is great fun for dogs and humans alike. You can also make use of his talents when you need a hole dug—to plant a tree, put in fence posts, or perhaps bury a treasure.

A BARK IN THE PARK

We had just moved our two horses to our new home in Tennessee the day before. I was working in my office, trying to get caught up on some of the work I had let slide during our move the prior weekend. Our four dogs had been particularly barky over the past week, as they adjusted to the stimuli of the new neighborhood, especially the profusion of squirrels who seemed to take great delight in tormenting them from the branches of the hickory trees that surround the house. I became fairly irritated by the constant interruptions because each time they barked, I felt compelled to stop what I was doing to go see if the cause was UPS, FedEx, or, hopefully, the moving van with all of our furniture. When the pack started up yet one more time, I was tempted to just firmly ask them to be quiet without checking on yet one more false alarm. Was I ever glad I didn't. This time when I got up to check, I discovered that the horses had found a breach in the pasture fence and were running down our driveway toward the road and possible disaster. At that moment of crisis, I was graphically reminded of what a blessing our dogs' voices can be.

If Dogs Were Meant to Be Quiet . . .

One of the more disgusting things humans sometimes do to their dogs is *debarking*. Dogs come with voices; it's up to us to train them not to be chatterboxes. Debarking a dog by severing his vocal cords is an abomination. If barking is particularly annoying to you, steer clear of the breeds that are known to be talkative, such as many of the herding breeds (Shelties are high on the list), lots of the toy dogs, and some of the terriers. Of course, barkiness seems to be related, at least in part, to outgoing, exuberant personalities—the dogs who are least vocal tend to be those who are most self-contained and aloof, like Chows, Basenjis (who, although they don't bark, do scream), and Akitas. So, if you like bouncy, outgoing dogs, you may have to tolerate some barking along with the bouncing.

You don't have to tolerate out-of-control nuisance barking, however. Personality and genetics aside, there is no excuse for the dog who yaps nonstop in his backyard, at his front window, or on-leash in public. Dogs who do are usually bored, lonely, frustrated, or convinced that it's their job to do sentry duty.

All Quiet on the Home Front

Resolving the root of the barking behavior is important. Simply slapping a no-bark electric shock collar (shudder) around the backyard dog's neck may stop the barking, but it does nothing to help the dog become less bored, lonely, or frustrated. My answer to the dog owner who asks how to get a dog to stop barking in the backyard day and night is simply to bring him indoors. This relieves his loneliness because:

- He is now more a part of the family
- It does away with boredom because there are more interesting things going on inside the house
- It shuts out the stimuli that frustrate him—like squirrels in the trees and cats on the fence
- It lifts the burden from his shoulders of feeling like he's the only member of the pack who is guarding the den

Indoors, you can let him know that you have things under control and he doesn't have to worry about them.

You can't eliminate barking completely, just like you don't expect to eliminate all inappropriate chewing or soiling. You still want Woofie to alert you if someone is breaking into the house, right? The problem is, he can't tell if the person walking up the sidewalk is a friend, burglar, or rapist. If you *did* succeed in eliminating all of his barking, he would have to sit idly by and watch your stereo system and valuable jewels walk out the front door in the hands of a stranger. Most of us *want* our dogs to let us know when someone is coming—we just want to be able to turn the barking off when we want. You can do this with a positive interrupt, or you can get more inventive and teach Woofie to bark on cue in order to teach him to *stop* barking on cue.

As calm and sweet as this Sheltie looks,
this breed has a reputation for being notoriously barky.
(Photo by H. L. Nieburg)

Positive Barking Interruption

To use the positive interrupt, begin by teaching Woofie that *over here* means "Turn toward me for a *click!* and a treat." Practice this on-leash with a small distraction, like sniffing a bush, until Woofie looks to you eagerly when he hears the Over Here cue. Now you can start using it when he barks. Arrange for a friend to come to your house at a prearranged time. Put Woofie on a leash prior to the friend's arrival, and when he starts to bark at the visitor, call his name and tell him "Over Here!" As soon as he stops barking and turns toward you for his treat, *click!* and tell him "Quiet. Good boy!" then *click!* again for the quiet and give him another treat. (I actually have my clients say "Thank you!" to their dogs when we do this, to remind them that we really do appreciate having our dogs alert us to unusual visitors and events.)

After Woofie has stopped barking and has gotten his *click!* and treat, signal to your friend to repeat whatever it is that gets Woofie to bark—walking up the sidewalk, knocking on the door, opening the door, or whatever. The more you repeat it, the less excited Woofie will be about the knock on the door and the quicker he will be to turn toward you on the Over Here cue. Of course, the next time someone comes to the door, Woofie will be excited all over again—it takes time and numerous repetitions of this exercise to get Woofie to give up his deeply ingrained, out-of-control barking behavior.

Remember that you are not using the Quiet cue to *make* your dog stop barking—you are waiting until he stops barking and then telling him that the behavior of not barking is called quiet. In time, when Woofie has learned to associate the word with the behavior of being quiet, you will be able to get him to stop barking with the Quiet cue, but if you use it in the beginning *while* he's barking, you will be teaching him that *quiet* actually *means* "bark." In fact, I honestly believe that a lot of dogs think their owners are barking *with* them when they are actually yelling at them to shut up!

I avoid teaching dogs to bark on cue if they don't already bark a lot, but for those who are problem barkers, it can be a superb solution to the barking behavior challenge. Getting the bark on cue is the easy part—barky dogs are usually more than willing to offer the behavior. You probably already know what stimulates Woofie to bark. If it's a knock on the door, then knock on the door, *click!* when he barks, and feed him a treat. If this works, do it again, but say "Speak!" or "Who's there?" just before you knock. When he barks, *click!* and treat. Because he likes to bark anyway, in very short order he will probably bark for you on just the verbal cue, without the knock. Aside from using this exercise to teach Woofie to be quiet on cue, it can also be useful for self-protection. I had one client who taught her dog that What Do You Want? was the cue to start barking. She could then use it if she felt threatened by an approaching stranger, and her very friendly dog would bark nonstop and quite convincingly keep the potential bad guy at a distance.

Now that you have the bark on cue, you can teach Quiet or Enough by clicking and rewarding a pause in the barking. Again, remember that in the beginning you won't be asking Woofie to stop barking with the verbal cue; you'll just be associating the *quiet* word with the cessation of barking. Eventually, when you know he has made the connection between the word and the behavior, you will be able to use the cue to ask him to stop barking.

Remember first to thank him for alerting you to something going on in the world. You never know when he might be trying to tell you that there's a burglar outside, that Timmy has fallen into the well, or that your horses are running down your driveway.

This lonely Airedale pup anxiously awaits her owner's return. (Photo by Pat Miller)

Chapter 21

One Is the Loneliest Number

Dogs are pack animals. They are genetically programmed to live in a social hierarchy and to bond and have relationships with other members of their pack, just like we are. This is a good thing—it's the primary reason we love our dogs as much as we do. It's why they are our best friends.

Dogs used to occupy a very utilitarian place in our lives. They went hunting with us. They herded the flocks and guarded the farm. They protected our grain supplies from rodents and our chickens from varmints. Although dogs also filled the role of our companions as they assisted us with our chores, only the very wealthy and the very weird kept dogs *solely* as companions. Over the last fifty years, however, the dog's role in society has changed dramatically. Although there are still plenty of dogs who hunt, herd, and guard, the vast majority of dogs in this country are now kept primarily as companions.

In many ways, this is a good thing for our canine pals. Today's owners are far more likely to invest in high-quality food and medical care for their dogs than in the past. We spend millions of dollars a year on treats, toys, beds, collars, leashes, brushes, shampoos . . . even hats, jackets, and boots for our furry friends. All things considered, dogs are living in the lap of luxury compared to their recent ancestors—except for one thing: Many owners today do a pretty poor job of meeting their dogs' social needs.

In her natural environment, a dog is with other members of her pack close to twenty-four hours a day, seven days a week, fifty-two weeks a year. She gets anxious when she is separated from the safety and security of her pack, in part because her subconscious knows that she is much more vulnerable when she is alone than when she has her buddies around to protect her. When we domesticated the dog, *we* became the pack.

One hundred years ago, Mom was home all day cooking dinner, cleaning the house, weeding the garden, gathering eggs from the henhouse, and hanging the laundry out to dry. In many families, Dad was home all day, too, plowing the fields, mending fences, and tending to the stock, with Shep hanging out at his heels. Most farms had several dogs, so Shep had her canine pack for companionship as well as her humans.

As our society industrialized, more families moved into cities and then into suburbs. Dad left the farm and went to work in an office or a factory. Shep stayed home with Mom and started spending more time in the house. Her canine pals were left behind on the farm—one dog is plenty for most people in town—so she became more dependent on human companions to meet her social needs. This arrangement was working pretty well for Shep until the 1970s, when Mom was empowered by the women's movement and went to work outside the home, too. Now Shep was left home alone . . . and lonely. Today, the home where Shep has companionship 24/7, or anywhere even near that, is the exception rather than the rule. Because of that, today's dogs are suffering from an epidemic of behavior problems that result from being left alone for one-third to one-half of the day or longer, without company or supervision. The worst of these behavior problems is separation anxiety.

CANINE SEPARATION ANXIETY

Separation anxiety (SA), the canine equivalent of a panic disorder, occurs in some dogs when they are separated from a person or persons with whom they are closely bonded. A less intense stress response in dogs over being left alone is called *isolation distress* (ID). Destructive behavior, excessive vocalization (barking, whining, crying, and screaming), and inappropriate elimination are the most common signs of ID and SA. Other symptoms can include anorexia, diarrhea, vomiting, depression, and excessive licking and drooling. Dogs who are generally anxious in nature are more likely to experience ID and SA than dogs who are calm and confident.

Because these can be difficult behavior problems to resolve, it is vitally important to take the time to accustom a young puppy to being left alone. Lots of families make it a point to adopt their new puppy when they know someone will be home for a period of time. Working puppy parents might take a week of vacation to help the pup settle into her new home. Families may adopt little Shep at the beginning of the summer, when the kids will be home and available to spend a lot of time with her. This is a good plan: An 8-week-old puppy *does* need a lot of time and attention in order to learn her lessons in housetraining, socialization, and good manners.

This good plan falls apart, however, when the doting new owners forget to teach Shep how to be left alone during this window of opportunity for intensive training and socialization. Often, in fact, the family unintentionally rewards and reinforces Shep's unease at being by herself, by responding to her whine or bark when the pup expresses her dismay at being left alone even for a moment. Shep quickly learns that crying brings the pack back to her, and an isolation/separation vocalization problem has begun. When everyone goes back to work or school and the crying doesn't work to bring the pack back, Shep works herself up into a state of panic. In her terror, she shreds the door frame, trying to escape and find the security of her family. Her fear also causes her to lose control of her bowels and bladder—another reaction to extreme stress.

When Mom gets home from work, she finds the house in a shambles. Upset and angry, she tells Shep in no uncertain terms what a bad dog she has been, then drags her out to the backyard so she can clean up the mess. Shep, wildly excited that someone has finally returned to rescue her, doesn't understand that she is being punished for something that happened hours ago. She is confused and frightened that her previously friendly pack mate has suddenly, and for no apparent reason, turned aggressive. So, on top of all her stress about being left alone, Shep adds another stressor—her humans are scary and unpredictable when they finally come home. This just makes her anxiety worse, and her destructive behavior escalates.

Crating a dog who suffers from these stress-related disorders usually only makes things worse. Although confinement is the ideal solution for the dog who is being destructive due to unsupervised juvenile high spirits, SA dogs may panic even *more* when left alone in very close quarters. Thus distinguishing between the two behavior challenges is important. Separation anxiety destruction tends to focus around doors and windows, evidence of the dog's desperate attempts to escape her solitary confinement. Shep literally fights tooth and nail to get free and rejoin her pack. Rowdy, adolescent high jinks are likely to be more widespread and less likely to include serious destruction at possible exits. Your rambunctious pup may empty wastebaskets and engage in pillow fights, shred the toilet paper, and sample a few shoes, but the destruction, although it may be massive, somehow feels less desperate.

If Shep tolerates relatively brief separations and can handle long stretches of time in the crate while the family is home in another room, chances are her destructive behavior is *not* ID or SA. If, however, Shep clings to your heels as you move around the house, panics if she is shut in another room for even a moment or two, and trashes the house if you step out for just five minutes, chances are that it's a true isolation/separation stress behavior. The manifestation of these behaviors, while disturbing, often can be controlled if you commit to a long-term behavior modification program and take the necessary steps to minimize her stress and manage her behavior.

BEHAVIOR MODIFICATION

A successful behavior modification program will use counterconditioning and desensitization to gradually help Shep become comfortable with being left alone. Your trainer should help you identify a complete list of Shep's stressors—all the things that contribute to her anxiety—and help you eliminate as many of those as possible to reduce her stress level. The primary one, of course, is your departure, but there are lots of puzzle pieces that lead up to you walking out the door. If you can desensitize Shep to the various pieces of the puzzle, she will be in a much calmer frame of mind when you *do* leave, and she'll be less likely to panic and destroy things. Here's a sample list of a dog owner's departure ritual on a typical workday:

- Get up.
- Take Shep out for jog-and-bathroom trip around the block.
- Feed Shep.
- Shower.
- Get dressed, except for shoes.
- Eat breakfast.
- Let Shep out in fenced yard for last-minute potty.
- Check e-mail.
- Let Shep back in.
- Put on shoes.
- Put on coat.
- Hug and kiss Shep good-bye.
- Pick up purse or briefcase.
- Pick up keys.
- Walk out door.
- Get in car.
- Start engine.
- Drive to work.

As you can see, numerous items on this list all broadcast to Shep that the dreaded isolation is pending. As each item occurs in its programmed order, Shep's anxiety rises a notch until she is whipped into a near frenzy of anxiety. The more each of the elements can be defused—that is, disassociated from the departure ritual—the lower Shep's level of accumulated stress will be when you actually walk out the door. If you normally go shoeless in the house, for example, and only put on your shoes to go outside, putting your shoes on is a clear signal to Shep that you are leaving soon. It is a *reliable predictor* of your departure. To defuse this, start putting on your shoes at various times during the day when you are home, even if you are not planning to leave. Do the same thing with the other predictors, such as putting on your coat and picking up your car keys, even walking out the door, getting in the car, and starting the engine. The less reliable each of these becomes as a predictor of your pending absence, the less anxiety will be added to Shep's stress load by the time you walk out the door.

It also helps to vary your morning routine as much as possible. Although you really do have to shower *before* you put your clothes on, there are other things you can make less predictable. Some mornings, shower first, then feed Shep, then get dressed. Put your coat on and then check your e-mail. Put your keys in your pocket *before* you eat breakfast. You get the idea. Oh, and eliminate the dramatic good-byes altogether—your emotion only arouses Shep more.

Home Alone

At the same time you are defusing Shep's predictors, you need to help her become brave about being left alone. You can use this same procedure to prevent isolation distress and separation anxiety in a puppy. It will be much easier in a baby dog, who has not already developed ID or SA. You will need to do this in tiny steps. You can start from a Sit/Stay. Use a tether or, if she will crate quietly with you near her, crate her, then *click!* and reward her for the Stay or for being calm on the tether or in her crate. (If she keeps breaking the Stay, use the tether or crate and work on the Stay some other time.)

Take one step away from her, *click!*, return, and feed her a treat. Gradually increase the distance between you and Shep, moving toward the doorway to another room as you do so, and giving clicks and treats generously along the way. If Shep starts showing signs of stress (panting, drooling, whining, and so on), you are going too fast. You want her to stay calm during this exercise. If taking one step away stresses her, take a half-step, or a three-inch step—whatever is small enough for her to handle. When you reach the doorway, take one step outside, *click!* when out of sight, and immediately return to the room and feed her a treat. If she tolerates you out of sight for one second, repeat this several times. Then increase very gradually the amount of time you stay out of sight before you *click!* and return. You may get to the doorway in one training session, or it may take you several. The key is to teach her that you always come back and that she gets rewarded for calm behavior during your absence, no matter how short. When you can go out the front door, get in your car, and drive away for twenty to thirty minutes, you are probably home free. Most SA destructive behavior will occur within the first half-hour of your departure.

Behavior-Management Tips

The difficulty with the ID/SA behavior modification program is that it can sometimes take months to reach the thirty-minute benchmark. Normal humans have to leave Shep alone for extended periods of time long before the program is finished. Meanwhile, every time she has an episode, it's a setback to the program. Here are some behavior-management tips that can help you get through the tough times:

- Spend fifteen to twenty minutes in a hard play session every morning to take the edge off Shep's energy level before you leave the house. End the session at least fifteen minutes before you leave so that she has time to settle down and relax before your departure.

- Provide as much exercise as possible at other times of the day as well. A dog who has a reservoir of pent-up energy is more stressed than one who is tired. A tired dog is usually a happier and better-behaved dog.

- *Be calm* when you leave and return. Dramatic good-byes and hellos raise Shep's anxiety level. If you find damage when you come home, calmly put Shep outside and clean up. Punishment for something that occurred out of your presence is totally ineffective and will only increase her anxiety about your homecoming, making the behavior worse. (Routinely removing valuable items from Shep's reach can help keep your anger and frustration levels down.)

- Give Shep a Kong toy or marrow bone filled with peanut butter or cheese just before you leave. This will take her mind off your departure and keep her occupied for that first half-hour when most destructive behavior occurs.

- Do not crate Shep unless you *know* she stays calm in the crate while you are gone. Dogs with separation anxiety can panic in close confinement and do serious damage to themselves. A room or garage with nothing in it that Shep can harm *may* suffice if she is comfortable there—you can test this by leaving her in the room for short periods with the Kong or marrow bone while you are home. If she is calm while you are there, she might be content to stay there while you are gone (but she may not).

- Try doggy day care. There are commercial operations that provide this service (be sure to check them out first—strange dogs should never be left loose together without someone in attendance), or you may be able to find a friend or neighbor who is home during the day and willing to Shep-sit for you.

- Adding a companion canine may have the same result as doggy day care, but you should only adopt another dog if you really want another for yourself as well as for Shep. Try borrowing a friend's dog first (one whom your dog likes) to see if it helps. If it does, you might be able to borrow your friend's dog on a regular basis as a long-term solution or until you find the right permanent companion for Shep. Be careful—addition of a canine companion doesn't always solve the problem; you could end up with *two* separation anxiety challenges instead of one.

- If inappropriate defecation is a problem, try feeding Shep only in the evenings until the separation anxiety is under control. (This strategy isn't appropriate for a young puppy, however.)

- If these measures don't work, you may want to consult with your veterinarian about using one of the very effective pharmaceutical products now available to reduce a dog's stress chemically while you continue your behavior-modification program to overcome her anxiety. Please note: These drugs will not cure Shep all by themselves—they *must* be used in conjunction with an appropriate training program in order to be truly effective.

- Seek the help of a competent trainer or behavior consultant to help you implement a behavior modification program. Most owners are not able to resolve serious SA problems without the counsel of a skilled animal-care professional.

Separation anxiety is not an easy problem to deal with, but it can be managed. A lot of dogs like Shep end up at animal shelters because their owners are unable or unwilling to do what is necessary to rescue them from the isolation hell that we had created for them in the first place. Your dog is fortunate to have a committed owner who is willing to find a way to make life less stressful for both of you.

Dogs with aggressive behaviors, such as this one, often have short life spans. (Photo by Sumner Fowler)

Chapter 22

A Biting Commentary

In a recent and disturbing incident in the Lookout Mountain (Tennessee) community, Murray the Golden Retriever attacked a woman who was walking past his house. He inflicted three bite wounds, one each on her leg, side, and buttocks. The victim, understandably, was at first terrified, then angry. In the brouhaha that followed, residents polarized into kill Murray and save Murray camps. Emotions ran high, and the judge's decision to release Murray to a training program for drug-sniffing dogs was not a popular one with those who felt that a dog who has inflicted a serious bite is too much of a threat to be allowed to live under any circumstances.

Murray was not a bad dog. He didn't deserve to die. Certainly, it would have been sheer folly to return Murray to the circumstances in which he had been previously kept to risk a repeat incident that could easily be more serious the next time. However, before inflicting a death sentence on a dog, it is important to understand dog behavior and to determine whether the risk of a future bite can be reasonably mitigated.

TOO MUCH STRESS = POSSIBLE BITING

Remember, all dogs can bite. And under the right set of circumstances, the gentlest, most loving dog can be induced to bite. A dog's teeth are important tools, and every dog is aware of their potential use as offensive or defensive weapons. Indeed, it is a miracle that people aren't bitten more often. I choose not to call dogs who bite aggressive dogs, but rather dogs with aggressive behaviors.

Even more important, every dog has a *bite threshold* (that is, a point beyond which, if pushed, he will bite). Some dogs' bite thresholds are low; some are high. Aggression is caused by stress. Each thing (*stimulus*) that causes a dog stress is a small building block (*stressor*) toward that dog's bite threshold. The lower a particular dog's bite threshold is and the more things that cause that dog stress, the more likely that dog is to bite. This is why Buddy the Beagle, who is normally great with kids, one day turned around and bit Johnny in the face. Enough building blocks combined at that moment to push Buddy past his bite threshold. Let's take a closer look at Buddy's stressors and figure out why Johnny was bitten. Buddy's stressors are:

- Small children under age 4 (Johnny is 7 years old)
- Thunder
- Men with beards
- Moderate to severe pain

On the day Johnny was bitten, his cousins were visiting. His cousins' family includes 11-month-old Shawn, 2-year-old Joey, and 3-year-old Brittany. The cousins have visited before, and there has never been a problem. However, since their last visit, Uncle Jack has grown a beard. Plus, there was a thunderstorm rumbling through the valley. In fact, it had been storming for three days straight. Finally, Buddy had a rotten tooth that his family was unaware of that was causing him a moderate amount of pain.

Buddy's bite threshold is fairly high, as is typical of Beagles. However, every single one of his building blocks were stacked together in that moment, and he just couldn't handle it. When Johnny went to retrieve little Shawn, who was crawling toward Buddy's bone, he bumped the side of Buddy's face and hit the rotten tooth. Seemingly out of nowhere, apparently "without provocation," as so many bite reports claim, Buddy snapped, catching Johnny in the face as he bent down to lift Shawn. In the aftermath, Buddy is banished to the backyard while the family ponders his fate.

If Buddy is lucky, the family will find a competent positive trainer or behavior consultant (one who does not use physical punishment) who will help them identify Buddy's stressors, guide them through a desensitization program so he is less stressed by the stimuli that currently upset him (to minimize the possibility of stressors pushing him past his bite threshold again), and help them figure out how to observe and manage his behavior so he is not compelled to bite if his stressors are building up. If he is not lucky, he is facing an unnecessary and tragic, one-way trip to the vet hospital or animal shelter and an appointment with the euthanasia needle—unnecessary and tragic because in Buddy's case, if it weren't for the rotten tooth, chances are he would never have bitten, even in the presence of several of his stressors.

The longer a dog's list of stressors, the more likely he is to eventually bite someone. This is why early and ongoing socialization is so critically important. In fact, thorough socialization may be the single best thing you can do to ensure that your dog has a long and happy life. Dogs who bite tend to meet untimely ends.

CLASSIFICATIONS OF AGGRESSION

There are a dozen or more commonly recognized classifications of aggression, including status-related aggression, fear-related aggression, maternal aggression (a mom protecting her puppies), play aggression (when a dog's level of arousal escalates during play and turns into aggression), displaced aggression, pain aggression, territorial aggression, possession aggression, protection aggression, barrier aggression, and redirected aggression. In each category, an underlying stressor is responsible for the dog's aggressive response. For example, in a case of status-related aggression a higher-ranking dog could be stressed by what he feels is an inappropriate response by a lower-ranking dog (remember that rank is fluid!). A dog may be stressed by the presence of a stranger/intruder on his property (territorial aggression), because he thinks you're about to take away his bone (possession aggression), or in the case of a mother dog because she thinks someone is threatening her puppies (maternal aggression). Most dogs who display aggressive behavior fall into more than one of these categories.

Chances are good that Murray's bites were a result of a combination of barrier aggression and pain aggression. Dogs who are kept on chains and behind wire or electronic (underground) fences are constantly visually stimulated into a state of arousal whenever someone or something (a person, another dog, a cat or squirrel, the mail carrier, a child on a skateboard or bicycle, a car) passes by. They see an intruder, they bark, and the intruder leaves.

What may have initially been friendly barking increases in intensity, and dogs bark more aggressively as they realize that they have the power to make intruders leave. (The "intruder" was going to leave anyway, but the dog does not know that; he thinks he made it happen.) The aggressive behavior is reinforced day after day with each success, and the aggression escalates. Now add the electric shock collar that is part and parcel of the underground pet fence. When the dog pushes the boundary limits of the fence, he gets shocked in the neck. Now he associates the pain of the shock with the passersby, and he's really aroused! Not only are they intruding, requiring him to keep chasing them off, but now they're fighting back and hurting him. When he does finally burst through the fence or snap his chain, woe to the unlucky person who happens to be passing by at that moment! It's no wonder that tying a dog up is one of the most effective ways of making him aggressive, and that electronic shock fences have been associated with numerous cases of barrier and pain-induced aggression.

California is one of several states that have passed laws limiting the circumstances under which dogs can be chained or tethered. Such laws recognize that tethering or chaining dogs is cruel and fosters aggression.

CLASSIFICATIONS OF BITES

Dr. Ian Dunbar, a well-known veterinarian, dog trainer, and behaviorist, has developed a six-level system of classifying bites:

- **Level 1 Bite**—Harassment but no skin contact. This is the so-called *snap*. Don't kid yourself. A snap is a bite from a dog with high bite inhibition. It is a lovely warning signal, telling us we need to identify the dog's stressors and either desensitize him or manage his behavior to avoid exposing him to the things that cause him undue stress.

- **Level 2 Bite**—Tooth contact on skin but no puncture. Again, this is a bite from a dog with high bite inhibition, and a warning that the dog is serious. It's a very good idea to remove the dog's stressors at this point, before he graduates to the next level.

- **Level 3 Bite**—Skin punctures, one to four holes from a single bite (all punctures shallower than the length of the canine tooth).

- **Level 4 Bite**—One to four holes, deep black bruising with punctures deeper than the length of the canine (which means the dog bit and clamped down), or slashes in both directions from the puncture (the dog bit and shook his head).

- **Level 5 Bite**—Multiple-bite attack with deep punctures, or multiple-attack incident.

- **Level 6 Bite**—Killed victim and/or consumed flesh.

With few exceptions, dogs who inflict level 6 bites are—and should be—euthanized. Level 5 biters are also a huge risk to human safety and should probably be euthanized unless there are compelling mitigating circumstances (for example, the dog was being tortured or the victim was a rapist attacking the dog's owner). Level 3 and 4 dogs need serious behavior modification in conjunction with immediate and significant changes in management and environment to remove any present risk. The behavior of level 1 and 2 biters can—and should—usually be modified with relative ease and the guidance of a behavior consultant without making major environmental changes.

All dogs can bite. Many who do are wonderful and well-loved companions the vast majority of the time. When a dog bites, it's usually due to the failure of his human to be observant and recognize the dog's signs of stress, to properly manage and modify behavior to shorten a dog's stressor list, and to control the environment to protect a dog from his stressors. Rarely is killing the dog the best or only solution to a biting dog challenge. Compassion for the victims (human *and* nonhuman), knowledge and understanding of human and animal

A classic recipe for aggression: keeping your dog on a chain.
(Photo by Sumner Fowler)

behavior, and a willingness to explore and pursue realistic and safe alternatives can map the path to a positive, appropriate, and life-affirming resolution for all concerned.

Murray got lucky. The save Murray camp had him evaluated by a behavior consultant (me!), and we determined that he was basically a sound, friendly dog who had been placed in an untenable situation. One of his supporters contacted a state law-enforcement agency, whose staff leapt at the chance to work with Murray to see if he would be a likely drug-sniffing dog candidate. As a backup plan, supporters also got a commitment from Golden Retriever Rescue to take Murray and place him in an appropriate environment should he fail drug-sniffing school. Thanks to people who understood dog behavior and were willing to advocate for the dog, the judge sided with the save Murray folks, and Murray was given a second chance to lead a long and productive life.

The author's Australian Kelpie, Katie, guards her owner from a visiting Basset Hound. (Photo by Pat Miller)

Chapter 23

The Green-Eyed Monster

Dusty, our nine-pound Pomeranian, stood over his dinner dish, eating his daily dinner ration as quickly as his tiny mouth would allow. Katie the Kelpie and Tucker the Cattle Dog mix, forty-five and seventy-five pounds respectively, always inhaled their meals and finished first, then hovered like vultures over Dusty, hoping he'd leave a few kibbles in the bowl—which he often did. By sheer virtue of their size, they could have easily bullied Dusty away from his dish and taken what they so obviously coveted. But if they hovered too near, Dusty issued a comical, pint-sized growl, and the two big dogs backed off until he finished.

RESOURCE GUARDING

Dusty was *resource guarding*—a perfectly normal survival skill that allows smaller, weaker, and lower-status dogs to keep possession of a highly valued object even when that object is the target of a larger and stronger dog's desire. The bigger dog acknowledges the smaller dog's possession rights and, thus, helps maintain harmony in the pack, although because he is bigger and stronger, he technically could—and occasionally does—assert his position of higher status to insist that the lower-ranked dog give up the prize.

Later that evening, my husband, Paul, was playing a rousing game of growly-butt-scratch with Tucker in the den. Katie, hearing the commotion from the dining room, charged into the den and effectively broke up the game by making ugly faces at Tucker and biting his heels. When Tucker was put in his place, Katie ran to Paul with her ears back, eyes squinting adorably, demanding attention for herself with a burst of irrepressible Kelpie energy. (I fondly describe Kelpies as Border Collies on caffeine.) Although this looked a lot like jealousy, and, indeed, we might call it that, Katie was also resource guarding. Paul's attention is a very valuable resource. Katie wanted it for herself and was willing to aggress on the considerably larger, often higher-ranking Tucker to get it. Because Tucker was an easygoing guy, he was willing to defer to Katie and give up his game with Paul rather than generate conflict.

In a more serious example of resource guarding, a potential client called me, shaken, because her Chow had bitten her badly the day before when she leaned down next to his food bowl to pick up a scrap of paper. She needed stitches, Bear is in bite quarantine, and she and her husband are debating whether or not to have him euthanized.

Natural behavior or not, resource guarding is a serious problem when it results in open aggression, especially aggression toward humans. It is a particularly dangerous behavior around children, because they tend to disregard our warnings about leaving Gimme alone when she's eating or chewing on a toy. Kids are also good at not heeding Gimme's warning signs when she stiffens and growls to signal that she is serious about defending her possession rights. Because a child is so much lower to the ground than an adult, if Gimme does feel compelled to back up her warning with teeth, those teeth are likely to end up in the child's face. Not a good outcome for either party!

If your dog's resource-guarding behavior is serious, I cannot stress enough the importance of working with a dog-training professional. Few nonprofessional dog owners have the knowledge, courage, or skills to modify serious aggression without assistance, and someone could be badly hurt in the meantime. Don't take any chances. If you are at all in doubt about your ability to work with your dog's behavior, seek qualified help.

Prevention, Prevention, Prevention

Resource guarding, like so many other behavior challenges, is a natural, normal dog behavior that just isn't acceptable in human society. It's also much easier to prevent than cure. If you have the advantage of working with a puppy or a dog who does not already display unacceptable guarding behavior, you can take steps to ensure that she doesn't start. You want her to know that good things come *from* humans, and that on those occasions when you *must* take something away, she gets something even better! Teaching Gimme, the Give exercise described in chapter 13, Core Exercise "4.4—Give" will lay the foundation for this important concept. You can build on this foundation by working with Gimme at her mealtimes in a four-week resource-guarding program.

Begin by setting her dish on the counter and putting her kibble in it. During week one, feed her the entire meal by hand, one kibble at a time. Have other family members take turns feeding her, and even allow an occasional visitor to do it so that she really gets the concept that humans *deliver* resources. Be sure to include children in the mix—you want her to realize that having small humans around her food bowl is a *good* thing.

In week two, set Gimme's empty food bowl on the floor and put her meal in a second dish on the counter. Now drop a few kibbles into her dish, and while she is eating those, drop a few more. You want her to realize that when a human hand approaches her bowl it is not coming to take her food away; instead, *more* food is coming. Again, have all the family participate, and include an occasional friend in the mealtime ritual.

During week three, put her bowl on the floor with about ¼ of her meal already in it. As she eats, continue to add more kibble, and occasionally add something really wonderful, like a slice of hot dog, chicken, or roast beef. Now you are teaching her that not only does the approaching hand bring *more* food, it actually brings *better* food. By now she should be pretty well convinced that having humans around her food bowl is a wonderful idea.

In the final week of your food bowl training, continue to drop kibble into her bowl as she eats. Now, assuming that she is showing absolutely no signs of food guarding when you reach toward her bowl, pick the bowl up while at the same time you drop pieces of her really wonderful treat on the floor. The message you're giving to Gimme is that food bowl going away = really wonderful food on the ground. While you have the food bowl in your hand, put a few more pieces of the really wonderful treat in it and set it back down on the ground after she has finished the treats you dropped. You are simply reinforcing the concept that having humans mess with her food bowl is good—it returns to her with even better stuff in it.

If you, and others, for the rest of Gimme's life, continue to occasionally drop great stuff in her bowl while she is eating, she will always recognize humans near her bowl as a *good* thing and should never develop a food-guarding problem.

Modifying Resource Guarding

What if Gimme already has a food-guarding problem? Management of her resource-guarding behavior is critically important. For Gimme's sake, as well as for the safety of any potential victims, don't leave food, food bowls, and other high-value items lying around. If Gimme guards her feeding area even when her bowl is put up, she should routinely be fed in an out-of-the-way location, where unsuspecting visitors are not likely to travel. If her resource guarding is unpredictable or extends to toys, furniture, and humans, she needs to be safely secured in her crate when guests are visiting, especially if children are present.

The first step toward changing Gimme's resource-guarding behavior is a good positive-training class. A good trainer will be able to work with you, without using physical punishment, to teach basic exercises that will help reduce

Gimme's resource guarding. Training opens the channels of communication and strengthens the relationship between you and your dog.

The more dogs you have, the more important it is for pack harmony that you train them. Good verbal control of your dogs identifies you as benevolent pack leader in their eyes and greatly enhances your ability to intervene peacefully and appropriately when necessary.

If Gimme is just beginning to show signs of mild resource guarding and has never actually inflicted a bite, you may be able to modify her behavior yourself. Anything more serious than that, however, requires the guidance of a dog-training professional. While the training class is teaching the two of you how to communicate better, you can begin a Say Please program at home. *Say Please* means that Gimme must earn everything she wants, whether it is her dinner kibble or a favorite chew toy. She must realize that everything of value comes from you, and that it is yours to bestow upon her or not at your whim. This means that she sits or lies down for your attention, petting, treats, eye contact, and praise. She sits for a treat. She sits to go outside. She sits to have her leash put on. She lies down by your feet to be petted when you are sitting on the sofa.

You can also begin the food bowl guarding program described earlier in this chapter—with a few changes. As long as Gimme is showing signs of stress around her bowl when you approach—hackles up, stiffening legs, eating faster, growling, or snapping—only *one* adult family member does the feeding program. The four-week program for puppies, outlined above, will likely take much longer with an adult dog who already has food-guarding issues. Do not move on to the next week's lesson until she is doing the first week's procedure without any signs of stress, no matter how long that takes. When she is doing week two procedures well for the first adult, a second adult family member can begin week one procedures. Do not add children or visitors until she has completed the entire program and is completely comfortable with the week four procedures with all of the adults in the family. Keep in mind that this could take months.

For now, Gimme cannot have items that are so valuable that they easily trigger an aggressive response, such as rawhide chews or pig ears. If she growls at you from the middle of the mattress when you try to get in bed, her new sleeping spot must be in a closed crate. If she snaps at your boyfriend from your lap when he tries to get cozy, she is no longer allowed on the sofa. If she snaps at you when you try to invite her off the bed or sofa, use treats to lure her off, and, if necessary, attach a light houseline to her collar so you can lead her off without putting your hand in the strike zone. (A houseline is a light cord long enough to get the job done that you leave on your dog only when you're there to supervise, to be sure she doesn't get tangled.) Then figure out how to block off her access to forbidden territory so you don't have to keep removing her.

PAWS OFF MY PERSON!

It might be cute that little Chica the Chihuahua tries to bite your boyfriend when he kisses you, but it could get in the way of a long-term relationship, and it certainly won't be cute when you have to drive your boyfriend to the emergency clinic for stitches in his lip! Unfortunately, what you may initially perceive as an adorable attempt on your dog's part to claim your exclusive attention could end up in a one-way trip for the dog to the euthanasia room when the behavior escalates to a level that draws blood.

A dog's guarding of her human resource—jealousy—is a dangerous behavior that needs to be addressed. Dogs do what feels good, or, as behaviorists say, behavior is reward driven. If your dog is doing something that you want to change, at some level it is rewarding to her. Find out what the reward is and you are well on your way to changing the behavior. Think what it is that you do when your dog starts guarding you. Most people instinctively turn their attention toward the aggressor and yell at her or try to soothe her. Your attention is a huge reinforcer. Even *negative* attention (like yelling) is reinforcing—in your dog's mind, something is better than nothing. So instead of directing your attention to your dog, figure out how to remove the reward, make the good thing go away—and there's a good chance the behavior will diminish and eventually stop. In the case of jealousy, the good thing is you, or your attention.

Remember: Negative punishment means a good thing goes away—it does not involve the use of physical punishment. The easiest way to accomplish this is to have the human who is being resource-guarded remove himself from the dog's presence or, alternatively, remove the dog from the human's presence. When Chica growls at the boyfriend, her owner says cheerfully, "Too Bad!" and stands up—and Chica is gently deposited on the floor. If she continues to act out from the floor, she gets another pleasant "Too Bad!" and goes in her crate or on her tether for a timeout. The *too bad* is an important no-reward marker used to mark the behavior for which Chica is getting the timeout. Like the *click!* of the clicker, it communicates instantly and clearly to the dog so she knows which behavior is making the good thing—in this case Mom, lap, sofa, or Chica's freedom—go away.

The Too Bad is delivered in a cheerful tone of voice. You are not trying to intimidate Chica into behaving; you are simply showing her that the consequence of her misbehavior is that all the good stuff goes away. The timeout is short—a few minutes in duration, so Chica can have another chance to make a more acceptable behavior choice. If she repeatedly acts aggressive from the sofa or her owner's lap, then she loses those privileges for a longer period, until a long-term Say Please program has a positive effect on Chica's behavior.

DOGGONE IT!

Negative punishment also works well when Chica is guarding her human resource (you) from other dogs. Again, you remove yourself from her presence, or vice versa. This may be as simple as walking into another room and closing the door behind you so that she can't follow, and returning a few minutes later. It may, however, require crating or tethering. If you think the other dog contributed to the scuffle, as is often the case, then both dogs get the benefit of the timeout. It is also important to initiate other good management practices, including instituting very clear structure in terms of acceptable behavior; practicing responsible management by keeping the dogs separated as necessary; and using counterconditioning to teach the dogs that they are not a threat to each other, but rather a predictor of good things. For example, your dog only gets special treats and attention in the presence of the other dog, and is ignored when the other dog is not present.

This Greyhound owner and mom-to-be wisely prepares
her dogs in advance for her baby's arrival.
(Photo by Pat Miller)

Chapter 24

And Baby Makes Three

A tragic number of dogs lose their previously happy homes when the first human baby joins the family and usurps Lady's role as the favored "only child." What makes this even more of a tragedy is that it doesn't have to happen. Wise parents-to-be take steps to ensure that Lady will accept her baby brother or sister with little or no resistance, and thus successfully avoid the *Lady and the Tramp* syndrome.

DOGS AND BABIES

As with most training challenges, the sooner you start, the better. Many couples are childless for years before the blessed event occurs. It is more difficult to convince an 8-year-old Lady to accept the little bundle of joy if she's never been around babies than it is if Mom and Dad have gone out of their way to make good things happen whenever babies were around. This is a good thing to do even if you are absolutely positive you never will have children of your own. There are babies and children all around us, and having Lady bite Aunt Meggie's new baby during family Thanksgiving dinner at your house is guaranteed to put a damper on the festivities.

Puppy Steps

If possible, start when Lady is a puppy. Find a baby. If you don't have a family member, friend, or neighbor with one, go to the community park at least once a week on nice, sunny days. There are always mothers and babysitters with babies and toddlers at parks. (Be sure to keep Lady on a leash, scoop her poop, and obey all other dog-related park regulations.)

You have already taught Lady to sit, lie down, walk politely on a leash, and not jump on people, so she is very well behaved in this social environment. Your job is to continue to *click!* and reward her for her superlative behavior and to make sure that no one frightens or hurts her. Between the ages of 4 weeks and 4 months, a puppy passes through her *critical socialization period,* during which she learns what is safe and what is not safe in the world. You want her to think that having children around is not only safe, but that it also means *lots and lots* of great treats.

Don't be stingy here—leave Lady's dinner kibble at home. Instead, get out the hot dogs, cheese, steak, chicken—whatever Lady likes best—and keep feeding her one tiny piece at a time. You don't even need to *click!* her for this; you're not trying to change or teach a *behavior*; you're trying to influence the way that her brain responds to the presence of children. (This is called *classical conditioning*, like Pavlov's salivating dogs.) We just want Lady to realize that the presence of babies and small children is a reliable predictor of *wonderful treats*. Use Lady's all-time favorite treat, and give her this treat *only* in the presence of children. I have to admit, if I got a bowl of chocolate chip cookie dough ice cream *every* time small children were around, and *only* when they were around, I might like them better myself!

You can also have the babies' parents or babysitters and some well-behaved small children feed treats to Lady and pet her gently so that she realizes that not only do good things *happen* when kids are around, some of the good things actually *come from* the children. In Lady's eyes, that makes kids even better! If you teach the adults and children that Lady has to sit before she gets the treat, you are also reinforcing her no-jumping zone behavior around little humans— another good thing to do in preparation for the eventual arrival of your own human puppy.

While you are doing this, be careful to protect Lady from children who may hurt or frighten her, intentionally or otherwise. If she has a traumatic experience with a child during this time—that is, if a child hurts or scares her—she could easily decide that children are *very bad things* and dislike them forever. You definitely don't want that!

If Lady is already beyond 4 months, it's not too late to help her like children, it's just not as easy. You may need to go to the park two or three times a week, or even every day. If she is wary of children, sit at a distance where she appears comfortable (take along a folding chair), and feed her treats. You may recall that this is called *counterconditioning*—changing the way a dog's brain reacts to a stimulus, in this case, the presence of children, from negative to positive. When Lady seems to be happily anticipating her visit to the park/treat bar, gradually start moving the chair closer to the kiddie activities. You may recall that this is called *desensitization*—gradually bringing the stimulus (children) closer and closer without reactivating the dog's fear or distrust of them. If your dog is fearful of children, you *should not* have them attempt to feed her until your counterconditioning and desensitization program is well down the road and she's realizing that children are good and valuable predictors of fantastic treats.

Remember: This can take a long time! Don't expect to accomplish it all in one session. It can take weeks, even months, of dedicated work to convince a dog who has previous negative associations with children to decide that noisy, hyperactive little humans are really good things to have around. That's why it's easier to start with puppies. That's also why, if you are starting with an adult dog, you need to begin the baby-preparation process early, preferably before Junior is even a gleam in Mom and Dad's eyes.

Before Baby's Arrival

Let's assume Lady already likes kids (lucky—or wise—you!) and the little bundle is on the way. You are still not off the hook. You need to be sure that Lady is going to continue to like kids even after Junior arrives. Dogs are stressed by change, and stress causes aggression. Things are sure going to change when Junior arrives, and aggression around the new baby is absolutely unacceptable.

You can make the change smoother by doing it gradually. This creates less stress all at once, and also avoids having Lady associate all of the changes with the arrival of the baby. If Lady's crate and toy box are now in the spare room that is going to become the nursery, evict her now, not the week before the baby is due. Find her another wonderful spot to call her own—perhaps a corner in the master bedroom—*not* the backyard or the laundry room in the basement. The goal here is to maintain her quality of life while making the necessary accommodations for the baby. If Lady sleeps with you on *your* bed and won't be allowed to do so postbaby, put a wonderfully comfortable dog bed or crate for her in the corner of your bedroom and start making her sleep in it *now*. Make it very rewarding for her by giving her favorite treats and toys to her when she is on her bed, even lying on it with her. If necessary, tether her near her bed at night so she can't slide up onto yours while you are sound asleep. Prevent her access to your bed when you are not there by closing the bedroom door or putting boxes or other objects on the bed so she can't get up.

Maybe Mom has an evening ritual of cuddling on the sofa with Lady during the evening news. If that's going to be replaced with a nursing Junior ritual, change it now. Teach Lady that cuddle time happens when Mom gets on the floor with her, instead, and make sure Mom gives the dog a reasonable amount of quality cuddle time on her turf. Or gradually have Dad take over dog-cuddling duties, since he can't nurse Junior.

Put up baby gates *now* if you plan to restrict your dog's access to certain parts of the house after the baby arrives. If possible, rather than shut her out, use the Go to Your Spot exercise (see chapter 13, Core Exercise 4.1—"Go to Your Spot") to teach her to stay in one spot on her rug in the nursery when you are changing diapers or putting Junior down for a nap. The more Lady can continue to be part of the family and family routines, the happier she'll be. The happier she is, the less stressed she is, and the less likely that there will be any aggression problems related to Junior's arrival.

Scrutinize your daily routine. Identify rituals and places that could create conflict when baby moves in. Does Lady like to race you up and down the stairs, body-slamming you in the process? Practice your Stay exercise so she will park at the top of the stairs until you can walk all of the way down safely (with your arms full of a pretend baby wrapped in a towel to make it seem real). Does she get underfoot in the kitchen? That's another good opportunity for go to Your Spot. Is she accustomed to riding shotgun in the passenger seat of the car? Have her start riding now in a travel crate in the back of the van or seat-belted safely in the back seat. Any other changes that you can identify and implement well in advance of the baby's arrival will make the transition smoother for you as well as your dog. It will be stressful enough for all of you when the time comes anyway!

After Baby's Arrival

Finally, the blessed event has happened. Mom rushes to the hospital for delivery, and Lady sits at home wondering what all the fuss is about. Dad comes home hours later, and even Lady can tell that something's changed. Dad just seems . . . different. And where, by the way, did he leave Mom?

Mom's gone for a few days, but Dad brings home a tiny blanket and lets Lady sniff it. It smells sort of like Mom, sort of like a vet hospital, but there's also a different human smell on it. Lady can tell it's a human puppy smell. Every so often Dad takes it out of its sealed plastic bag, shows it to the dog, and feeds her a cookie. By the time Junior comes home, Lady will have already begun to associate his scent with cookies!

A few days later, Mom and Junior come home. Dad holds Junior outside while Mom goes in and greets Lady. She knows that Lady is going to be very excited to see her after her absence, and she wants their reunion to be a positive one, without worrying that Junior might be accidentally hurt. A moment later, after the dog settles down, Dad comes in with Junior in his arms. If Lady tries to jump up to see the bundle, Dad turns his back. Mom is standing by with clicker and treats, and when the dog sits, Mom clicks and feeds her a goodie. Then Dad bends down and lets her sniff the baby. If Lady is gentle, Mom clicks and treats again. If Lady gets too excited, Dad calmly says "Off" (see chapter 12, Core Exercise "3.3—Leave It!") and turns slightly to block her with his body. As soon as the dog backs off, Mom clicks and treats, and continues to

It is critically important to teach your dog that good things
happen when the baby is around. (Photo by Meg Leader)

click! and reward Lady for being calm around Dad and Junior. Dad and Mom
swap baby and clicker, and Mom sits on the sofa. Now Dad clicks Lady for good
behavior, and Mom holds Junior and protects him from any oversolicitous
greeting that the dog may offer. Both parents carefully avoid verbal or physical
corrections—they want Lady to know that having the baby around is a *good*
thing. If she gets yelled at every time she tries to see the baby, she's more likely to decide that babies are *not* good.

DOGS AND KIDS

The Centers for Disease Control and Prevention in Atlanta, Georgia, report
that some 420,000 children were treated for dog bite injuries in 1994. A sta-
tistic like that can terrify new parents, but in reality, dogs and kids can be best
pals—providing parents take proper precautions:

- *Never* leave dogs, babies, and/or small children (under age 10—or older if the dog is large and active) together unsupervised. No matter how trustworthy the dog, a responsible adult must always be actively observing the interaction between dog and baby human(s). When a "Dog Mauls Toddler" tragedy occurs, it is invariably the fault of the adult who failed to supervise, not the fault of the dog.

- Give the dog an escape route. When Junior starts moving, he can be pretty determined and irritating. Lady should not have to tolerate toddler fingers in her eyes, ears, and mouth. Teach Lady how to jump over a low barrier to reach safety if she has had enough baby for the moment. Dogs who can't escape their tiny tormentors are more likely to bite in self-defense.

- Teach your dog bite inhibition so that if she does feel compelled to bite in self-defense, she will give an inhibited warning bite rather than a serious bite. (See chapter 22, "A Biting Commentary.")

- Teach your children to respect the dog. Children should handle dogs gently and kindly. As soon as Junior is old enough to understand, he needs to learn that it is not okay to hit, poke, kick, or pull Lady's ears or tail. He should also be taught that Lady's crate is her sanctuary—she is never to be disturbed there. Until he is old enough to understand, it is the responsibility of the supervising adult to prevent Junior from tormenting Lady.

- Teach your children basic dog safety tips:
  - Never approach an unfamiliar dog.
  - Never run away from a dog.
  - Never scream near a dog.
  - Stand still when an unfamiliar dog approaches.
  - Do not hug a dog unless an adult has told you that you can hug him.
  - Do not stare into a dog's eyes.
  - Do not disturb a dog who is sleeping, eating, resting in his crate, or with or near her puppies.
- Do not play with a dog unless supervised by an adult.

Do your training homework, socialize and supervise, and teach your kids good doggy manners, and Lady will be a household fixture and beloved family member for all of her remaining years.

Finding good dog-care professionals is as important as finding a good trainer. Just ask this Sheltie how much she loves her groomer. (Photo by Mary Bloom)

Epilogue

Choosing Your Animal-Care Professionals

Now that you have read this book, you probably have a good understanding of the importance of finding a dog-training professional whose philosophies are in alignment with yours. The same holds true for all your animal-care professionals, be they trainers, groomers, pet sitters, doggy day care providers, or veterinarians. The guidelines that follow were developed and published by the Association of Pet Dog Trainers (APDT), a nonprofit organization that promotes the use of positive training methods and provides educational opportunities for all trainers to learn more about the modern science of dog behavior and training. You can access the list of APDT member/trainers at the APDT Web site, www.apdt.com, to find an APDT trainer in your geographical area. You will still need to screen your prospective trainer carefully; not all APDT members have the same level of commitment to positive training tools and philosophies.

Although the APDT guidelines were written specifically to help dog owners select dog trainers, many of the suggestions included are also applicable for other dog-care professionals. When selecting the people who will be working with you and your dog, remember that you have the right and the duty to protect your dog from harm. Be true to your own philosophies, trust your instincts, and never let anyone do anything to your dog that you know could hurt him or damage the trust that the two of you share.

HOW TO CHOOSE A DOG-TRAINING PROFESSIONAL

Guidelines created by the Association of Pet Dog Trainers; reprinted with permission of the APDT.

1. Training your dog should be fun! A competent instructor will allow and encourage you to observe a class prior to making the decision to enroll. In a well-run class, dogs and people will be enjoying themselves and having a successful learning experience. Look for an instructor who is

approachable and who encourages participants to have a good time. If space permits, an instructor should welcome and encourage all family members and others who interact with the dog to attend class.

2. A skilled class instructor will

Provide a clear explanation of each lesson.

Demonstrate the behavior(s) that students will be teaching to their dogs.

Provide clear instructions and written handouts on how to teach the behavior(s).

Give students ample time in class to begin practicing the day's lesson.

Assist students individually with proper implementation of techniques.

3. A skilled and professional trainer will encourage dialogue and be courteous to both canine and human clients alike.

4. You want to be comfortable with the training tools and methods used by the instructor. A skilled and professional dog trainer employs humane training methods that are not harmful to the dog and/or handler and avoids the practices of hanging, beating, kicking, shocking, and all similar procedures or training devices that could cause the dog great pain or distress, or that have imminent potential for physical harm. You have the absolute right to stop any trainer or other animal-care professional who, in your opinion, is causing your dog undue harm or distress.

5. A conscientious trainer will stay informed about innovations in dog training and behavior tools and techniques. Check to see if the instructor is a member of any educational organizations such as the APDT, and whether s/he pursues ongoing educational opportunities.

6. A good instructor will take care to protect your dog's health in a group setting. Ask if dogs and puppies are required to be vaccinated prior to class and, if so, which vaccines are required. Make sure you and your veterinarian are comfortable with the vaccination requirements.

7. Current clients are a valuable source of information for you. Attending a group class gives you the opportunity to ask clients how they feel about their experience—if they are enjoying the class and feel that their training needs and goals are being met.

8. Because of variables in dog breeding and temperament and owner commitment and experience, a trainer cannot and should not guarantee the results of his/her training. However, an instructor can and should be willing to ensure client satisfaction with his/her professional services.

Appendix I

Doggy Day Planners

In this book, I have introduced a lot of behaviors for you to teach your dog in a short time. **Remember:** The bonus games are optional—you can pick and choose which ones you and your dog want to play. A doggy day planner can help you establish and maintain a training routine, keep track of where you and Buddy are in your curriculum, and provide you with a place to chart your progress. Sometimes when you're feeling a little frustrated, it can give you a big boost to look back to your notes from the preceding week or two and see how far Buddy has really come in a short time. I've created a couple of sample planner pages to show you how you might use them. Feel free to copy them, modify them, or make up your own to suit your needs.

WEEK 1 Exercises	Monday # of repetitions planned	Comments	Tuesday # of repetitions planned	Comments	Wednesday # of repetitions planned	Comments	Thursday # of repetitions planned	Comments	Friday # of repetitions planned	Comments	Saturday # of repetitions planned	Comments	Sunday # of repetitions planned	Comments
Turn On The Clicker	25 Planned	Buddy seemed to catch on after only a dozen.	N/A		N/A		N/A		N/A		N/A		N/A	
The Name Game	15 Planned	Got this one quickly, too, but still did 15.	10 Planned	Did 5, no distractions. Could hardly get him to look away!	10 Planned	Did 10-5 w/o distractions, 5 w/mild distractions. Did well.	10 Planned	Decided to just use this with other exercises rather than doing alone.	N/A		N/A		N/A	
Sit Happens	15 Planned	Wow! Started offering sits after only 3 clicks! Did 20. It was so fun!	10 Planned	Did 10 great ones. Seems to understand the verbal cues.	10 Planned	Did 10. Am starting random reinforcement up to 2 or 3 before click!	5 Planned	Did 5. Getting good response on just a verbal cue.	5 Planned	Started using with other exercises rather just doing alone.	N/A		N/A	
Down	10 Planned	Kept standing up at first. Finally got it with shaping.	10 Planned	Did 7. Started going down more easily on 3rd repetition.	10 Planned	Started using verbal cue first. Hasn't got it yet.	10 Planned	Did 6. Started offering downs on 3rd repetition. Did 3 more and gave Jackpot!	5 Planned	Did 5. All verbal with no luring. This is very cool.	5 Planned	Did 5. He's a Star!	5 Planned	Did a bunch extra. I love to see him "get it!"
Puppy Push-Ups	0 Planned	Don't want to start this until he is doing down easily.	5 Planned	Did 3 not very good ones. Still not real smooth on Down.	5 Planned	Did 5. Much better. Only stood up once Down is much smoother now.	5 Planned	Did 5. These are easy now. Still luring the Sits and Downs, though.	5 Planned	Did 10 - he likes these! Last three were with verbal Down.	5 Planned	Did 5. All verbal Downs, just a little body language help with Sits.	5 Planned	Did 5. Seems to have it. Next week we will work on more repetitions.
Stand By Me	10 Planned	Did 8. Easier than I thought!	5 Planned	Did 5. Faded hand lure and just used body.	5 Planned	Did 5. Trying to remember to use verbal cues first to fade body.	5 Planned	Did 5. Still need body cue. Working for longer stands before clicking.	5 Planned	Did 5. Got 2 responses to verbal cue with no body language.	5 Planned	Did 5. Only needed help on one - I should have paused longer.	5 Planned	Did a bunch extra. I love to see him "get it!"
Bonus Game: Spin and Twirl	5 Planned	Ooh, doesn't like this. Only shaped a 1/4 turn to the right.	5 Planned	Did 5 - Three 1/4 turns; two 1/2 turns.	5 Planned	Did 5. Getting better - four 1/2 turns and one full Spin! Jackpot!	5 Planned	Did 5 - one 1/2 turn and four full Spins. I think he's got it now.	5 Planned	Did 5 full spins. Finally! Started using the verbal cue.	5 Planned	Did 5 full turns to the right. Tried a few to the right; back to 1/4 turns.	5 Planned	Did 5 to the right. Two 1/2 turns and 3 full turns to the left.
Notes:														

WEEK 1 Exercises	Monday # of repetitions planned	Comments	Tuesday # of repetitions planned	Comments	Wednesday # of repetitions planned	Comments	Thursday # of repetitions planned	Comments	Friday # of repetitions planned	Comments	Saturday # of repetitions planned	Comments	Sunday # of repetitions planned	Comments
Turn On The Clicker														
The Name Game														
Sit Happens														
Down														
Puppy-Push-Ups														
Stand By Me														
Bonus Game: Spin and Twirl														
Notes:														

WEEK 2 Exercises	Monday # of repetitions planned	Comments	Tuesday # of repetitions planned	Comments	Wednesday # of repetitions planned	Comments	Thursday # of repetitions planned	Comments	Friday # of repetitions planned	Comments	Saturday # of repetitions planned	Comments	Sunday # of repetitions planned	Comments
Come														
On Target														
No Jumping Zone														
Let's Walk														
Bonus Game: Shake, Partner														
Bonus Game: Lefty/Righty														
Bonus Game: High Five														
Bonus Game: Wave														
Notes:														

WEEK 3 Exercises	Monday # of repetitions planned	Comments	Tuesday # of repetitions planned	Comments	Wednesday # of repetitions planned	Comments	Thursday # of repetitions planned	Comments	Friday # of repetitions planned	Comments	Saturday # of repetitions planned	Comments	Sunday # of repetitions planned	Comments
Wait														
Take It!														
Leave It														
Bonus Game: Ring the Bell														
Bonus Game: Sitting Pretty														
Bonus Game: Jumping Jiminy														
Notes:														

WEEK 4 Exercises	Monday # of repetitions planned	Comments	Tuesday # of repetitions planned	Comments	Wednesday # of repetitions planned	Comments	Thursday # of repetitions planned	Comments	Friday # of repetitions planned	Comments	Saturday # of repetitions planned	Comments	Sunday # of repetitions planned	Comments
Go To Your Spot														
Relax														
Stay														
Give														
Bonus Game: Weave														
Bonus Game: Score!														
Bonus Game: Let Us Pray														
Notes:														

WEEK 5 Exercises	Monday # of repetitions planned	Comments	Tuesday # of repetitions planned	Comments	Wednesday # of repetitions planned	Comments	Thursday # of repetitions planned	Comments	Friday # of repetitions planned	Comments	Saturday # of repetitions planned	Comments	Sunday # of repetitions planned	Comments
Swing Your Partner														
Temptation Alley														
Up and Over														
Bonus Game: Playing "Possum"														
Bonus Game: Roll Over														
Bonus Game: Tug														
Notes:														

WEEK 6 Exercises	Monday # of repetitions planned	Comments	Tuesday # of repetitions planned	Comments	Wednesday # of repetitions planned	Comments	Thursday # of repetitions planned	Comments	Friday # of repetitions planned	Comments	Saturday # of repetitions planned	Comments	Sunday # of repetitions planned	Comments
Well, Excuse Me!														
Long Distance Down														
Dropped Leave It														
Bonus Game: Cross Your Paws														
Bonus Game: Crawl On Your Belly														
Bonus Game: Bravo														
Notes:														

Appendix II

Delicious Treats and Delightful Rewards

TREAT REWARDS

More often than not, when someone tells me that his dog is not motivated by food, it's because he hasn't gotten very creative about the kinds of treats he has offered to his furry friend. Even a dog who is not eating due to stress can often be tempted with superscrumptious offerings. In fact, food treats are a key element in the desensitization and counterconditioning programs that you can use to *reduce* a dog's stress, so it's critically important that you find foods that are irresistible enough to tempt your dog to eat.

You may need to think outside the box and shop in human food aisles to find treats that are truly tempting to your dog's palate—dry dog cookies generally can't compete with all the delicious distractions of the real world. Some of my favorites include sliced hot dogs or Vienna sausage (you can microwave them to make them less slimy); various kitty treats; trail mix; frozen Italian meatballs; chopped bologna; peanut butter; cream cheese; small cubes of cheddar cheese; chicken—boiled or, even better, fried; liver—freeze-dried or fried; minced steak or roast beef; and the several brands of meat rolls produced for dogs. Squeeze cheese is a favorite of mine for exceptionally fussy dogs, and baby food in a jar usually works with even the most reluctant dog. I let dogs lick baby food from the tip of a spoon or my finger, right out of the jar, or from a squeeze tube (sold at camping supply stores).

The sky's the limit when it comes to the kinds of food rewards you can offer your dog. Although meat treats tend to appeal to the greatest number of dogs, I know dogs who will work for bits of French toast, Cheerios, croutons soaked in salad dressing, and cheese-filled tortellini. Still others are mesmerized by small chunks of apple and carrot. Anything your dog absolutely *loves* to eat will serve you well as a primary motivator for training purposes.

One word of caution: A dog's digestive system simply cannot tolerate certain foods. Many dogs love chocolate, but many have ended up spending the holidays in the emergency clinic after consuming a handful of chocolate Santas or Easter Bunnies. Other dogs devour onions, if given the chance, with similar results. Both chocolate and onions can kill a dog if consumed in even moderate quantities. Grapes and raisins have also been implicated in numerous dog deaths. If you want to experiment with exotic treat tests, run your proposed list past your veterinarian first to make sure you aren't including anything harmful to your dog.

LIFE REWARDS

Life rewards are things other than food that your dog loves. Generally, the more reliably your dog has learned a behavior, the more you can use life rewards in place of treat rewards. Treat rewards are useful because your dog can eat them quickly and get back to work; life rewards can interrupt the flow of your training—you have to stop and let your dog play with the ball, or chase the squirrel. On the other hand, you can run out of treats long before you wear out a tennis ball, and for dogs who love a life reward *more* than a treat, the life reward can be a more important primary motivator than food. It's worth getting creative to figure out how to use toys, games, and other activities in your dog's training. Lots of dogs will turn up their noses at treats if there is a tennis ball in the offing. Some life rewards are

- Chasing a ball or a Frisbee
- Chasing squirrels or birds (in a safe environment)
- Going outside or coming inside
- Digging a hole
- Chewing a chew toy
- Playing tug of war or chase
- Taking a walk or going for a car ride
- Swimming
- Playing with other dogs
- Anything else your dog loves to do

Appendix III

Canine Activity Contact Information

AGILITY

American Kennel Club
5580 Centerview Drive, Suite 250
Raleigh, NC 27606-3389
Phone: 919-233-9767
Web site: www.akc.org

Australian Shepherd Club of America
6091 East State Highway 21
Bryan, TX 77808
Phone: 979-778-1082
Web site: www.asca.org

National Committee for Dog Agility
Attention: Bud Kramer
401 Bluemont Circle
Manhattan, KS 66052

North American Dog Agility Council
P.O. Box 1206
Colbert, OK 74733
Web site: www.nadac.com

United Kennel Club
100 East Kilgore Road
Kalamazoo, MI 49002
Phone: 269-343-9020
Web site: www.ukcdogs.com

ANIMAL-ASSISTED THERAPY

Delta Society
875–124th Ave. NE #101
Bellevue, WA 98005-2531
Phone: 425-679-5500
Web site: www.deltasociety.org

Love on a Leash
P.O. Box 4115
Oceanside, CA 92052
Phone: 760-740-2326
Web site: www.loveonaleash.org

Therapy Dogs International
88 Bartley Rd.
Flanders, NJ 07836
Phone: 973-252-9800
Web site: www.tdi-dog.org

CANINE FREESTYLE

World Canine Freestyle Organization
P.O. Box 350122
Brooklyn, NY 11235
Phone: 718-332-8336
Web site: www.worldcaninefreestyle.org

Canine Freestyle Federation
Web site: www.canine-freestyle.org

CANINE GOOD CITIZEN TESTS

American Kennel Club
5580 Centerview Drive, Suite 250
Raleigh, NC 27606-3389
Phone: 919-233-9767
Web site: www.akc.org

DOG CAMPS

Camp Gone to the Dogs (Vermont)
PO Box 25
Readington, NJ 08870
Phone: 888-364-3293
Web site: www.campgonetothedogs.com

Camp Winnaribbun
P.O. Box 50300
Reno, NV 89513
Phone: 775-348-8412
Web site: www.campw.com

EARTHDOG TRIALS

American Kennel Club
5580 Centerview Drive, Suite 250
Raleigh, NC 27606-3389
Phone: 919-233-9767
Web site: www.akc.org

American Working Terrier Association
Web site: www.dirt-dog.com

FLYBALL

North American Flyball Association
1400 West Devon Ave., #512
Chicago, IL 60660
Phone: 800-318-6312
Web site: www.flyball.org

FRISBEE FLYING DISCS

Skyhoundz
1015 Collier Rd. NW Suite C
Atlanta, GA 30318
Phone: 404-350-9343
Web site: www.skyhoundz.com

International Disc Dog Handlers Association
1690 Julius Bridge Rd.
Ball Ground, GA 30107
Phone: 707-735-6200
Web site: www.iddha.com

HERDING

American Border Collie Association
82 Rogers Rd.
Perkinston, MS 39573
Phone: 601-928-7551
Web site: www.americanbordercollie.org

American Herding Breed Association
Web site: www.ahba-herding.org

Australian Shepherd Club of America
6091 East State Highway 21
Bryan, TX 77808
Phone: 979-778-1082
Web site: www.asca.org

Border Collie Club of America
2005 Sussex Dr.
Mt. Dora, FL 32757
Web site: www.bordercolliesociety.com

Working Kelpies, Inc.
442154 E. 140 Rd.
Bluejacket, OK 74333
Phone: 918-784-2643
Web site: www.kelpiesinc.com

LOST PET RESCUE

Missing Pet Partnership/Pet Hunters International
P.O. Box 2457
Clovis, CA 93613
Phone: 559-292-4334
Web site: www.lostapet.org or www.pethunters.com

LURE COURSING

American Kennel Club
5580 Centerview Drive, Suite 250
Raleigh, NC 27606-3389
Phone: 919-233-9767
Web site: www.akc.org

American Sighthound Field Association
Web site: www.asfa.org

National Open Field Coursing Association
Web site: www.nofca.org

OBEDIENCE

American Kennel Club
5580 Centerview Drive, Suite 250
Raleigh, NC 27606-3389
Phone: 919-233-9767
Web site: www.akc.org

Australian Shepherd Club of America
6091 East State Highway 21
Bryan, TX 77808
Phone: 979-778-1082
Web site: www.asca.org

Mixed Breed Dog Club of America
Web site: http://members.tripod.com/mbdca

United Kennel Club
100 East Kilgore Road
Kalamazoo, MI 49002
Phone: 269-343-9020
Web site: www.ukcdogs.com

RALLY OBEDIENCE

American Kennel Club
5580 Centerview Drive, Suite 250
Raleigh, NC 27606-3389
Phone: 919-233-9767
Web site: www.akc.org

APDT Rally Obedience
31 Revere Avenue
Maplewood, NJ 07040
Phone: 800-738-3647
Web site: www.apdt.com/po/rally

SEARCH-AND-RESCUE

California Rescue Dog Association
Web site: www.carda.org

National Association of Search and Rescue
Phone: 877-893-0702
Web site: www.nasar.org

North American Search Dog Network
Web site: www.nasdn.org

Search Dog Foundation
206 N. Signal St. Suite R
Ojai, CA 93023
Phone: 888-459-4376
Web site: www.searchdogfoundation.org

TRACKING

American Kennel Club
5580 Centerview Drive, Suite 250
Raleigh, NC 27606-3389
Phone: 919-233-9767
Web site: www.akc.org

Australian Shepherd Club of America
6091 East State Highway 21
Bryan, TX 77808
Phone: 979-778-1082
Web site: www.asca.org

WATER RESCUE

Newfoundland Club of America
Web site: www.ncanewfs.org

WEIGHT PULLING

International Weight Pull Association
Web site: www.iwpa.net

Appendix IV

Resources

BOOKS

Alexander, Melissa. *Click for Joy*. Waltham, MA: Sunshine Books, Inc., 2003.

Aloff, Brenda. *Canine Body Language, a Photographic Guide*. Midland, MI: Brenda Aloff, 2002.

Aloff, Brenda. *Aggression in Dogs: Practical Management, Prevention and Behavior Modification*. Wenatchee, WA: Dogwise Publishing, 2005.

Book, Mandy, and Cheryl Smith. *Right on Target! Taking Dog Training to a New Level*. Wenatchee, WA: Dogwise Publishing, 2006.

Donaldson, Jean. *The Culture Clash*. Berkeley, CA: James & Kenneth Publishers, 1996.

Donaldson, Jean. *Dogs Are from Neptune*. Montreal: Lasar Multimedia Productions, 1998.

Donaldson, Jean. *Mine!* San Francisco, CA: San Francisco SPCA, 2002.

Donaldson, Jean. *Fight!* Kaysville, UT: Kinship Communications, 2004.

Dunbar, Ian. *How to Teach a New Dog Old Tricks*. Berkeley, CA: James & Kenneth Publishing, 1998.

King, Trish. *Parenting Your Dog*. Neptune City, NJ: T.F.H. Publications, Inc., 2004.

McConnell, Patricia, Ph.D. *The Other End of the Leash*. New York: Ballantine Publishing Group, 2002.

McConnell, Patricia, Ph.D. *Feisty Fido*. Black Earth, WI: McConnell Publishing, Ltd, 2003.

McConnell, Patricia, Ph.D. *The Cautious Canine*. Black Earth, WI: McConnell Publishing, Ltd, 2005.

McConnell, Patricia, Ph.D. *For the Love of a Dog; Understanding Emotion in You and Your Best Friend*. New York: Ballantine Publishing Group, 2006.

McDevitt, Leslie. *Control Unleashed: Creating a Focused and Confident Dog*. South Hadley, MA: Clean Run Productions, 2007.

Miller, Pat. *Positive Perspectives: Love Your Dog, Train Your Dog*. Wenatchee, WA: Dogwise Publishing, 2004.

Miller, Pat. *Positive Perspectives Volume 2; Know Your Dog, Train Your Dog*. Wenatchee, WA: Dogwise Publishing, 2008.

Owens, Paul. *The Dog Whisperer: A Compassionate, Nonviolent Approach to Dog Training*. Holbrook, MA: Adams Media Corporation, 1999.

Pelar, Colleen. *Living With Kids and Dogs Without Losing Your Mind*. Springfield, VA: C&R Publishing LLC, 2005.

Pryor, Karen. *Don't Shoot the Dog: The New Art of Teaching and Training*. New York: Bantam Books, 1999.

Reid, Pamela J., Ph.D. *Excel-Erated Learning: Explaining in Plain English How Dogs Learn and How Best to Teach Them*. Berkeley, CA: James & Kenneth Publishers, 1996.

Richmond, Mardi, and Melanee L. Barash. *Ruffing It: The Complete Guide to Camping with Dogs*. Loveland, CO: Alpine Publications, 1998.

Ryan, Terry. *Coaching People to Train Their Dogs*. Sequim, WA: Legacy Canine, 2005.

Spector, Morgan. *Clicker Training for Obedience: Shaping Top Performance—Positively*. Waltham, MA: Sunshine Books, 1999.

Wilde, Nicole. *Help For Your Fearful Dog*. Santa Clarita, CA: Phantom Publishing, 2006.

VIDEOS/DVDS

Bow Wow, Take 2, by Virginia Broitman. Take a Bow . . . Wow, Doswell, VA.

Clicker Fun Series (*Click & Go, Click & Fetch, Click & Fix*), by Deb Jones. Canine Training Systems, Littleton, CO.

Clicker Magic, by Karen Pryor. Sunshine Books, Waltham, MA.

Clicker Training for Dogs, by Karen Pryor. Sunshine Books, Waltham, MA.

Dog Training for Children, by Ian Dunbar. James & Kenneth Publishers, Berkeley, CA.

The Language of Dogs, by Sarah Kalnajs. Blue Dog Training & Behavior, Madison, WI.

New Puppy, Now What?, by Victoria Schade. Good Dog Obedience Training, Annandale, VA.

Puppy Love, by Karen Pryor. Sunshine Books, Waltham, MA.

Really Reliable Recall, by Leslie Nelson. Healthy Dog Productions, Washington, DC.

SIRIUS Puppy Training, by Ian Dunbar, Ph.D., MRCVS. James & Kenneth Publishers, 2140 Shattuck Avenue #2406, Berkeley, CA 94704. Order from the publisher.

Take A Bow . . . Wow!, by Virginia Broitman & Sherry Lippman. Take A Bow. . . Wow, Doswell, VA.

PERIODICALS

The Whole Dog Journal
P.O. Box 420234
Palm Coast, FL 32142
Phone: 800-829-9165
E-mail: wholedogjl@palmcoastd.com

E-MAIL LISTS

Peaceablepaws: Send a message to: peaceablepaws-subscribe@ yahoogroups.com (Pat Miller's e-mail list).

ClickerSolutions: Send a message to: ClickerSolutions-subscribe@ yahoogroups.com.

WEB SITES

The Association of Pet Dog Trainers

www.apdt.com (includes a trainer referrals list, with many positive trainers— but be careful, not all APDT members are positive)

Clicker Training Web Sites

www.clickertrain.com
www.clickertraining.com
www.clickerteachers.net

The International Association of Animal Behavior Consultants

www.iaabc.org (includes listing of certified animal behavior consultants)

Karen Pryor

www.clickertraining.com

Patricia McConnell

www.patriciamcconnell.com

Peaceable Paws

www.peaceablepaws.com (Pat Miller site)

Truly Dog Friendly

www.trulydogfriendly.com (Trainers who have made a commitment to using positive, nonviolent training methods)

Appendix V

Glossary of Training Cues and Terms

TRAINING CUES

All Done (or **Free, Release, Okay, You're Free, Go Play, At Ease, Free Dog**): You are released from whatever I was asking you to do.

Attention (or **Pay Attention, Watch, Watch Me**): Look at me.

Click (or a **mouth click, finger snap,** the words ***"Yes," "Click,"*** *or* ***"Tick"***): What you were doing at the exact moment you heard the click is earning you a food reward.

Come (or **Here, Close**): Run quickly to me. (You might also want it to mean "and sit right in front of me.")

Dog's Name: Look at me and wait for further instructions.

Down: Lie down on the ground (not get off something or someone).

Excuse Me (or **Reverse**): Walk backward.

Good Dog: General praise—not a reward marker!

Heel: Walk by my left side with your shoulder even with my knee.

Jackpot: Exceptionally good effort—you are earning extra rewards!

Leave It: Whatever you are touching or paying attention to, leave it alone; get off someone or something; don't touch.

Let's Walk: Walk with me without pulling on the leash, or walk closely with me with no leash, but not necessarily in the heel position.

No: What you are doing is very bad or dangerous—stop immediately! (Use very sparingly, just for life-threatening situations, and when you do use it, say it like you mean it!)

Oops (or **Wrong, Mistake, Sorry**): The behavior you are doing will not earn you a reward. (This is referred to as a no-reward marker and is also used sparingly.)

Relax: Lie flat on your side.

Sit (not **Sit Down**): Put yourself in the sitting position from whatever position you are in now.

Stand: Stand still on all four legs.

Stay: Don't move from the position I left you in until I release you.

Take It: Take food or an object into your mouth (the beginning of teaching a dog to retrieve).

Touch: Touch your nose to a designated target.

Wait: Pause. Stop moving, either until I leave or until I release you. (This is less formal than stay.)

TRAINING TERMS

Aversive: Anything the dog doesn't like.

Capturing: Marking and rewarding a complete behavior offered spontaneously by the dog.

Correction: Punishment.

Cue: A word or signal that asks the dog to perform a behavior.

Elicited behaviors: Behaviors that occur in response to encouragement or assistance from the trainer.

Fading: Gradually reducing the use of food or some other prompt to elicit a behavior.

Fluent: When a dog understands a behavior cue and performs the behavior reliably on cue at least 90 percent of the time.

Imitation: Learning through watching and copying the behavior of others.

Life reward: Something other than food that is highly rewarding to the dog, such as chasing a ball, going for a walk, swimming, going out, coming in, going for a ride in the car. (Life rewards are variable because what is very rewarding to one dog may be very aversive to another.)

Luring: Using a piece of food to encourage the dog to offer you the goal behavior so you can mark and reward it.

Modeling: Physically assisting the dog into the desired position.

Negative: Something is taken away.

Negative punishment: The dog's behavior makes something good go away, behavior decreases.

Negative reinforcement: The dog's behavior makes something bad go away, behavior increases.

No-reward marker: A signal—a sound or word such as *Oops*—that tells the dog that her behavior did not earn a reward.

Offered behaviors: Behaviors that the dog offers spontaneously, without trainer encouragement.

Positive: Something is added.

Positive punishment: The dog's behavior makes something bad happen, behavior decreases.

Positive reinforcement: The dog's behavior makes something good happen, behavior increases.

Punishment: Anything that decreases the likelihood of a behavior happening again.

Reinforcement: Anything that increases the likelihood of a behavior happening again.

Reinforcer/reward: Anything the dog likes.

Reward marker: A signal—a sound or word such as *click* or *Yes*—that tells the dog her behavior just earned a reward.

Shaping: Training a behavior by breaking it down into small steps, marking and rewarding each step until the dog has learned the entire behavior.

Throwing a behavior: When the dog deliberately, voluntarily, and emphatically offers a behavior in the hopes of being rewarded.

Index